2

I Don't Know Which Is Love

Tamamushi Oku

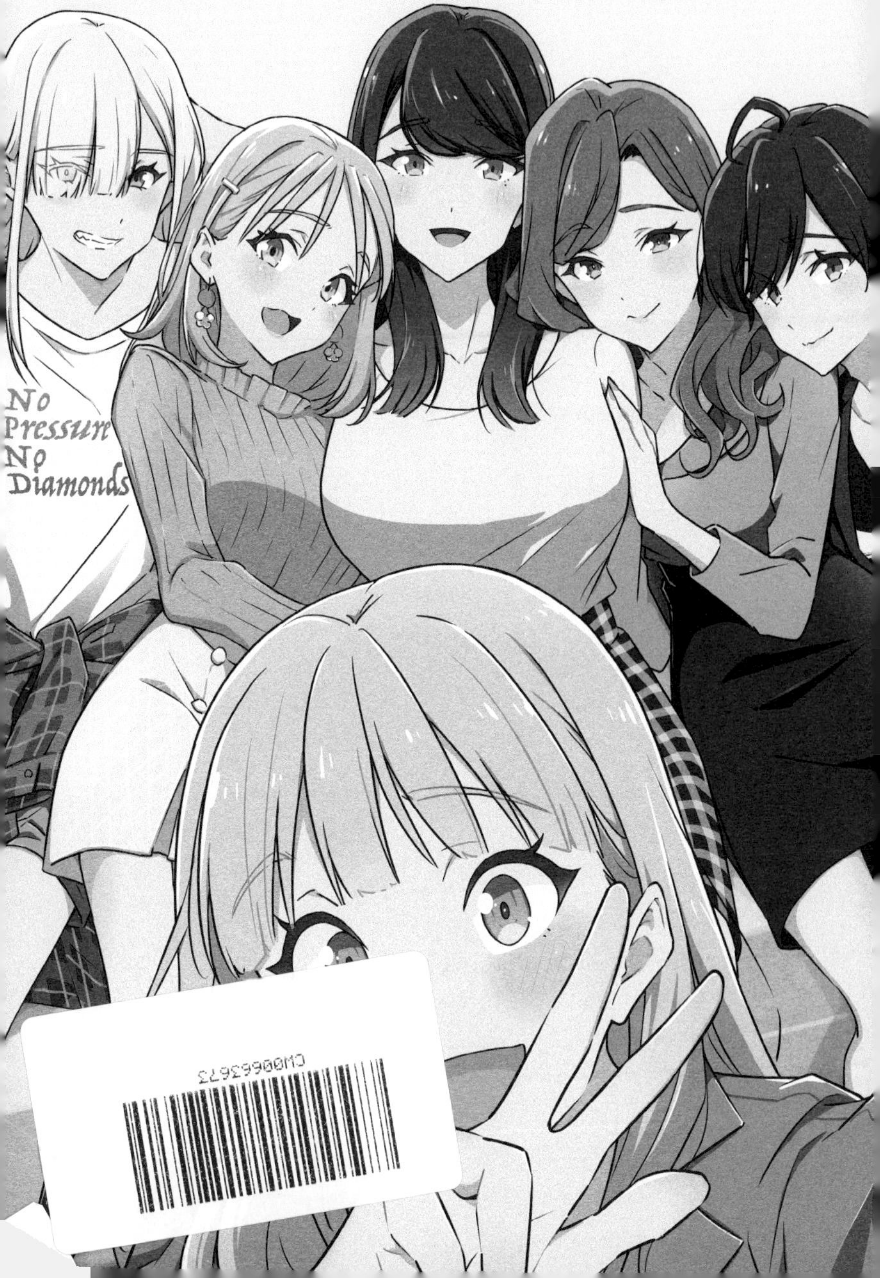
No
Pressure
No
Diamonds

contents

I Don't Know Which Is Love

Tamamushi Oku

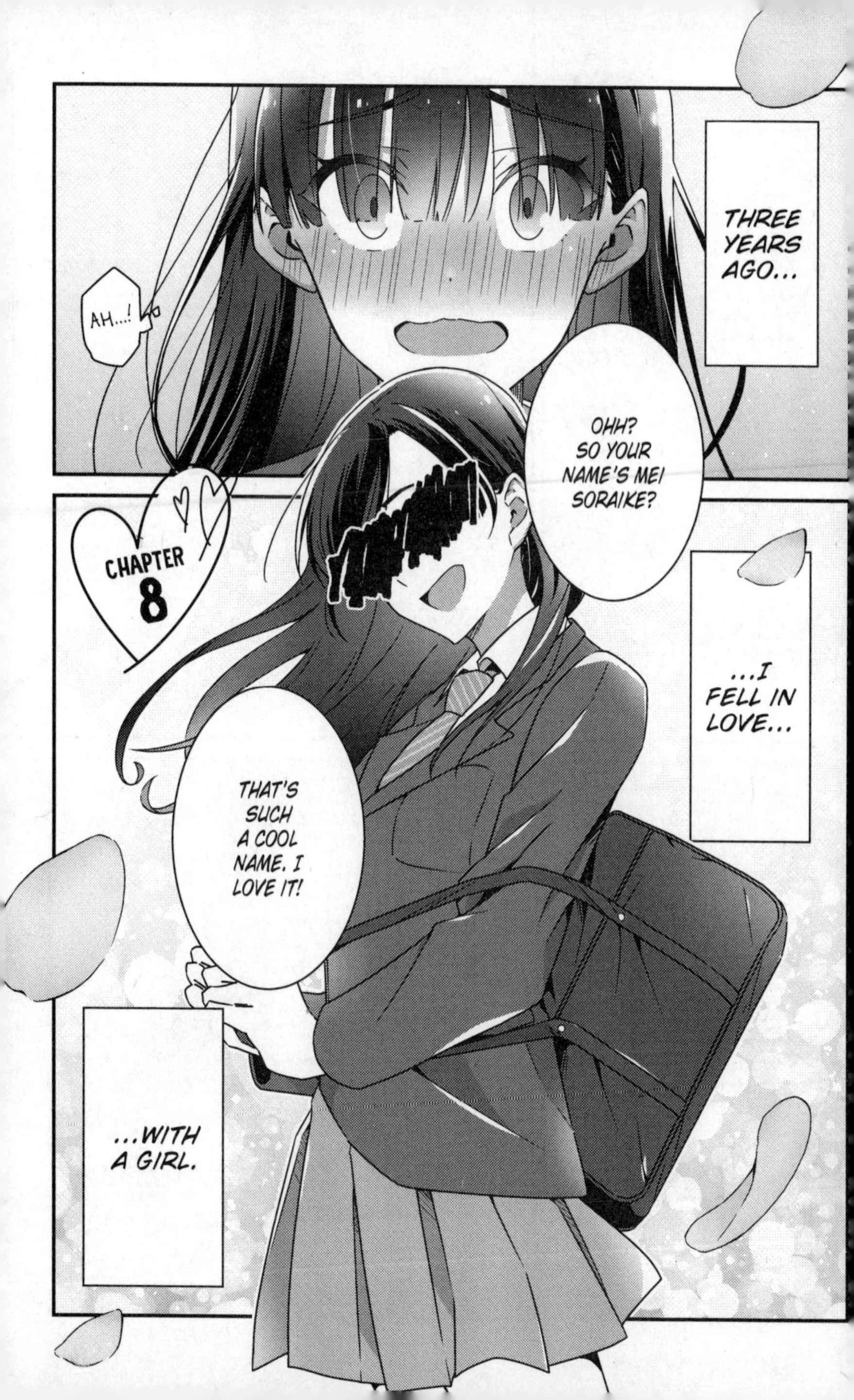
THREE YEARS AGO...
AH...!
OHH? SO YOUR NAME'S MEI SORAIKE?
...I FELL IN LOVE...
CHAPTER 8
THAT'S SUCH A COOL NAME. I LOVE IT!
...WITH A GIRL.

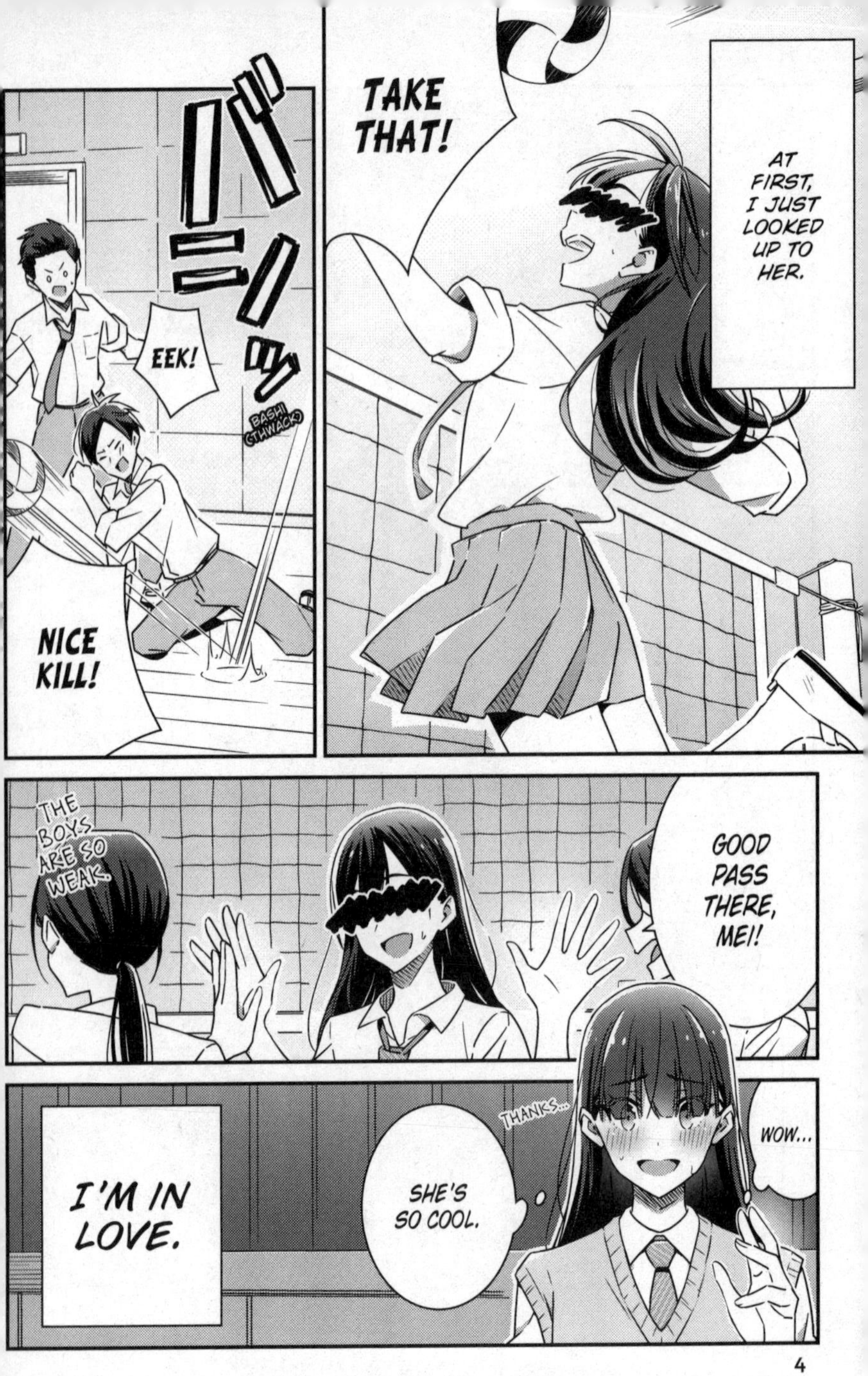
AT FIRST, I JUST LOOKED UP TO HER.
TAKE THAT!
EEK!
BASHI (THWACK)
NICE KILL!
GOOD PASS THERE, MEI!
THE BOYS ARE SO WEAK.
WOW...
THANKS...
SHE'S SO COOL.
I'M IN LOVE.

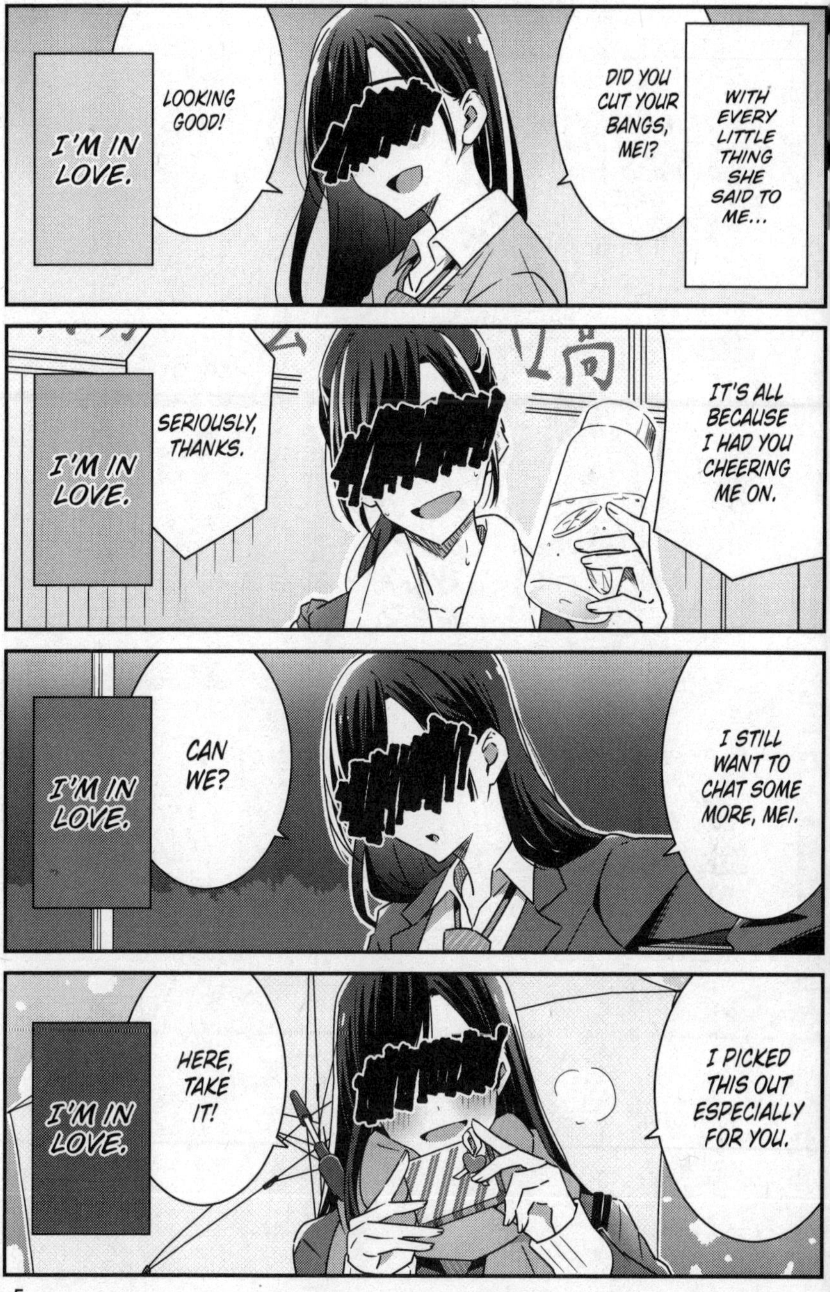
WITH EVERY LITTLE THING SHE SAID TO ME...
DID YOU CUT YOUR BANGS, MEI?
LOOKING GOOD!
I'M IN LOVE.
IT'S ALL BECAUSE I HAD YOU CHEERING ME ON.
SERIOUSLY, THANKS.
I'M IN LOVE.
I STILL WANT TO CHAT SOME MORE, MEI.
CAN WE?
I'M IN LOVE.
I PICKED THIS OUT ESPECIALLY FOR YOU.
HERE, TAKE IT!
I'M IN LOVE.

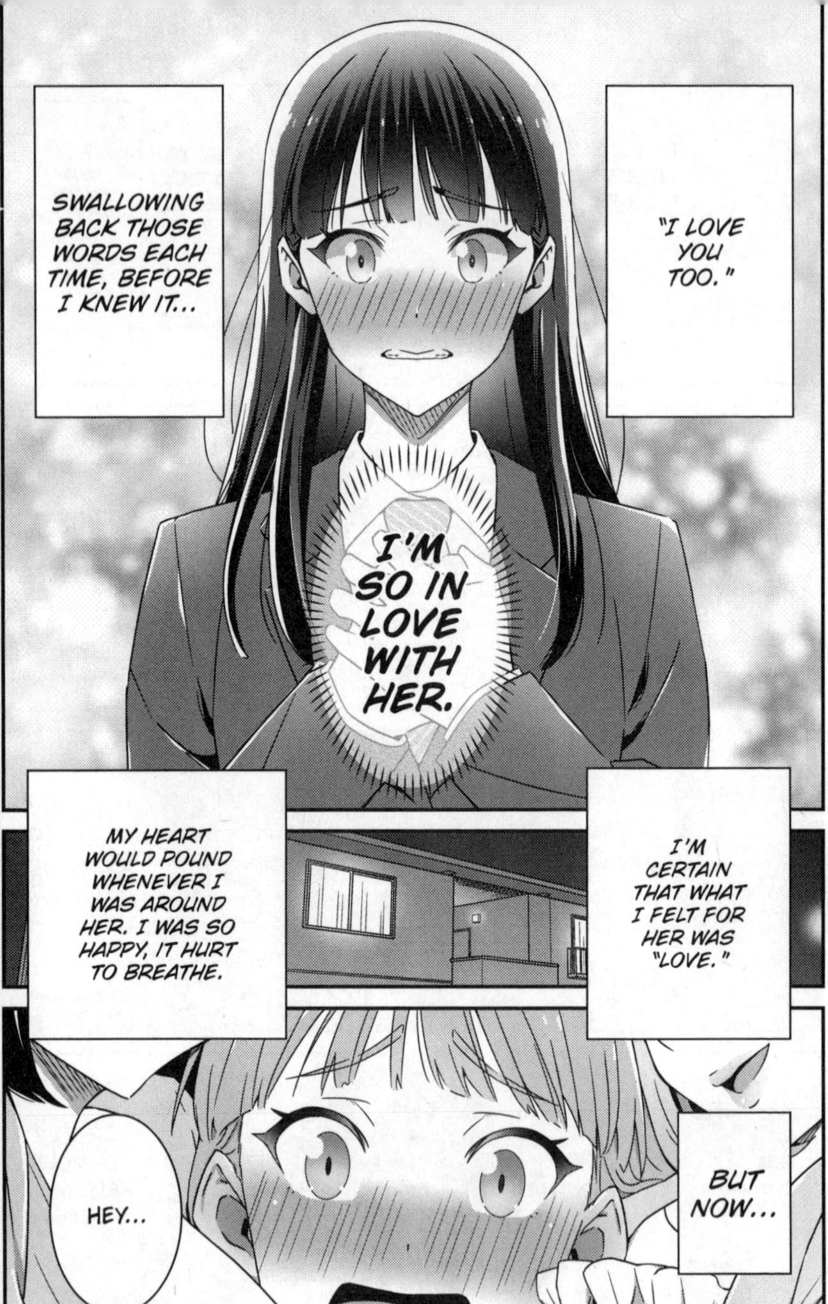
"I LOVE YOU TOO."
SWALLOWING BACK THOSE WORDS EACH TIME, BEFORE I KNEW IT...
I'M SO IN LOVE WITH HER.
I'M CERTAIN THAT WHAT I FELT FOR HER WAS "LOVE."
MY HEART WOULD POUND WHENEVER I WAS AROUND HER. I WAS SO HAPPY, IT HURT TO BREATHE.
BUT NOW...
HEY...

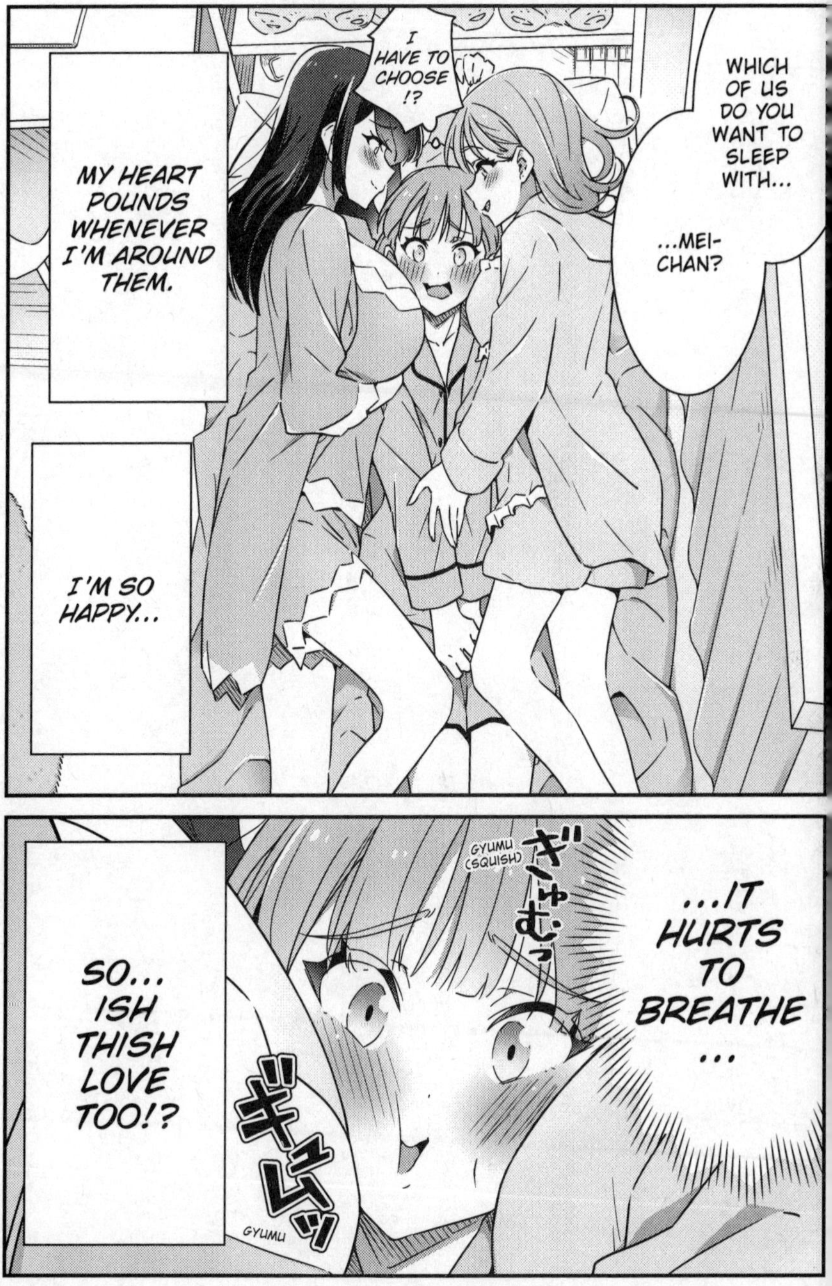
WHICH OF US DO YOU WANT TO SLEEP WITH...
...MEI-CHAN?
I HAVE TO CHOOSE!?
MY HEART POUNDS WHENEVER I'M AROUND THEM.
I'M SO HAPPY...
ぎゅむっ
GYUMU (SQUISH)
...IT HURTS TO BREATHE...
ギュムッ
GYUMU
SO... ISH THISH LOVE TOO!?

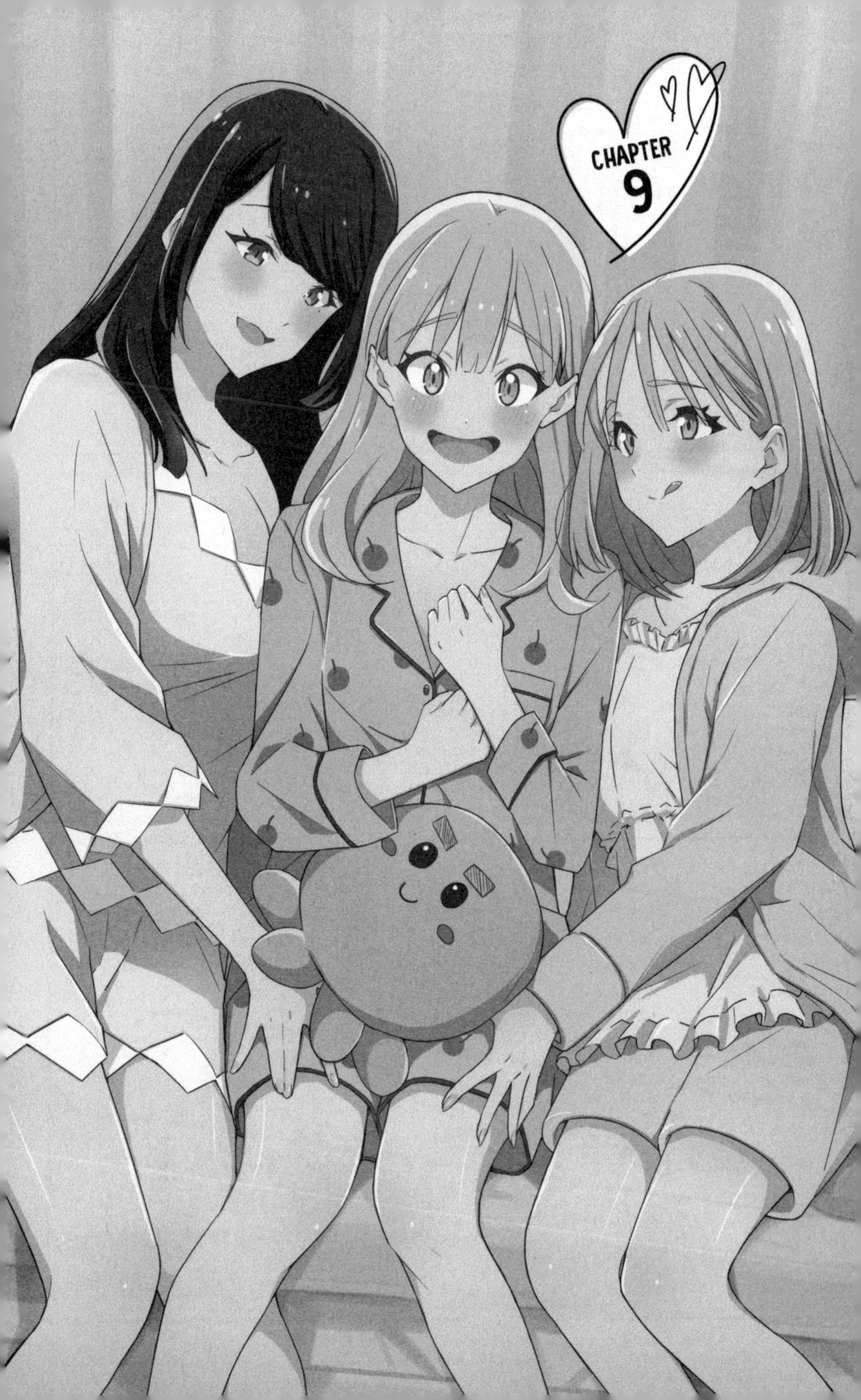
CHAPTER
9

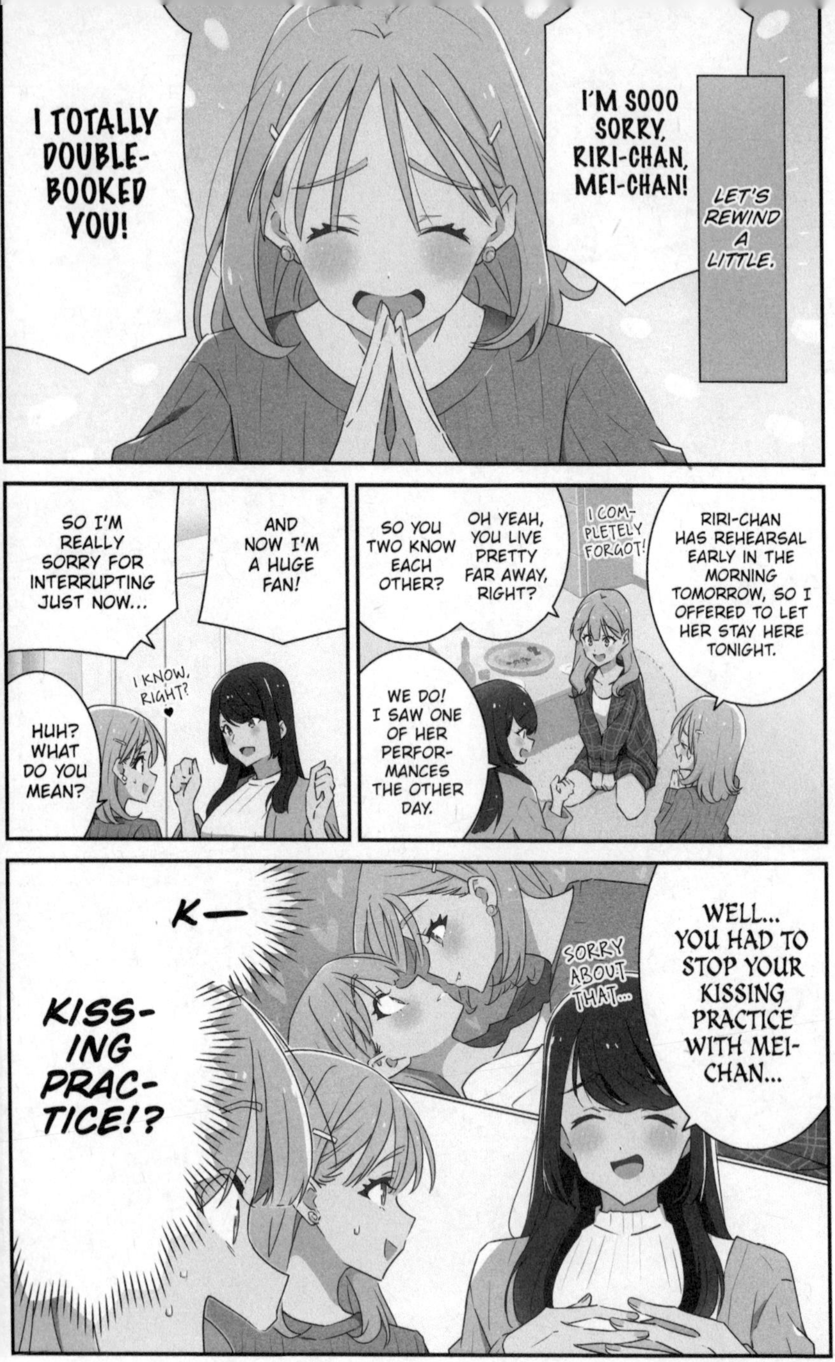
LET'S REWIND A LITTLE.
I'M SOOO SORRY, RIRI-CHAN, MEI-CHAN!
I TOTALLY DOUBLE-BOOKED YOU!
RIRI-CHAN HAS REHEARSAL EARLY IN THE MORNING TOMORROW, SO I OFFERED TO LET HER STAY HERE TONIGHT.
I COMPLETELY FORGOT!
OH YEAH, YOU LIVE PRETTY FAR AWAY, RIGHT?
SO YOU TWO KNOW EACH OTHER?
WE DO! I SAW ONE OF HER PERFORMANCES THE OTHER DAY.
AND NOW I'M A HUGE FAN!
SO I'M REALLY SORRY FOR INTERRUPTING JUST NOW...
I KNOW, RIGHT? ♥
HUH? WHAT DO YOU MEAN?
WELL... YOU HAD TO STOP YOUR KISSING PRACTICE WITH MEI-CHAN...
SORRY ABOUT THAT...
K—
KISSING PRACTICE!?

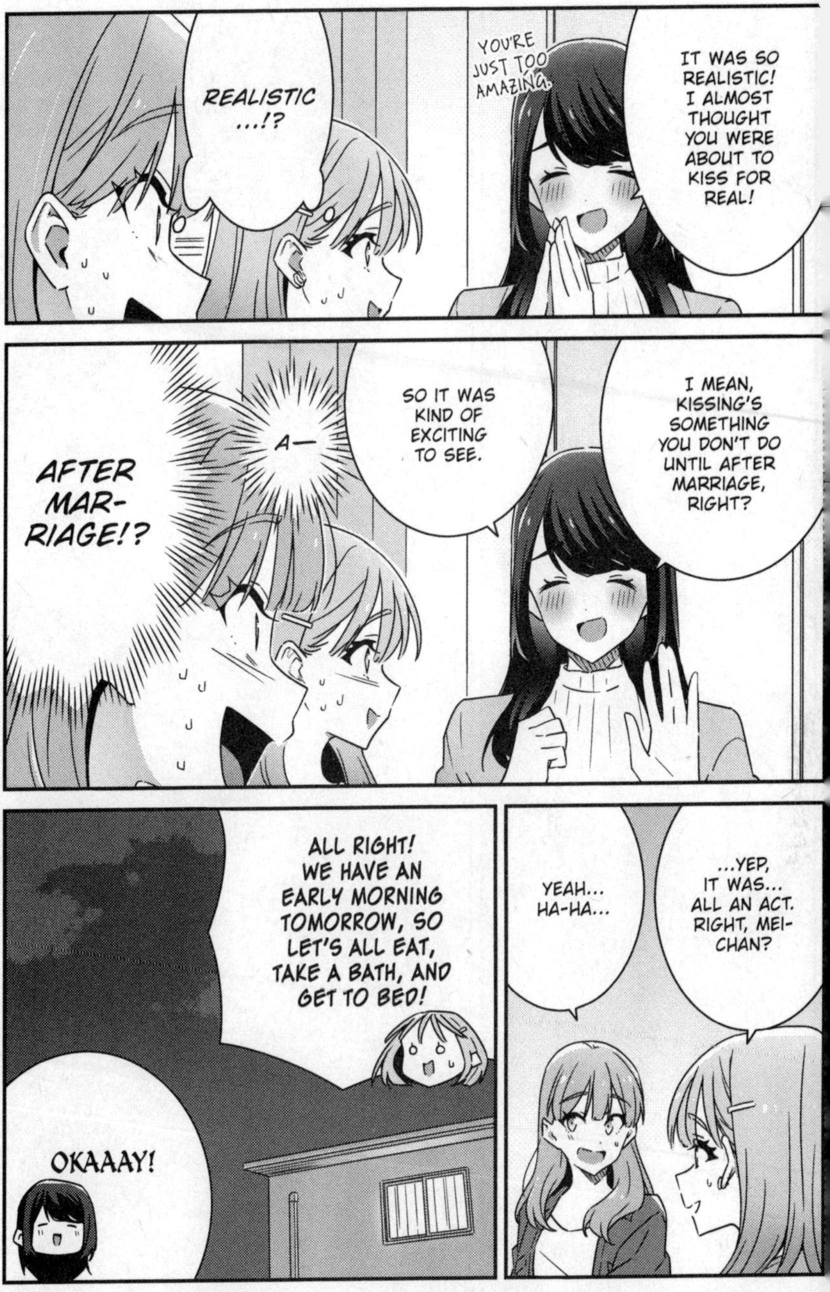
IT WAS SO REALISTIC! I ALMOST THOUGHT YOU WERE ABOUT TO KISS FOR REAL!
YOU'RE JUST TOO AMAZING.
REALISTIC ...!?
I MEAN, KISSING'S SOMETHING YOU DON'T DO UNTIL AFTER MARRIAGE, RIGHT?
SO IT WAS KIND OF EXCITING TO SEE.
A—
AFTER MAR-RIAGE!?
...YEP, IT WAS... ALL AN ACT. RIGHT, MEI-CHAN?
YEAH... HA-HA...
ALL RIGHT! WE HAVE AN EARLY MORNING TOMORROW, SO LET'S ALL EAT, TAKE A BATH, AND GET TO BED!
OKAAAY!

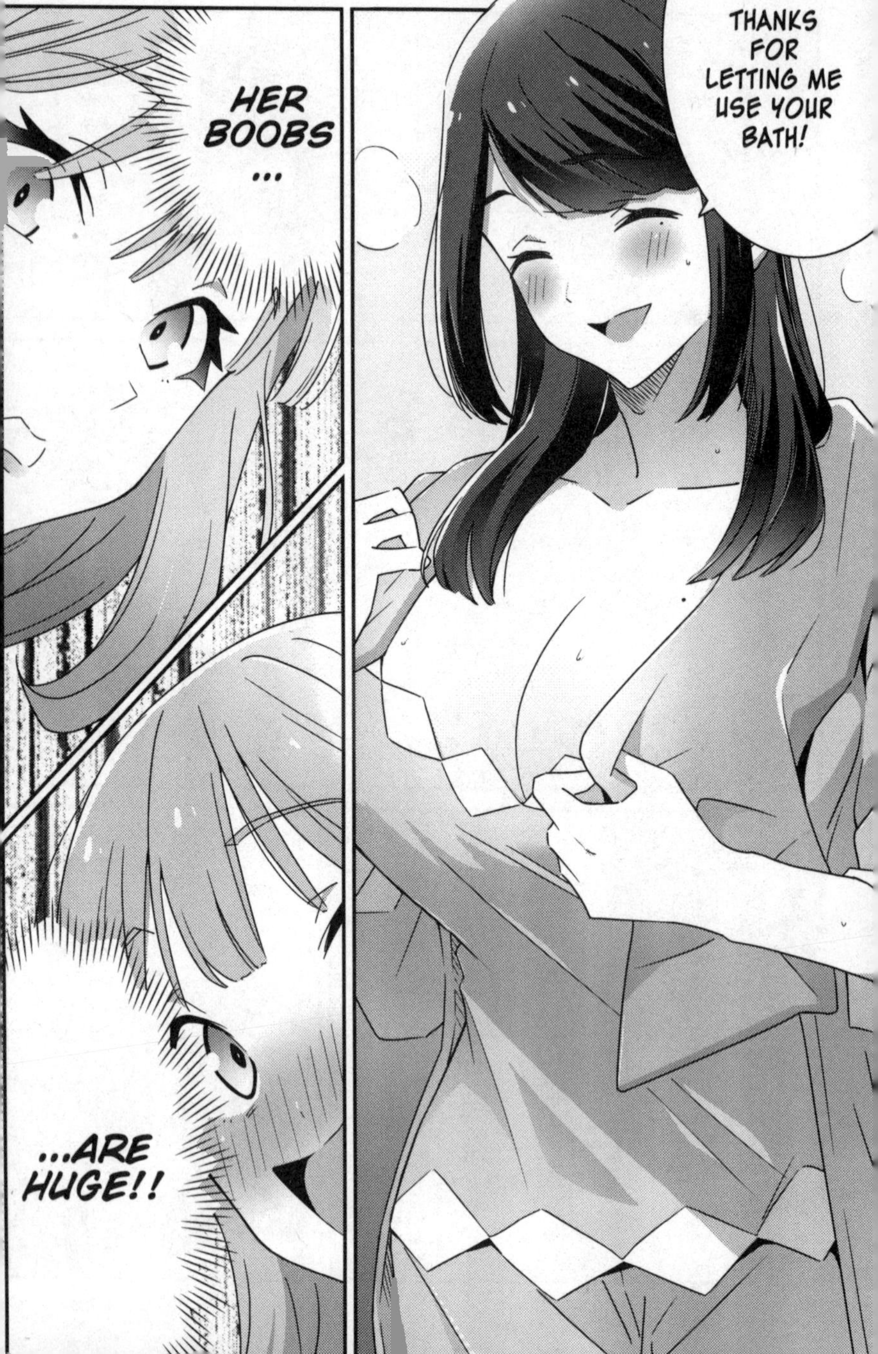
THANKS FOR LETTING ME USE YOUR BATH!
HER BOOBS ...
...ARE HUGE!!

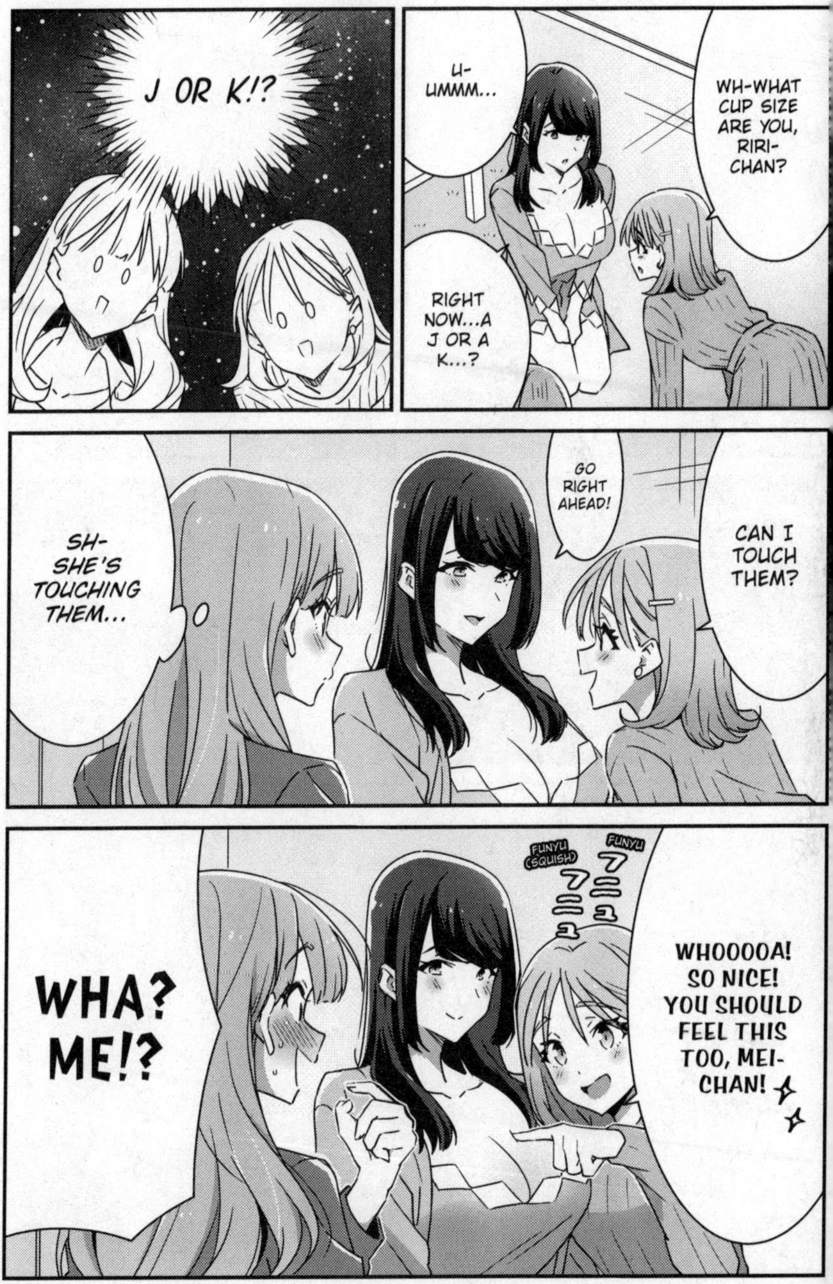
WH-WHAT CUP SIZE ARE YOU, RIRI-CHAN?
U-UMMM...
RIGHT NOW...A J OR A K...?
J OR K!?
CAN I TOUCH THEM?
GO RIGHT AHEAD!
SH-SHE'S TOUCHING THEM...
FUNYU
フニュ
FUNYU (SQUISH)
フニュ
WHOOOOA! SO NICE! YOU SHOULD FEEL THIS TOO, MEI-CHAN!
WHA? ME!?

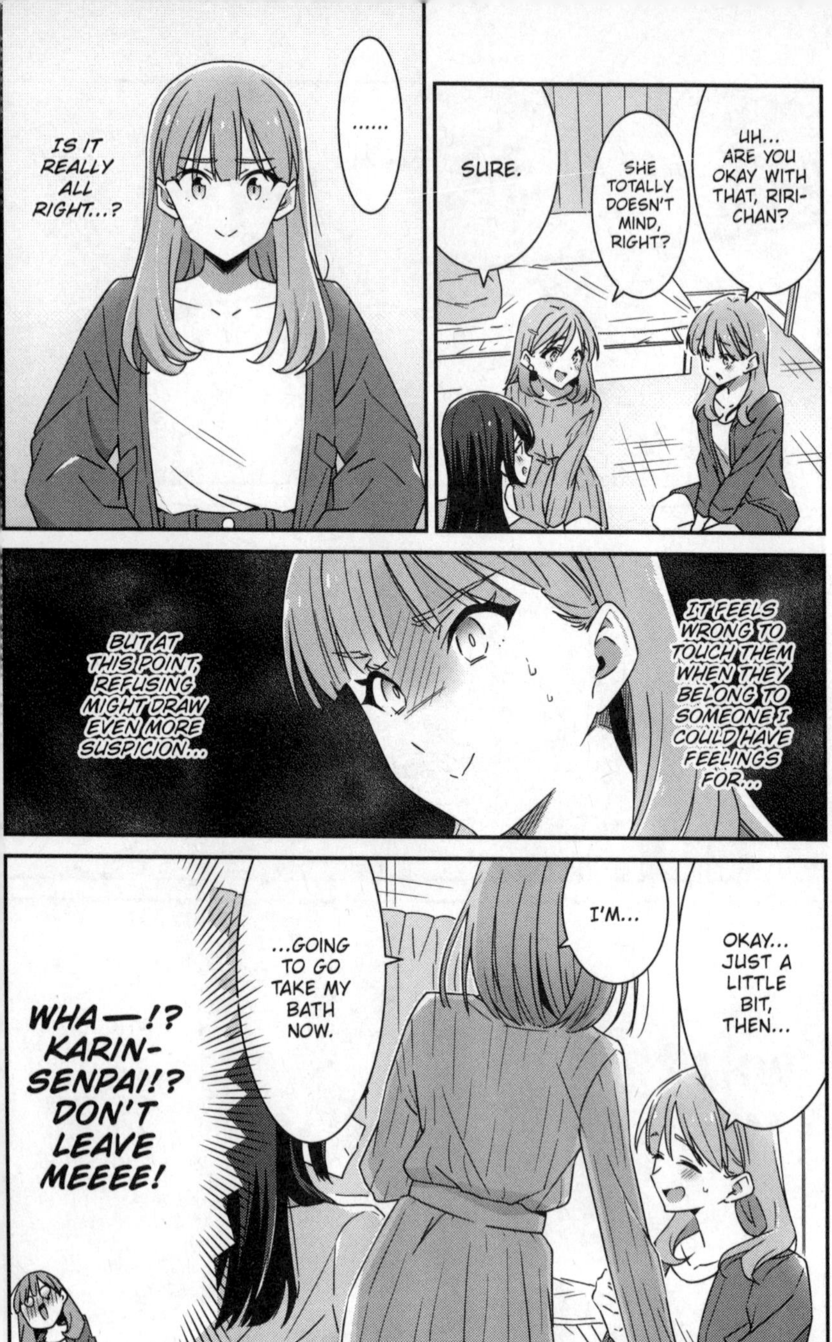
UH... ARE YOU OKAY WITH THAT, RIRI-CHAN?
SHE TOTALLY DOESN'T MIND, RIGHT?
SURE.
......
IS IT REALLY ALL RIGHT...?
IT FEELS WRONG TO TOUCH THEM WHEN THEY BELONG TO SOMEONE I COULD HAVE FEELINGS FOR...
BUT AT THIS POINT, REFUSING MIGHT DRAW EVEN MORE SUSPICION...
OKAY... JUST A LITTLE BIT, THEN...
I'M...
...GOING TO GO TAKE MY BATH NOW.
WHA—!? KARIN-SENPAI!? DON'T LEAVE MEEEE!

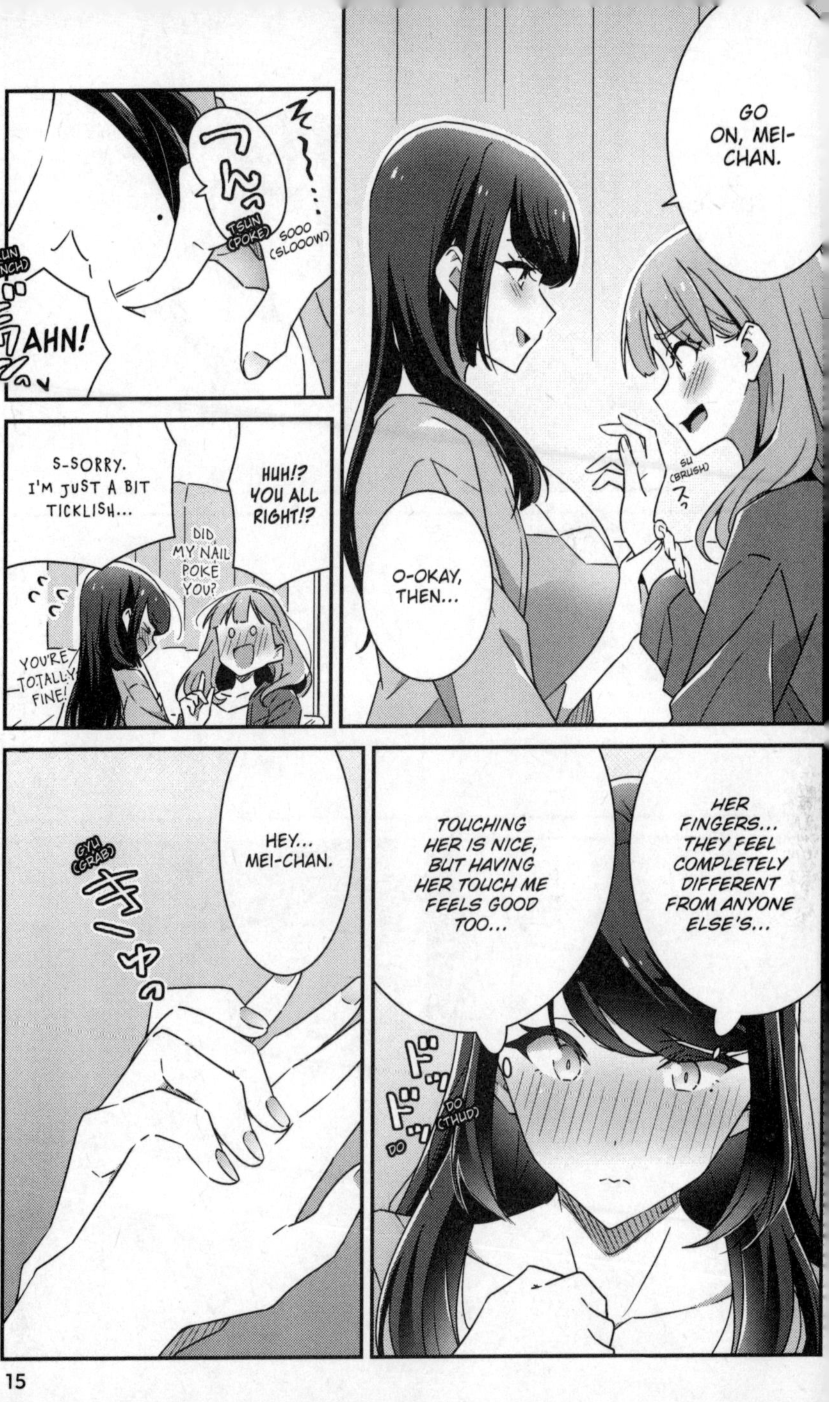
GO ON, MEI-CHAN.
SU (BRUSH)
O-OKAY, THEN...
SOOO (SLOOOW)
TSUN (POKE)
BIKUN (FLINCH)
AHN!
HUH!? YOU ALL RIGHT!?
DID MY NAIL POKE YOU?
S-SORRY. I'M JUST A BIT TICKLISH...
YOU'RE TOTALLY FINE!
HER FINGERS... THEY FEEL COMPLETELY DIFFERENT FROM ANYONE ELSE'S...
TOUCHING HER IS NICE, BUT HAVING HER TOUCH ME FEELS GOOD TOO...
DO (THUD)
DO
HEY... MEI-CHAN.
GYU (GRAB)

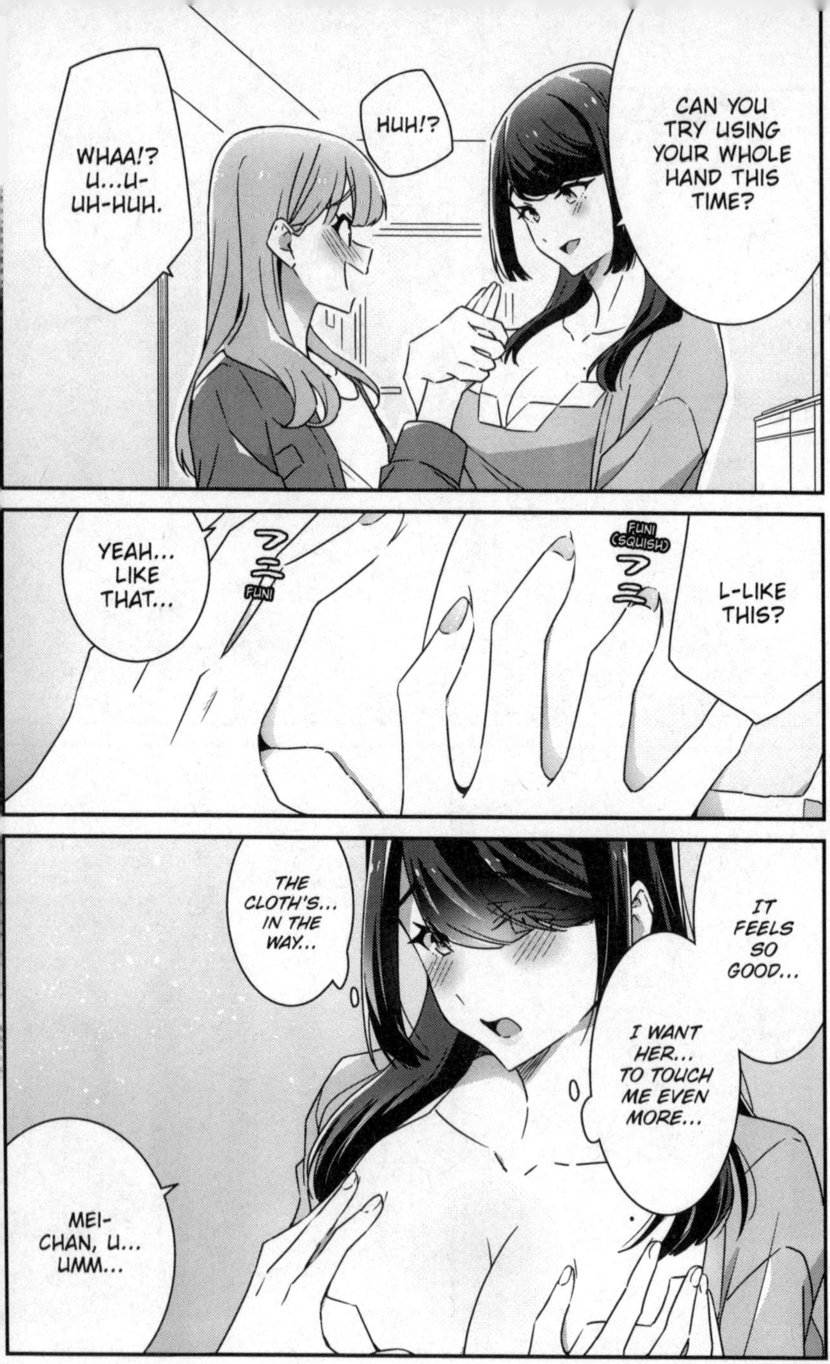
CAN YOU TRY USING YOUR WHOLE HAND THIS TIME?
HUH!?
WHAA!? U...U- UH-HUH.
L-LIKE THIS?
FUNI (SQUISH)
FUNI
YEAH... LIKE THAT...
IT FEELS SO GOOD...
I WANT HER... TO TOUCH ME EVEN MORE...
THE CLOTH'S... IN THE WAY...
MEI- CHAN, U... UMM...

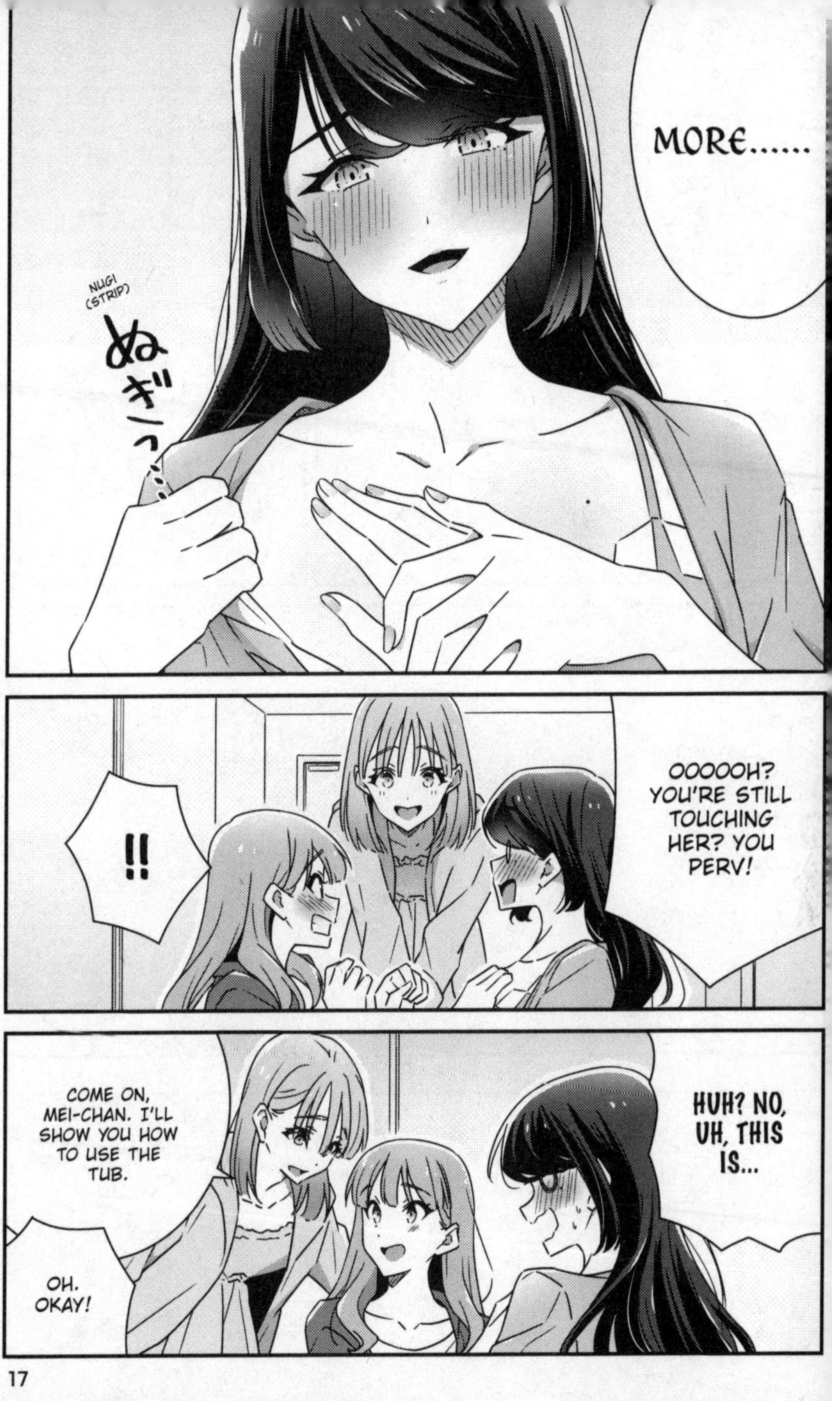

MORE......
NUGI (STRIP)
ぬギっ...
OOOOOH? YOU'RE STILL TOUCHING HER? YOU PERV!
!!
HUH? NO, UH, THIS IS...
COME ON, MEI-CHAN. I'LL SHOW YOU HOW TO USE THE TUB.
OH. OKAY!

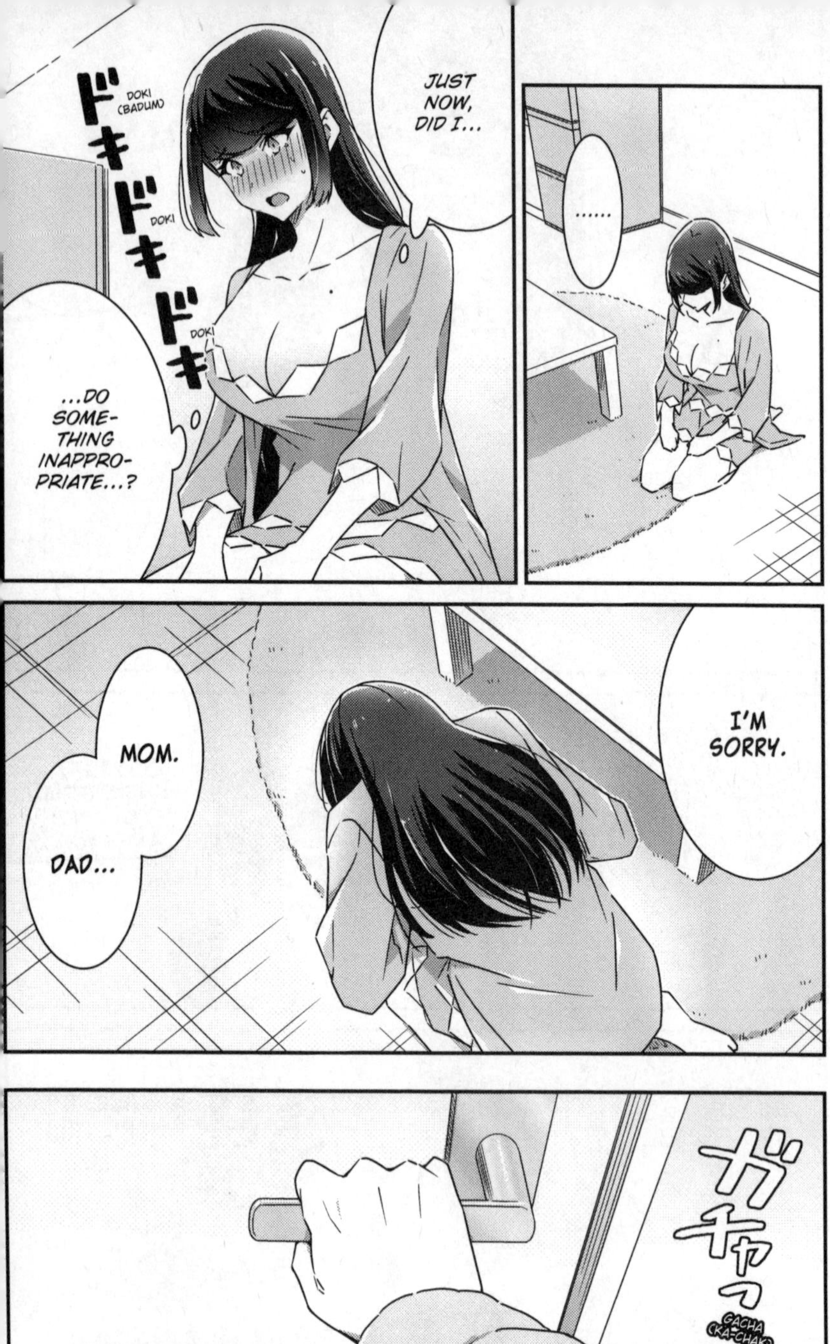
......
JUST NOW, DID I...
ドキ DOKI (BADUM)
ドキ DOKI
ドキ DOKI
...DO SOMETHING INAPPROPRIATE...?
I'M SORRY.
MOM.
DAD...
ガチャッ GACHA (KA-CHAK)

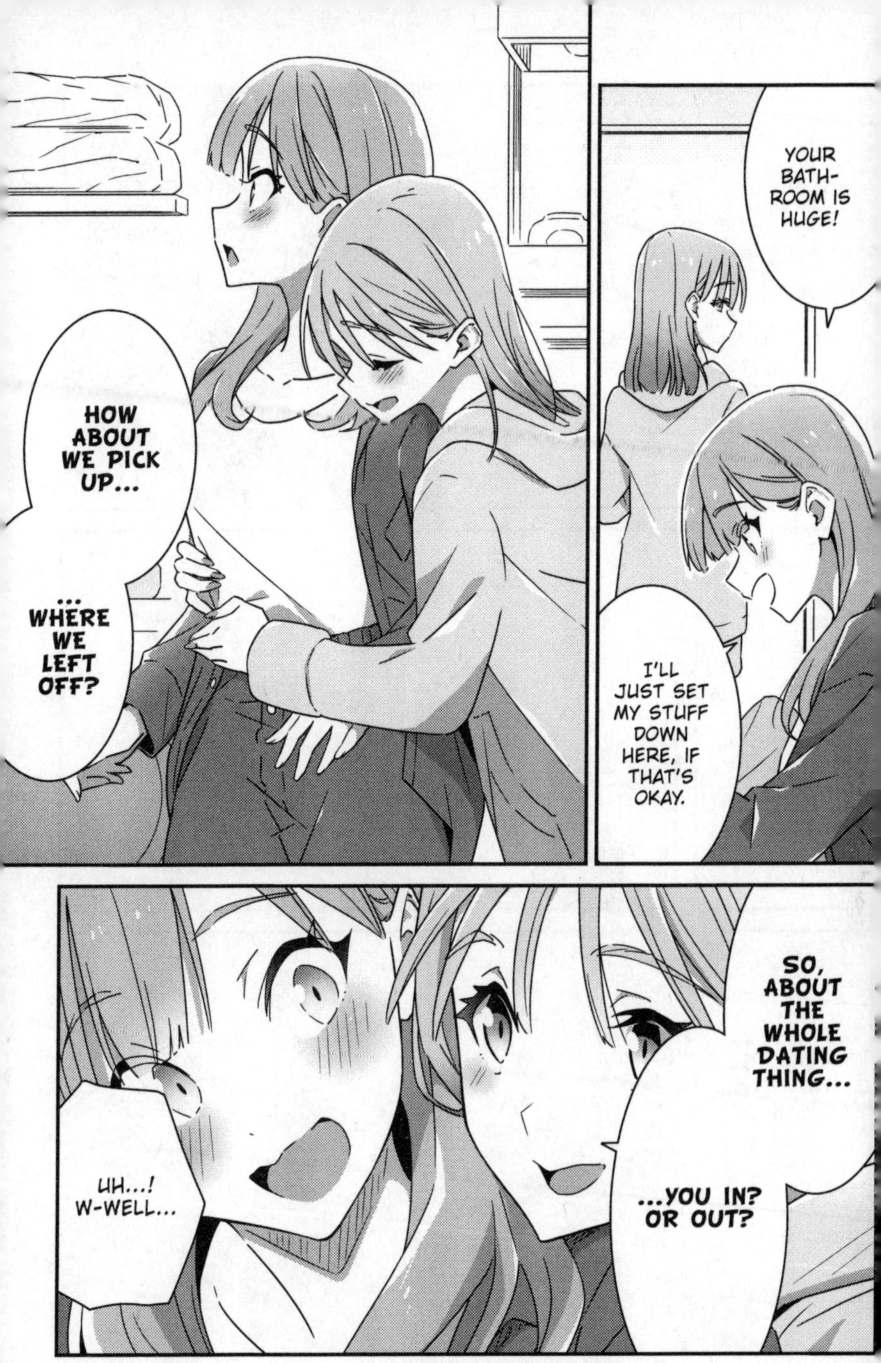
YOUR BATH-ROOM IS HUGE!
I'LL JUST SET MY STUFF DOWN HERE, IF THAT'S OKAY.
HOW ABOUT WE PICK UP...
...WHERE WE LEFT OFF?
SO, ABOUT THE WHOLE DATING THING...
...YOU IN? OR OUT?
UH...! W-WELL...

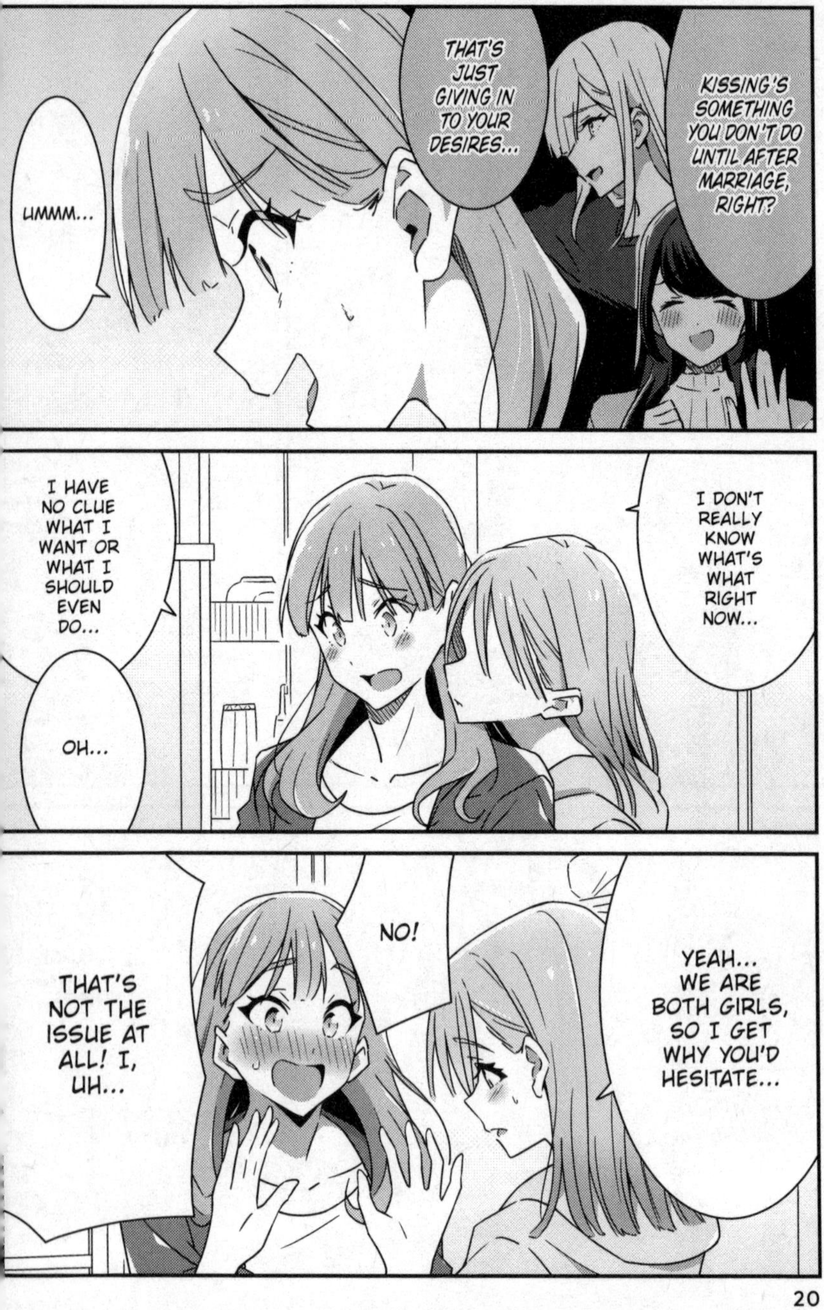
KISSING'S SOMETHING YOU DON'T DO UNTIL AFTER MARRIAGE, RIGHT?
THAT'S JUST GIVING IN TO YOUR DESIRES...
UMMM...
I DON'T REALLY KNOW WHAT'S WHAT RIGHT NOW...
I HAVE NO CLUE WHAT I WANT OR WHAT I SHOULD EVEN DO...
OH...
YEAH... WE ARE BOTH GIRLS, SO I GET WHY YOU'D HESITATE...
NO!
THAT'S NOT THE ISSUE AT ALL! I, UH...

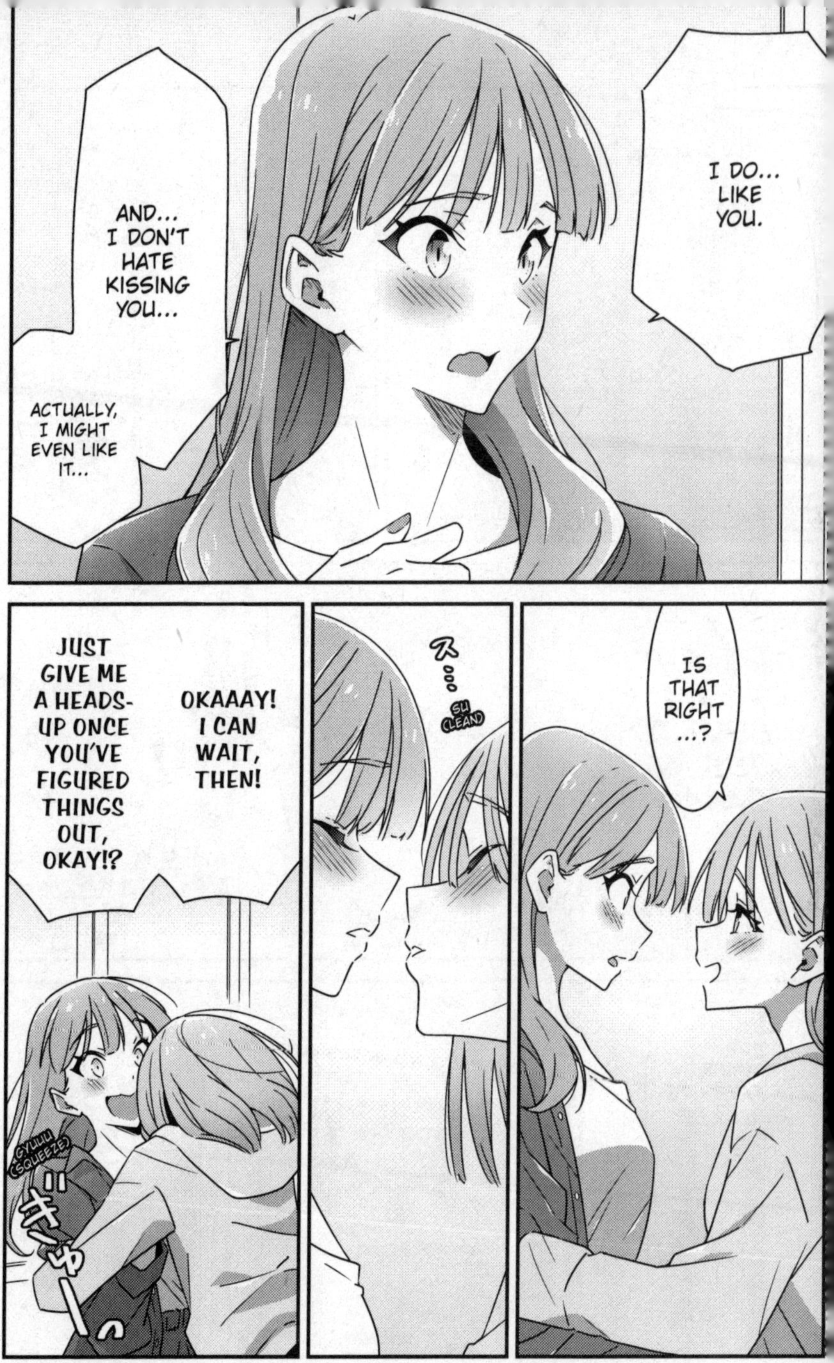
I DO... LIKE YOU.
AND... I DON'T HATE KISSING YOU...
ACTUALLY, I MIGHT EVEN LIKE IT...
IS THAT RIGHT ...?
ス...
SU (LEAN)
OKAAAY! I CAN WAIT, THEN!
JUST GIVE ME A HEADS-UP ONCE YOU'VE FIGURED THINGS OUT, OKAY!?
ぎゅー
GYUUU (SQUEEZE)

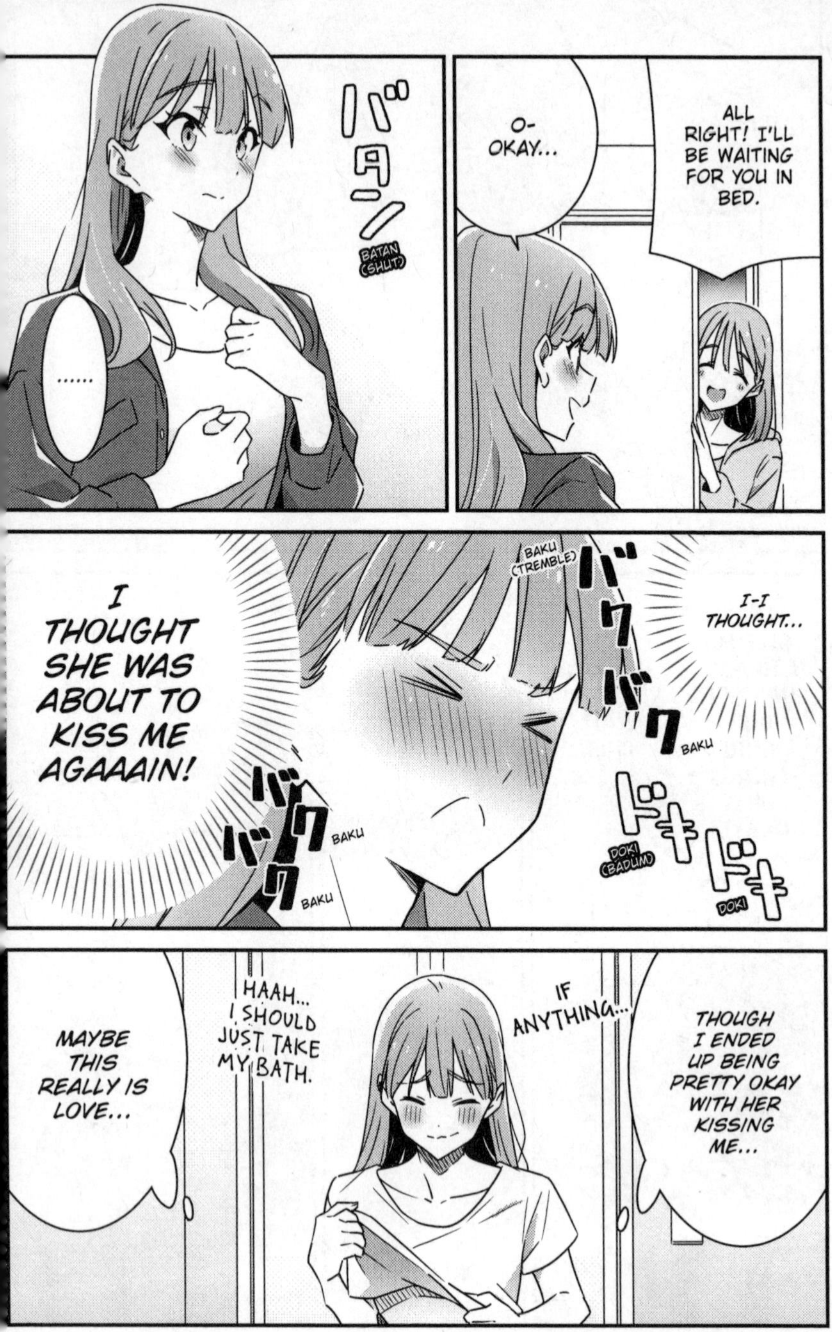
ALL RIGHT! I'LL BE WAITING FOR YOU IN BED.
O-OKAY...
BATAN (SHUT)
......
I-I THOUGHT...
BAKU (TREMBLE)
BAKU
DOKI (BADUM)
DOKI
I THOUGHT SHE WAS ABOUT TO KISS ME AGAAAIN!
BAKU
BAKU
THOUGH I ENDED UP BEING PRETTY OKAY WITH HER KISSING ME...
IF ANYTHING...
HAAH... I SHOULD JUST TAKE MY BATH.
MAYBE THIS REALLY IS LOVE...

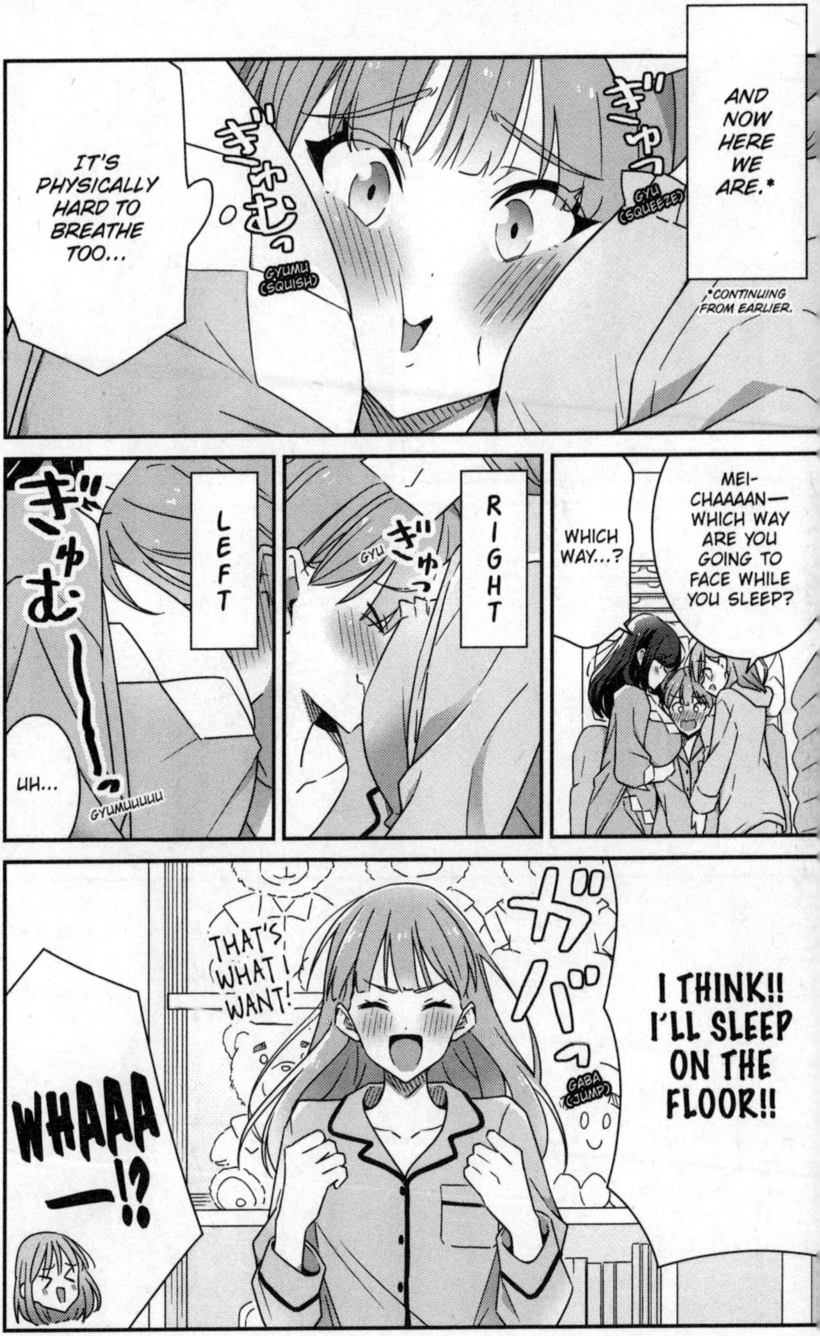
AND NOW HERE WE ARE.*
ぎゅっ
GYU (SQUEEZE)
ぎゅむっ
GYUMU (SQUISH)
IT'S PHYSICALLY HARD TO BREATHE TOO…
*CONTINUING FROM EARLIER.
MEI-CHAAAAN—WHICH WAY ARE YOU GOING TO FACE WHILE YOU SLEEP?
WHICH WAY…?
RIGHT
ぎゅっ
GYU
LEFT
ぎゅむ〜〜っ
GYUMUUUUU
UH…
I THINK!! I'LL SLEEP ON THE FLOOR!!
ガバっ
GABA (JUMP)
THAT'S WHAT I WANT!
WHAAA—!?

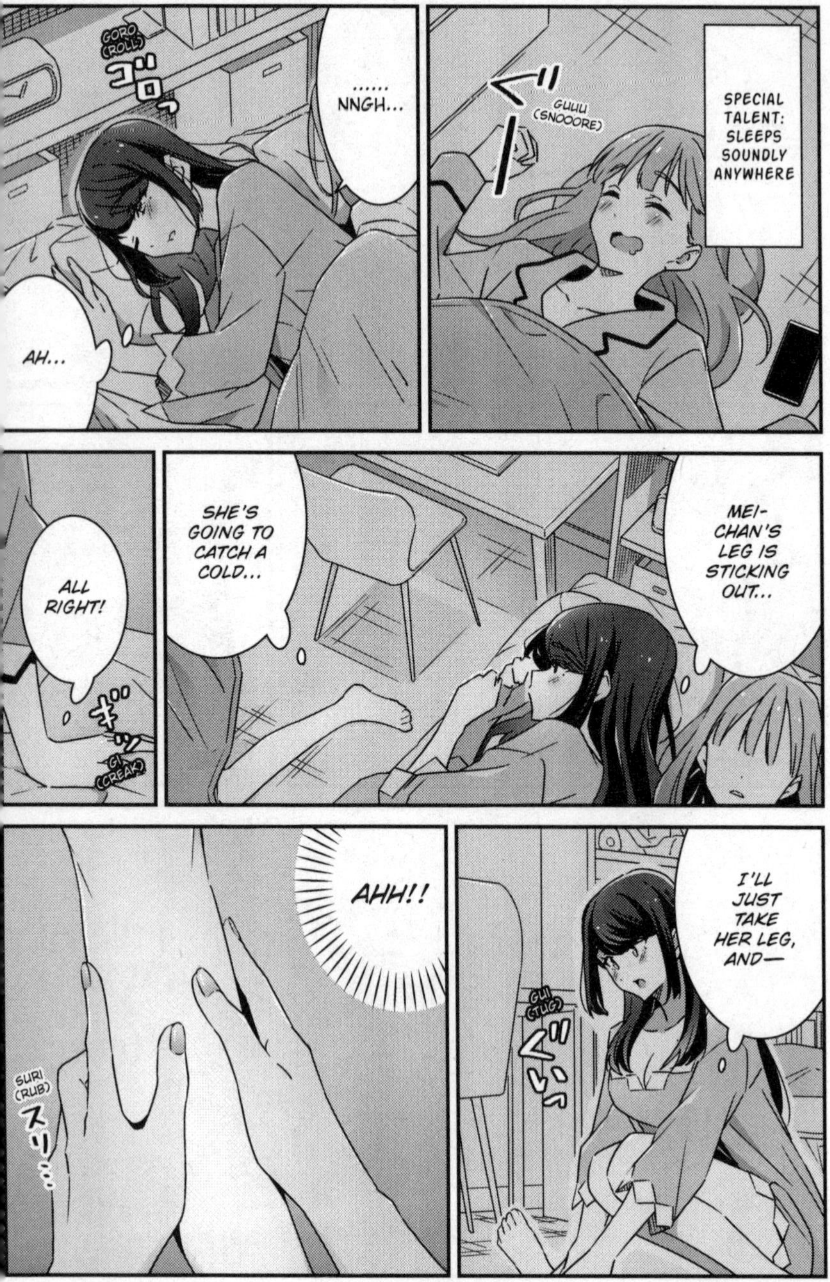
SPECIAL TALENT: SLEEPS SOUNDLY ANYWHERE
GUUU (SNOOORE)
GORO (ROLL)
ゴロッ
...... NNGH...
AH...
MEI-CHAN'S LEG IS STICKING OUT...
SHE'S GOING TO CATCH A COLD...
ALL RIGHT!
GI (CREAK)
ギッ
I'LL JUST TAKE HER LEG, AND—
GUI (TUG)
ぐいっ
AHH!!
SURI (RUB)
スリ...

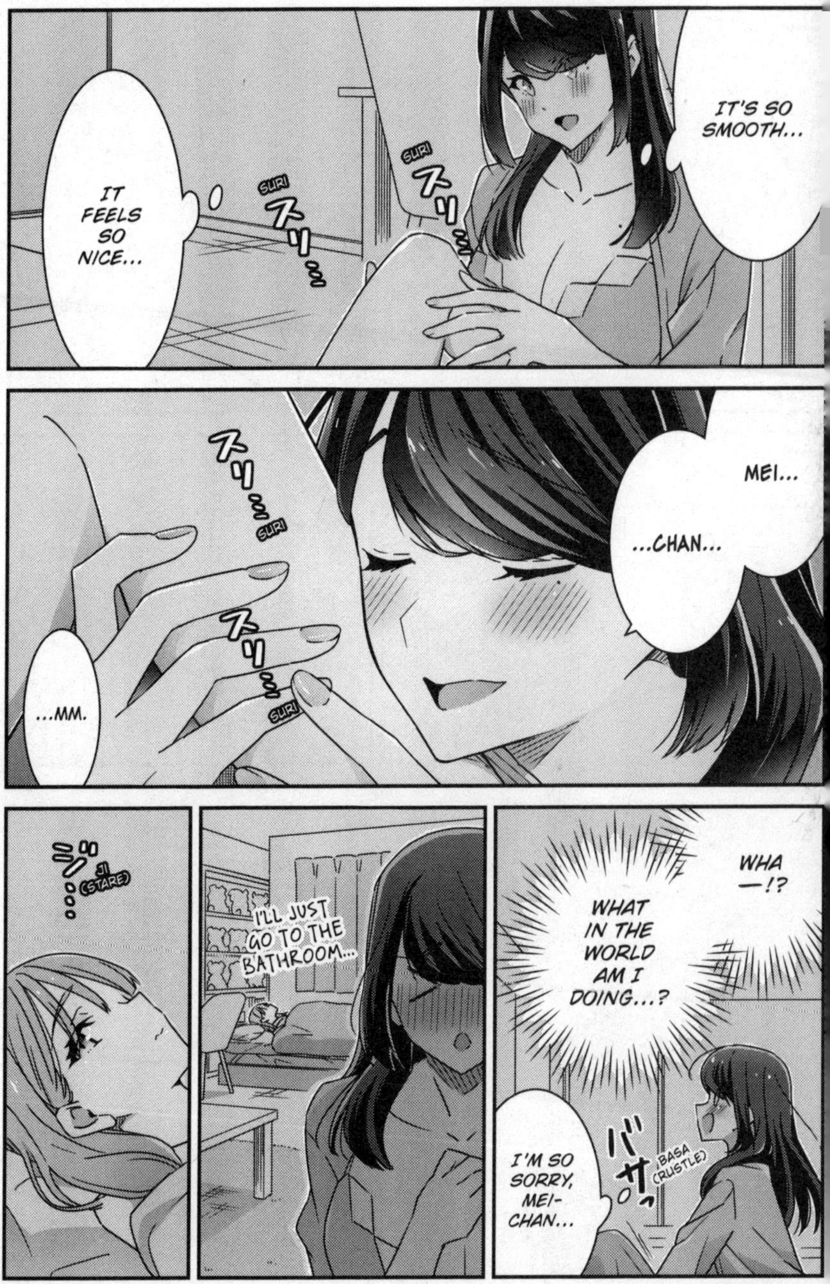
IT'S SO SMOOTH...
SURI
スリ...
SURI
スリ...
IT FEELS SO NICE...
MEI...
...CHAN...
スリ...
SURI
スリ...
SURI
...MM.
WHA—!?
WHAT IN THE WORLD AM I DOING...?
バサッ
BASA (RUSTLE)
I'M SO SORRY, MEI-CHAN...
I'LL JUST GO TO THE BATHROOM...
ジ...
JI (STARE)

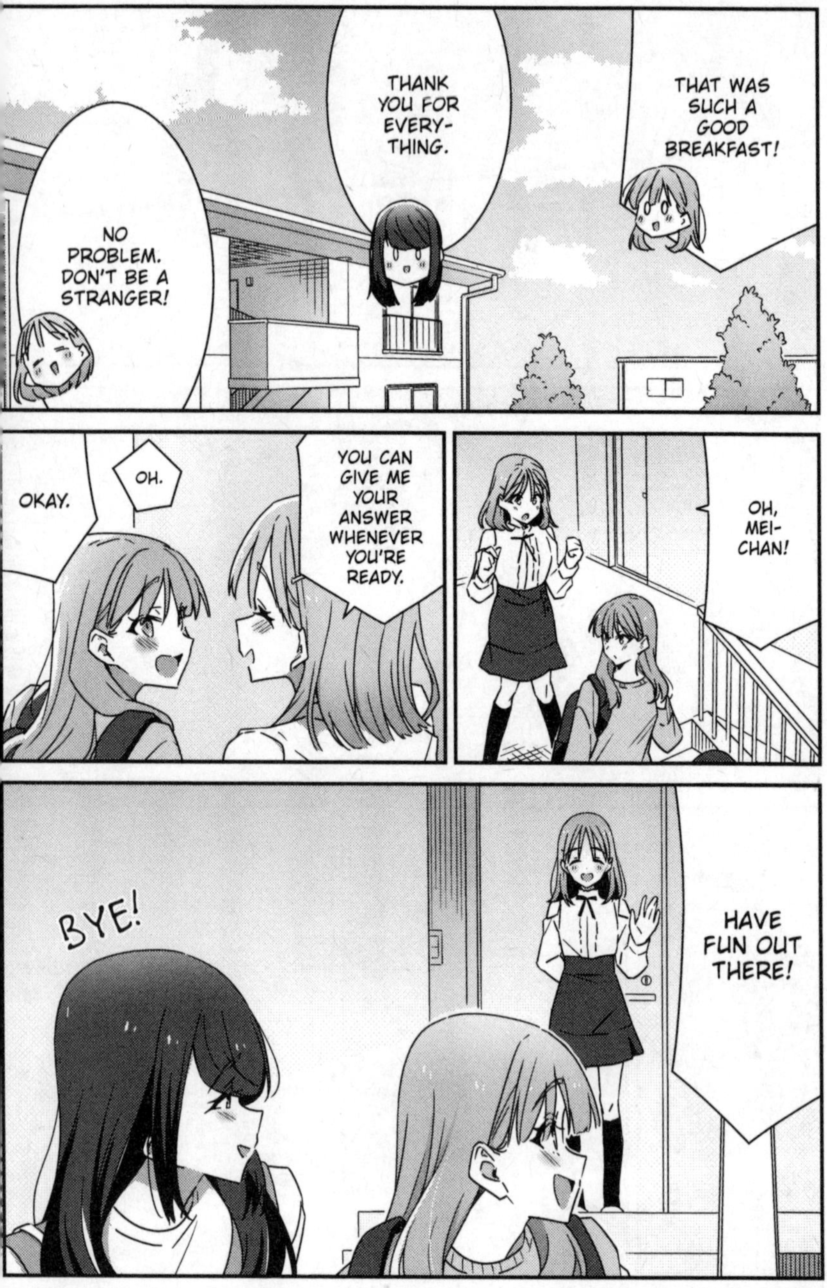
THAT WAS SUCH A GOOD BREAKFAST!
THANK YOU FOR EVERY-THING.
NO PROBLEM. DON'T BE A STRANGER!
OH, MEI-CHAN!
YOU CAN GIVE ME YOUR ANSWER WHENEVER YOU'RE READY.
OH.
OKAY.
HAVE FUN OUT THERE!
BYE!

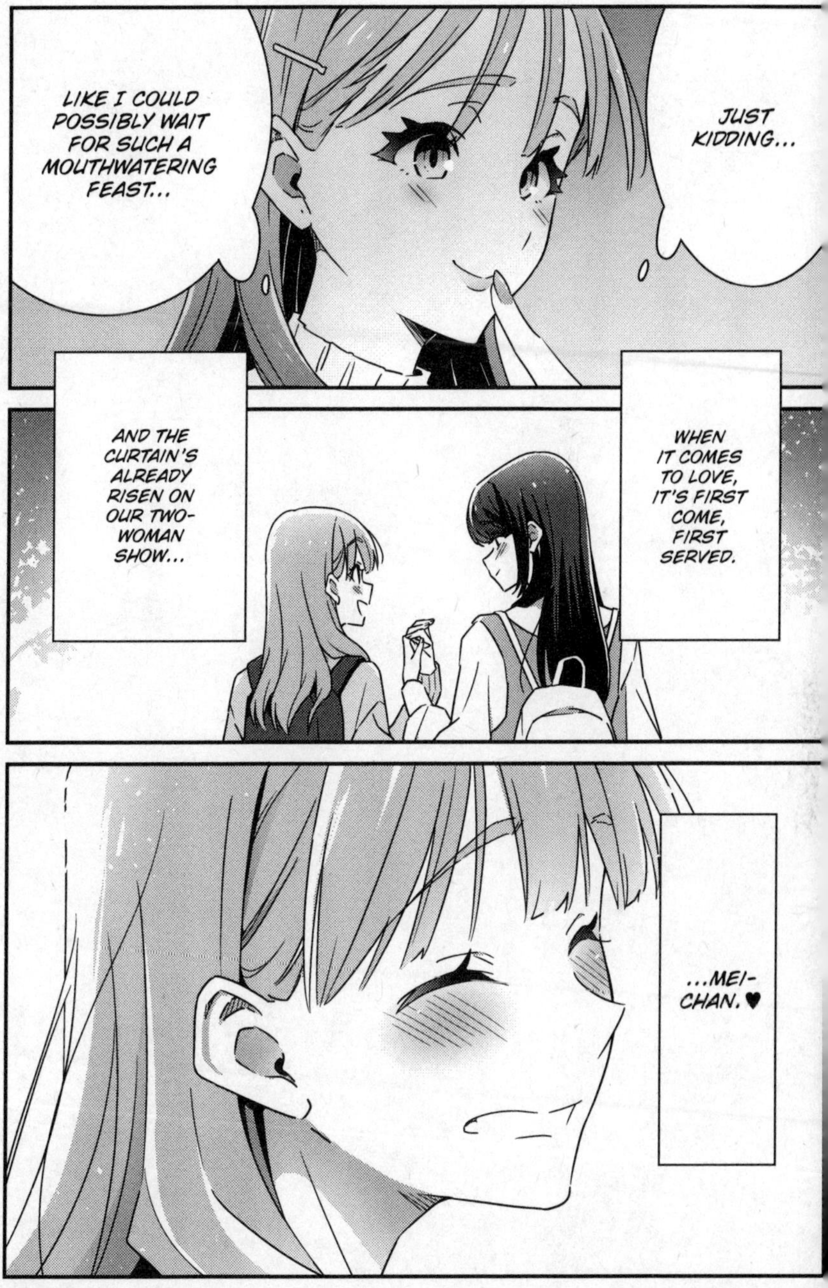
JUST KIDDING...
LIKE I COULD POSSIBLY WAIT FOR SUCH A MOUTHWATERING FEAST...
WHEN IT COMES TO LOVE, IT'S FIRST COME, FIRST SERVED.
AND THE CURTAIN'S ALREADY RISEN ON OUR TWO-WOMAN SHOW...
...MEI-CHAN.♥

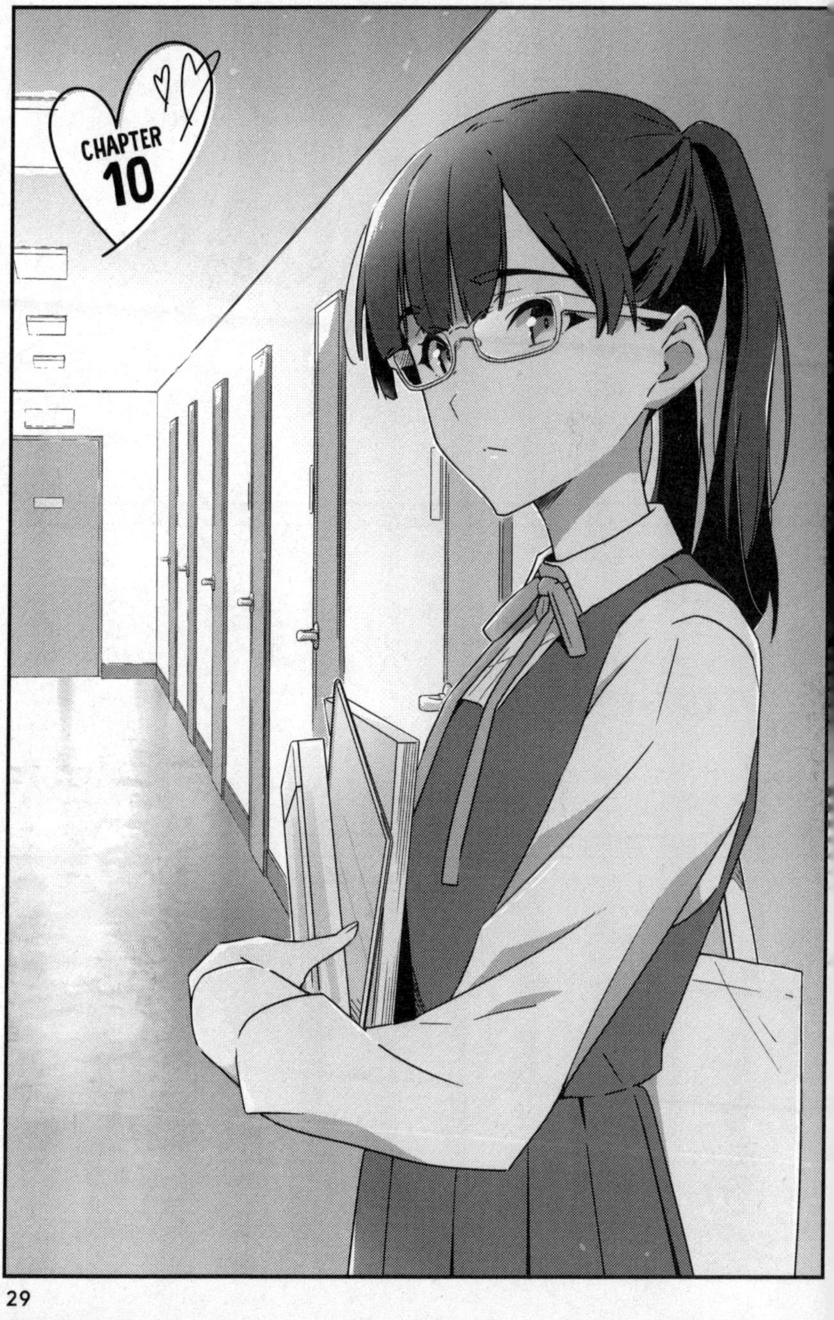
CHAPTER
10

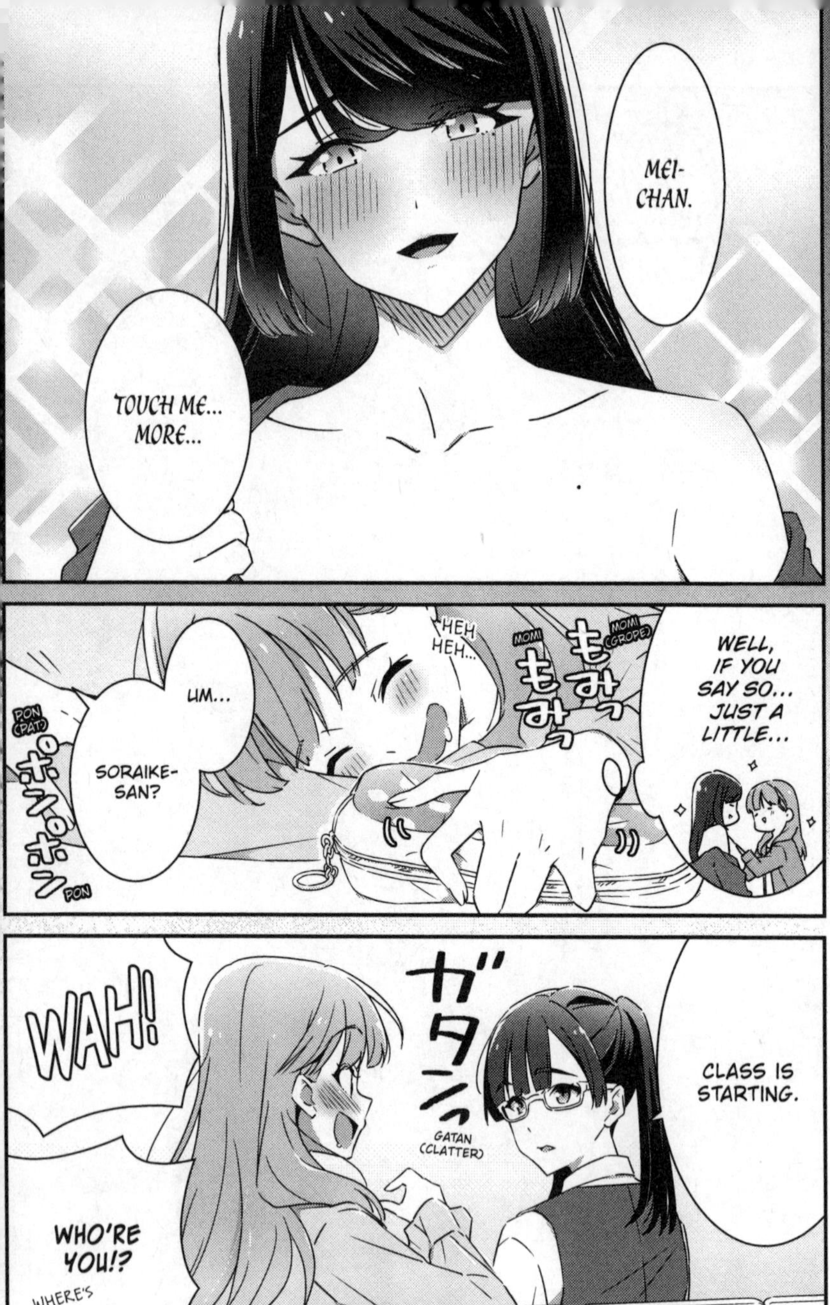
MEI-CHAN.
TOUCH ME... MORE...
WELL, IF YOU SAY SO... JUST A LITTLE...
MOMI (GROPE)
もみっ
MOMI
もみっ
HEH HEH...
UM...
SORAIKE-SAN?
PON (PAT)
ポンポン
PON
CLASS IS STARTING.
ガタンっ
GATAN (CLATTER)
WAH!
WHO'RE YOU!?
WHERE'S RIRI-CHAN!?

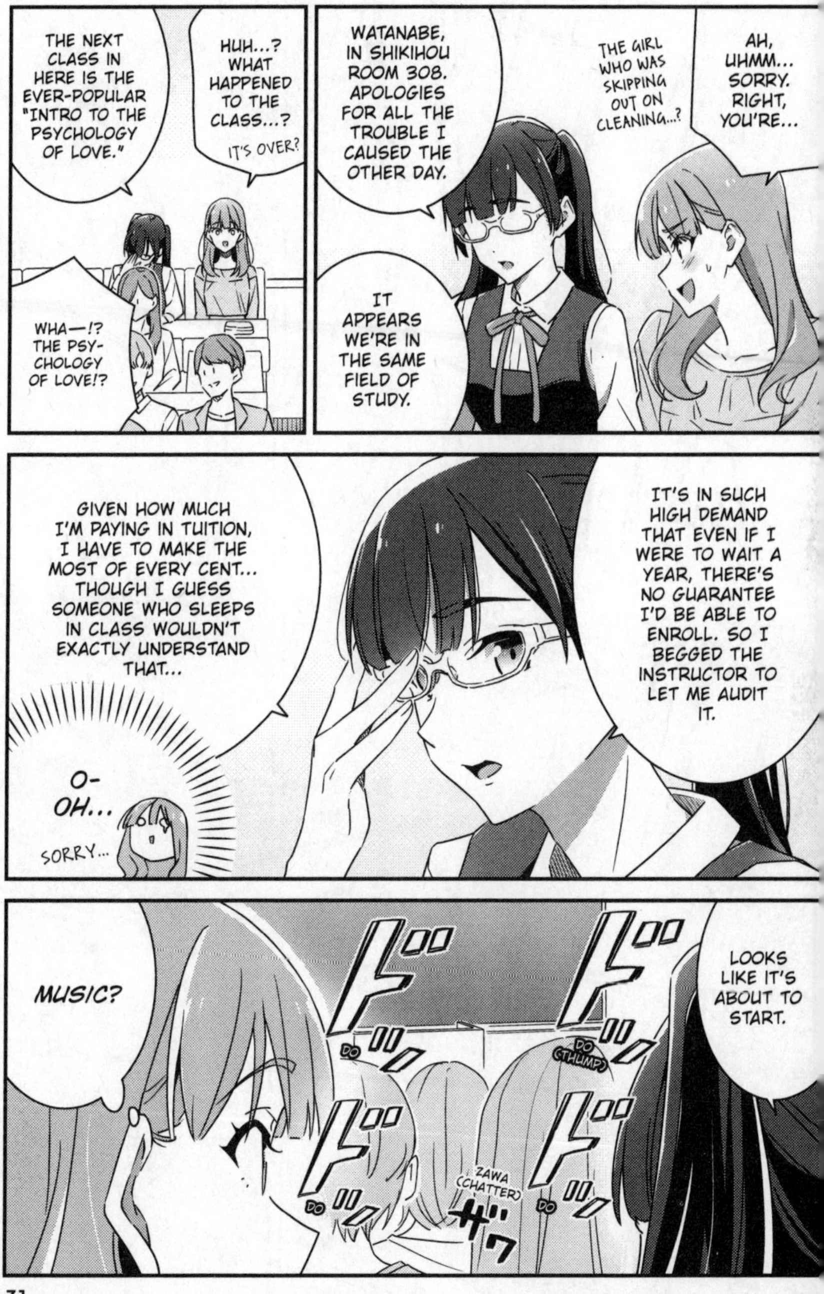
AH, UHMM... SORRY. RIGHT, YOU'RE...
THE GIRL WHO WAS SKIPPING OUT ON CLEANING...?
WATANABE, IN SHIKIHOU ROOM 308. APOLOGIES FOR ALL THE TROUBLE I CAUSED THE OTHER DAY.
IT APPEARS WE'RE IN THE SAME FIELD OF STUDY.
HUH...? WHAT HAPPENED TO THE CLASS...?
IT'S OVER?
THE NEXT CLASS IN HERE IS THE EVER-POPULAR "INTRO TO THE PSYCHOLOGY OF LOVE."
WHA—!? THE PSYCHOLOGY OF LOVE!?
IT'S IN SUCH HIGH DEMAND THAT EVEN IF I WERE TO WAIT A YEAR, THERE'S NO GUARANTEE I'D BE ABLE TO ENROLL. SO I BEGGED THE INSTRUCTOR TO LET ME AUDIT IT.
GIVEN HOW MUCH I'M PAYING IN TUITION, I HAVE TO MAKE THE MOST OF EVERY CENT... THOUGH I GUESS SOMEONE WHO SLEEPS IN CLASS WOULDN'T EXACTLY UNDERSTAND THAT...
O-OH...
SORRY...
LOOKS LIKE IT'S ABOUT TO START.
DO (THUMP)
DO
ZAWA (CHATTER)
DO
DO
MUSIC?

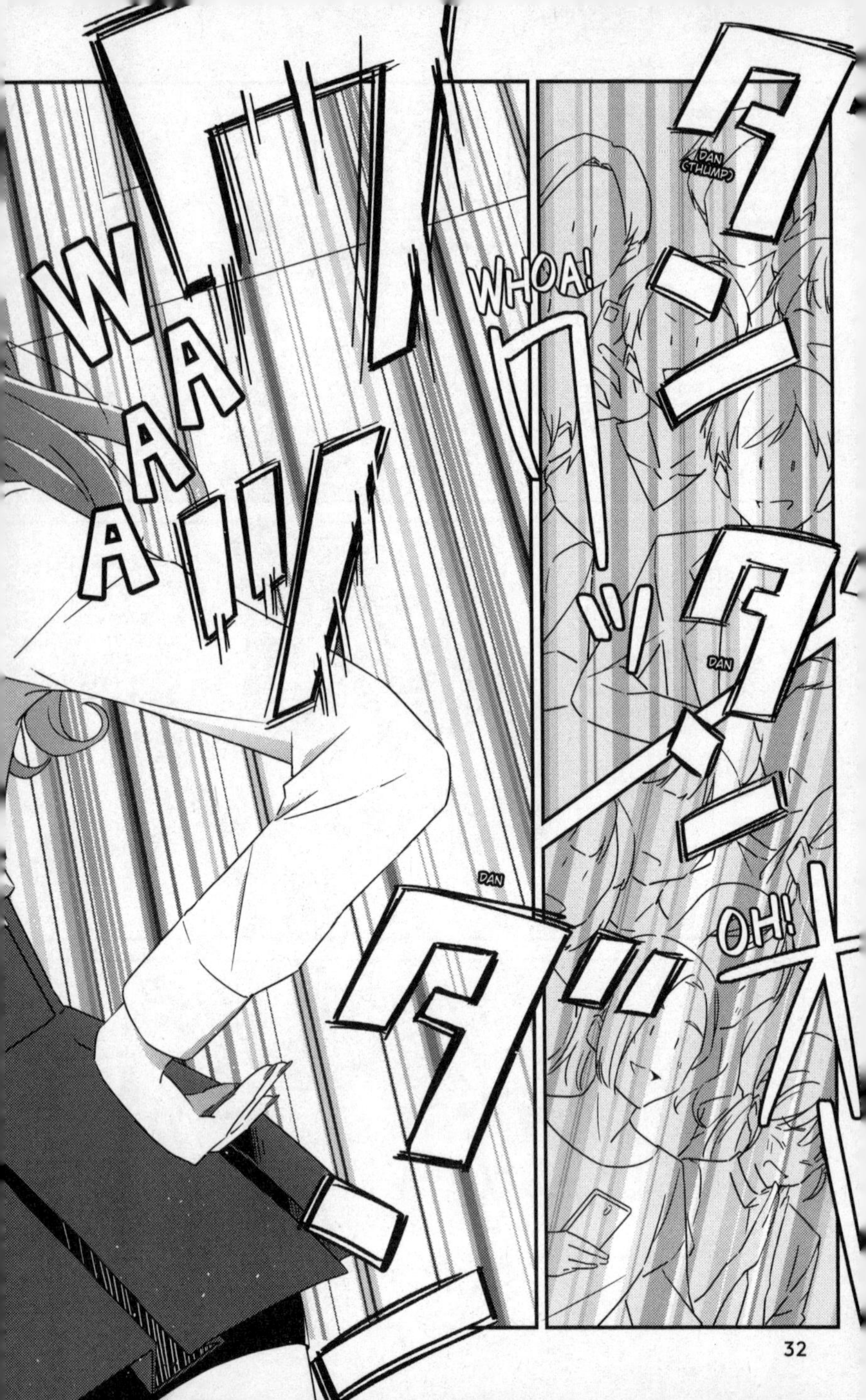
DAN (THUMP)
WHOA!
DAN
OH!
WAAA!!
DAN

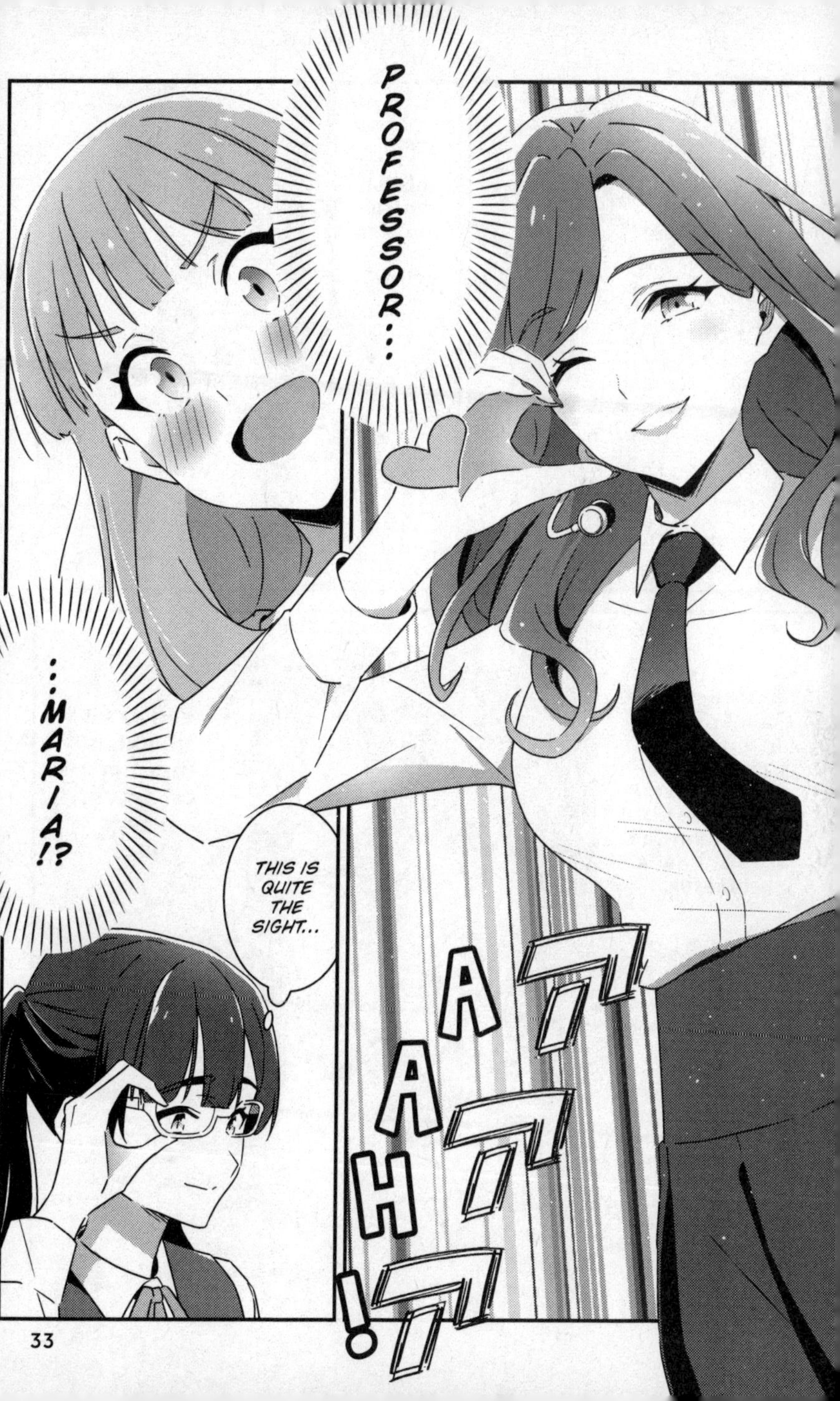
PROFESSOR...
...MARIA!?
AAH!
THIS IS QUITE THE SIGHT...

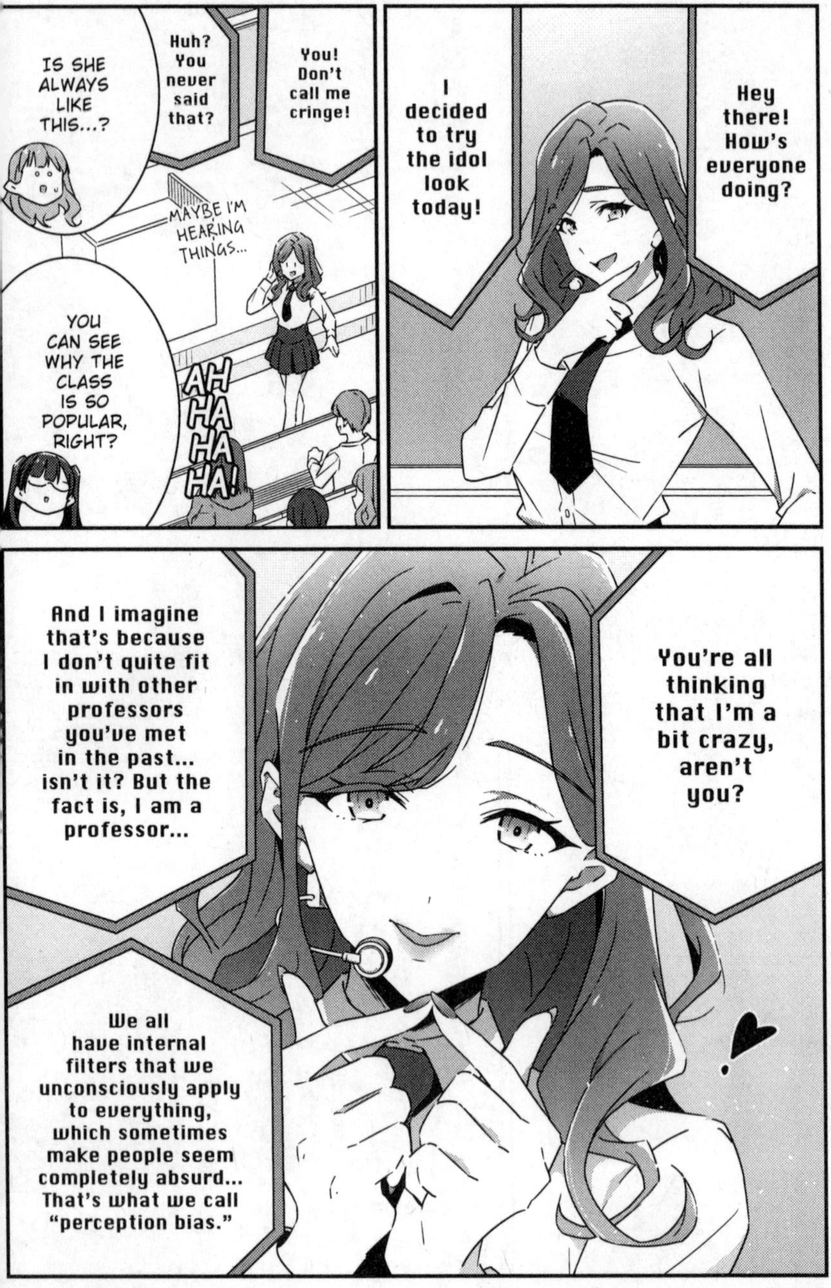
Hey there! How's everyone doing?
I decided to try the idol look today!
You! Don't call me cringe!
Huh? You never said that?
IS SHE ALWAYS LIKE THIS...?
MAYBE I'M HEARING THINGS...
AH HA HA HA HA!
YOU CAN SEE WHY THE CLASS IS SO POPULAR, RIGHT?
You're all thinking that I'm a bit crazy, aren't you?
And I imagine that's because I don't quite fit in with other professors you've met in the past... isn't it? But the fact is, I am a professor...
We all have internal filters that we unconsciously apply to everything, which sometimes make people seem completely absurd... That's what we call "perception bias."

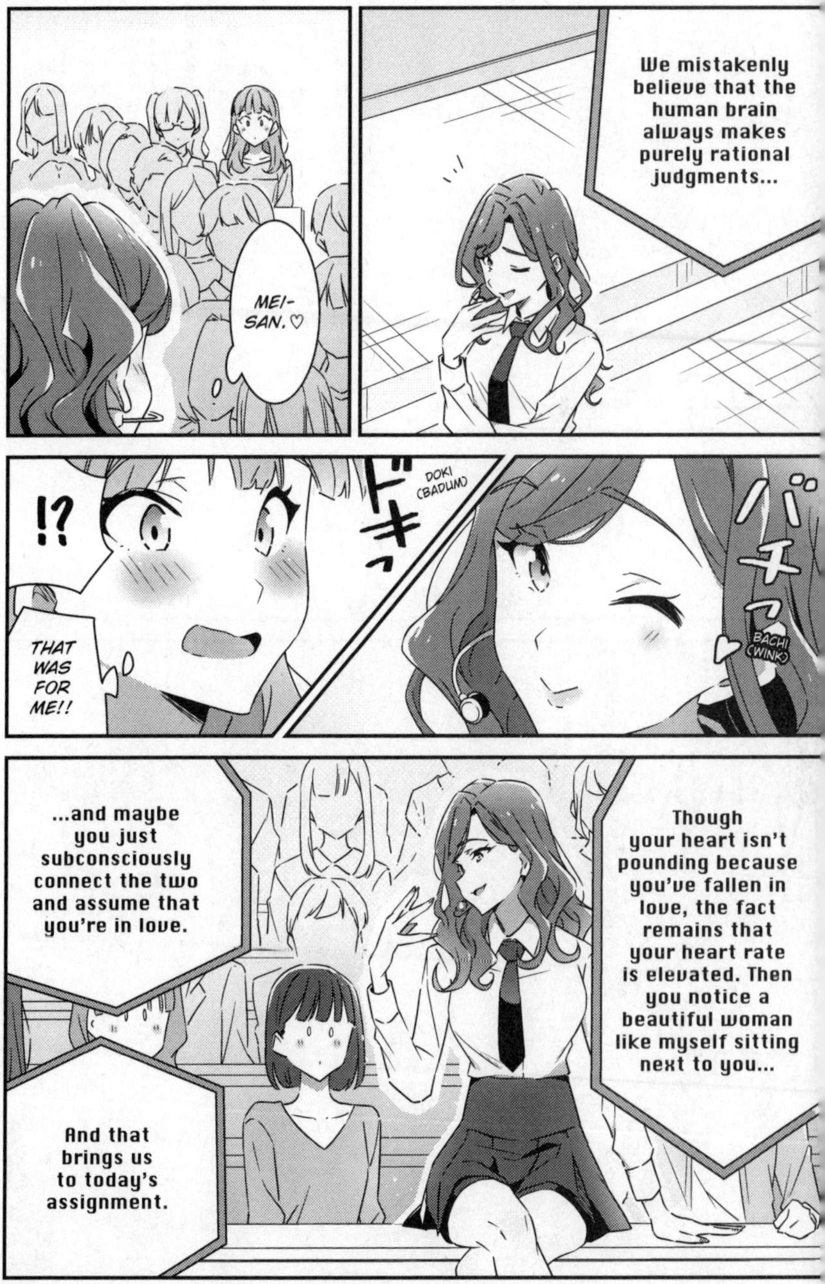
We mistakenly believe that the human brain always makes purely rational judgments...
MEI-SAN.♡
バチッ
BACHI (WINK)
ドキッ
DOKI (BADUM)
!?
THAT WAS FOR ME!!
Though your heart isn't pounding because you've fallen in love, the fact remains that your heart rate is elevated. Then you notice a beautiful woman like myself sitting next to you...
...and maybe you just subconsciously connect the two and assume that you're in love.
And that brings us to today's assignment.

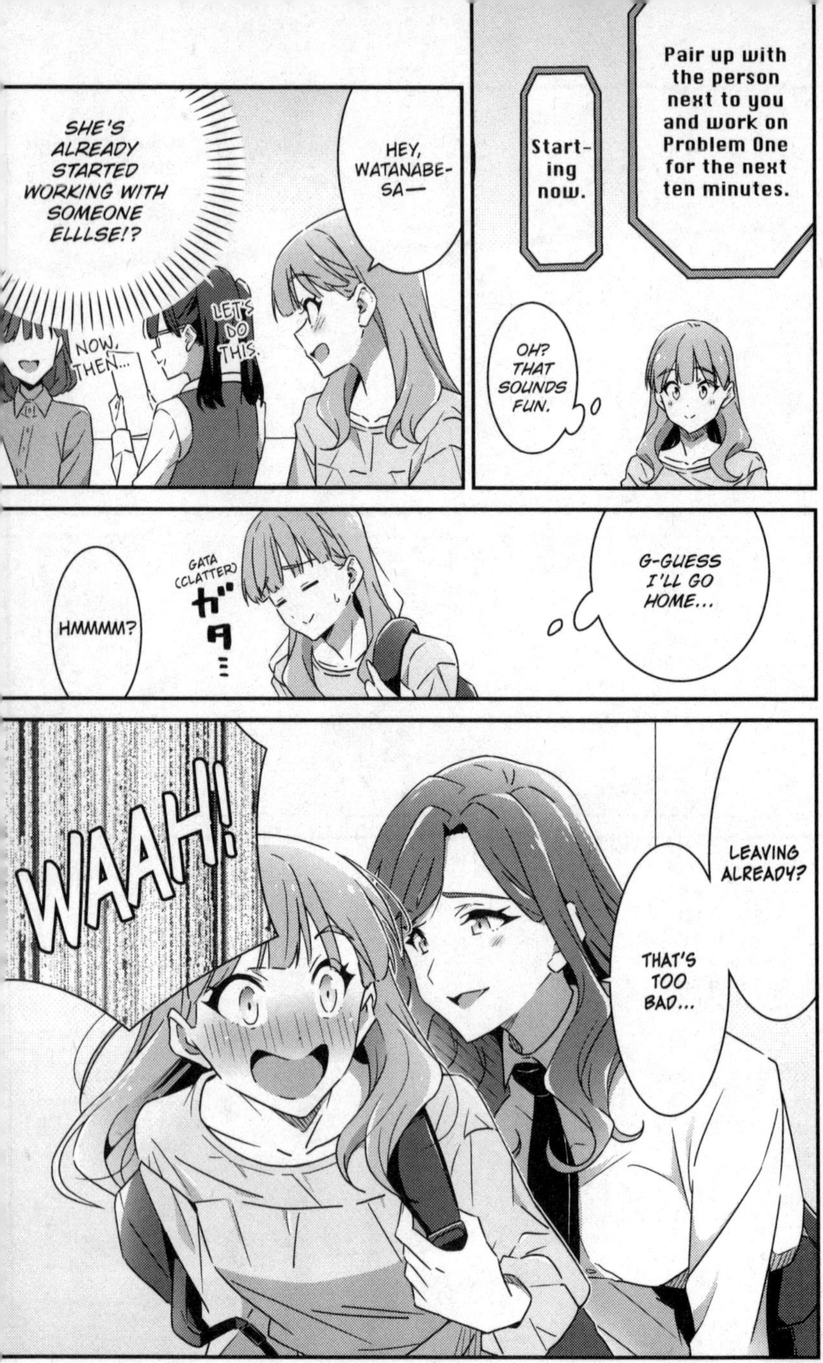
Pair up with the person next to you and work on Problem One for the next ten minutes.
Start-ing now.
OH? THAT SOUNDS FUN.
HEY, WATANABE-SA—
SHE'S ALREADY STARTED WORKING WITH SOMEONE ELLLSE!?
LET'S DO THIS.
NOW, THEN...
G-GUESS I'LL GO HOME...
GATA (CLATTER)
ガタ
HMMMM?
LEAVING ALREADY?
THAT'S TOO BAD...
WAAH!

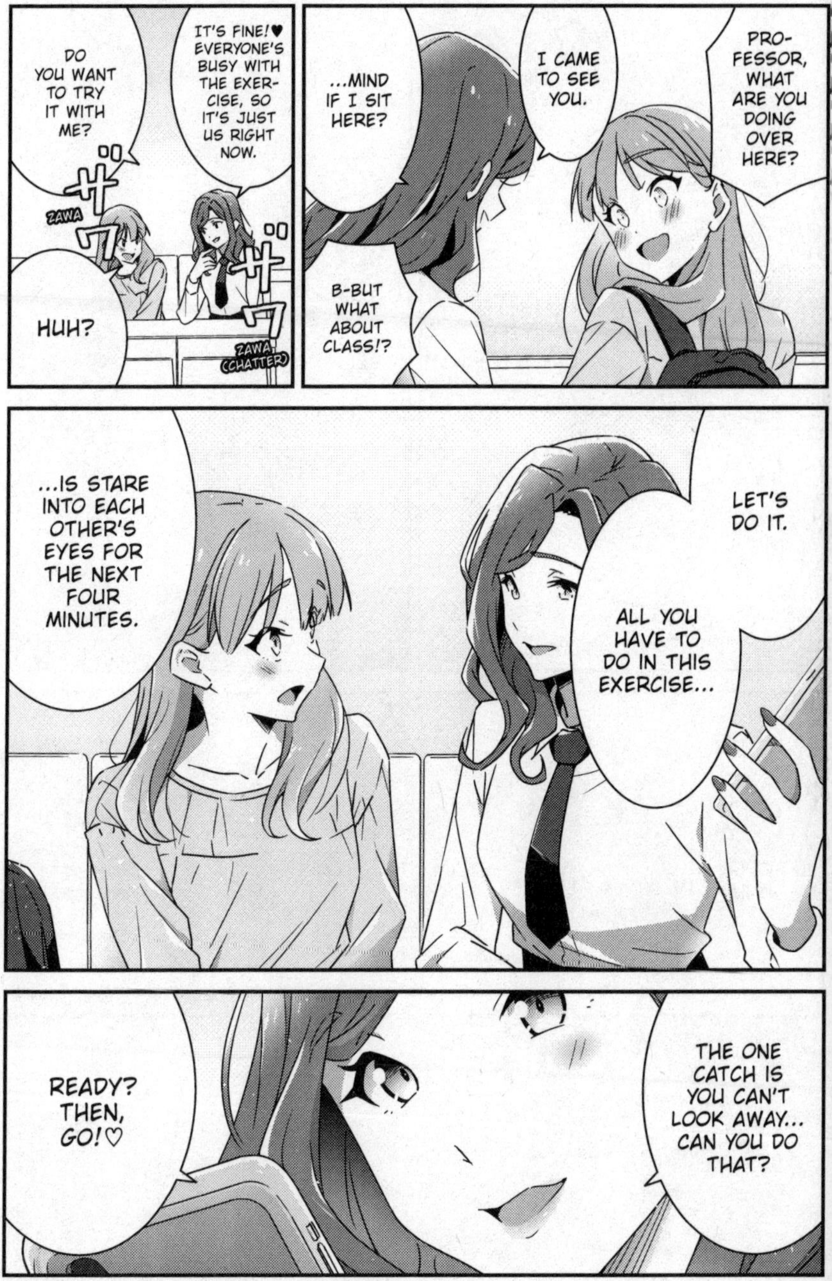
PRO-FESSOR, WHAT ARE YOU DOING OVER HERE?
I CAME TO SEE YOU.
...MIND IF I SIT HERE?
B-BUT WHAT ABOUT CLASS!?
IT'S FINE!♥ EVERYONE'S BUSY WITH THE EXER-CISE, SO IT'S JUST US RIGHT NOW.
DO YOU WANT TO TRY IT WITH ME?
ZAWA (CHATTER)
ZAWA
HUH?
LET'S DO IT.
ALL YOU HAVE TO DO IN THIS EXERCISE...
...IS STARE INTO EACH OTHER'S EYES FOR THE NEXT FOUR MINUTES.
THE ONE CATCH IS YOU CAN'T LOOK AWAY... CAN YOU DO THAT?
READY? THEN, GO!♡

URK!

...J (STARE)

COME, NOW!

BA (FWISH)

SHE'S JUST TOO PRETTY. I CAN'T STARE DIRECTLY AT HER.

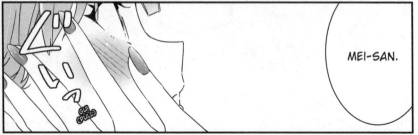

GUI (PULL)

MEI-SAN.

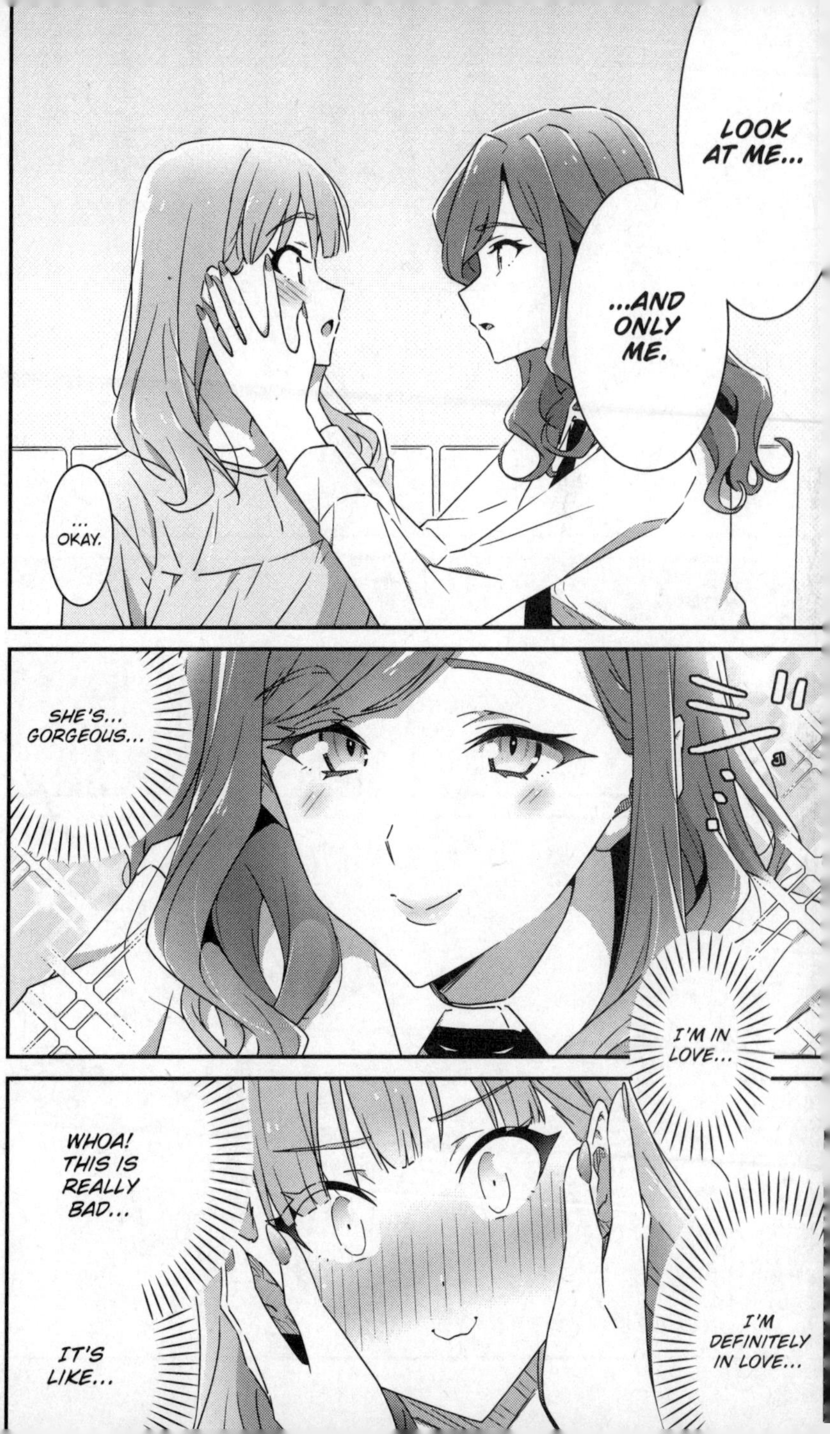
LOOK AT ME...
...AND ONLY ME.
... OKAY.
SHE'S... GORGEOUS...
I'M IN LOVE...
WHOA! THIS IS REALLY BAD...
I'M DEFINITELY IN LOVE...
IT'S LIKE...

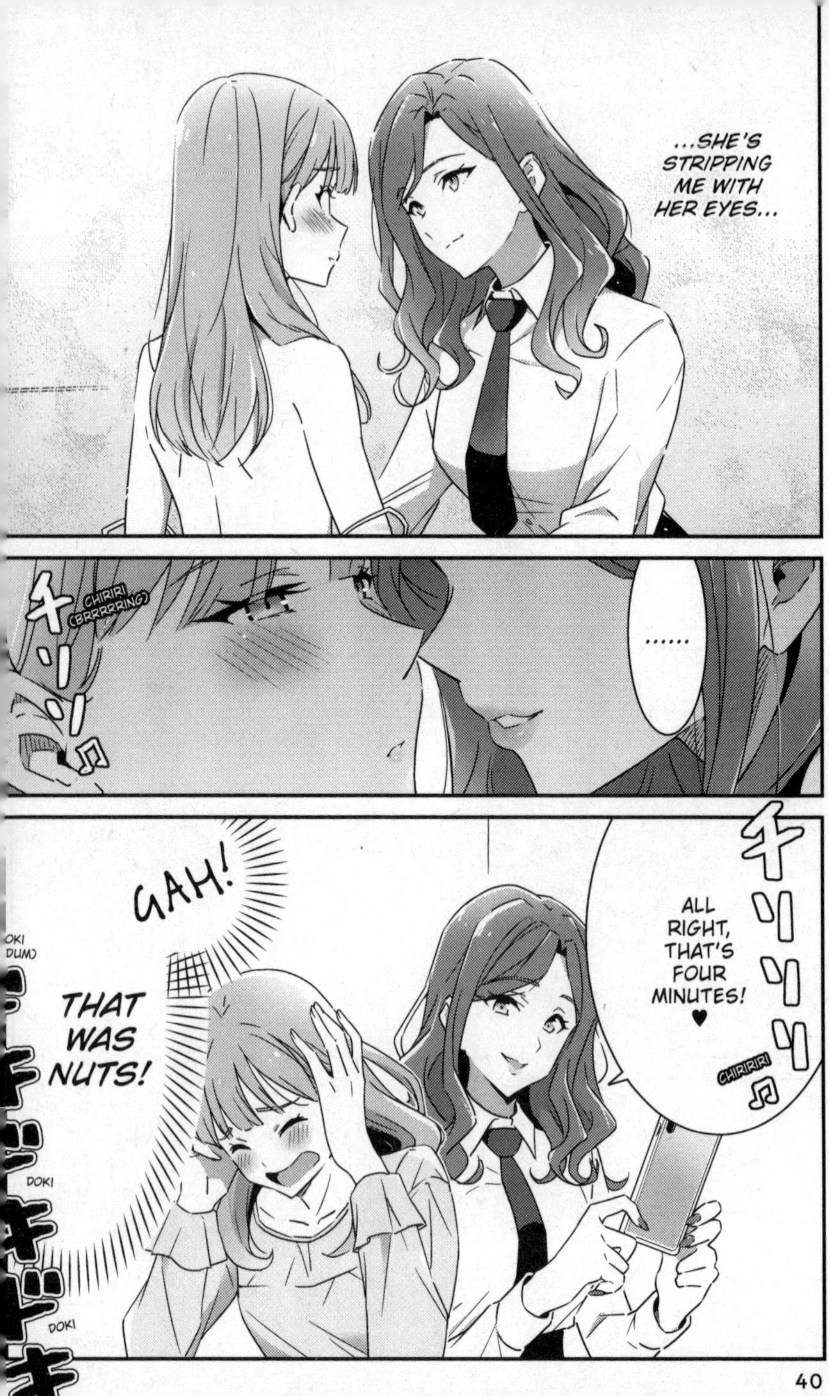
...SHE'S STRIPPING ME WITH HER EYES...
......
CHIRIRI (BRRRRRING)
CHIRIRI
ALL RIGHT, THAT'S FOUR MINUTES! ♥
GAH!
THAT WAS NUTS!
DOKI
DOKI

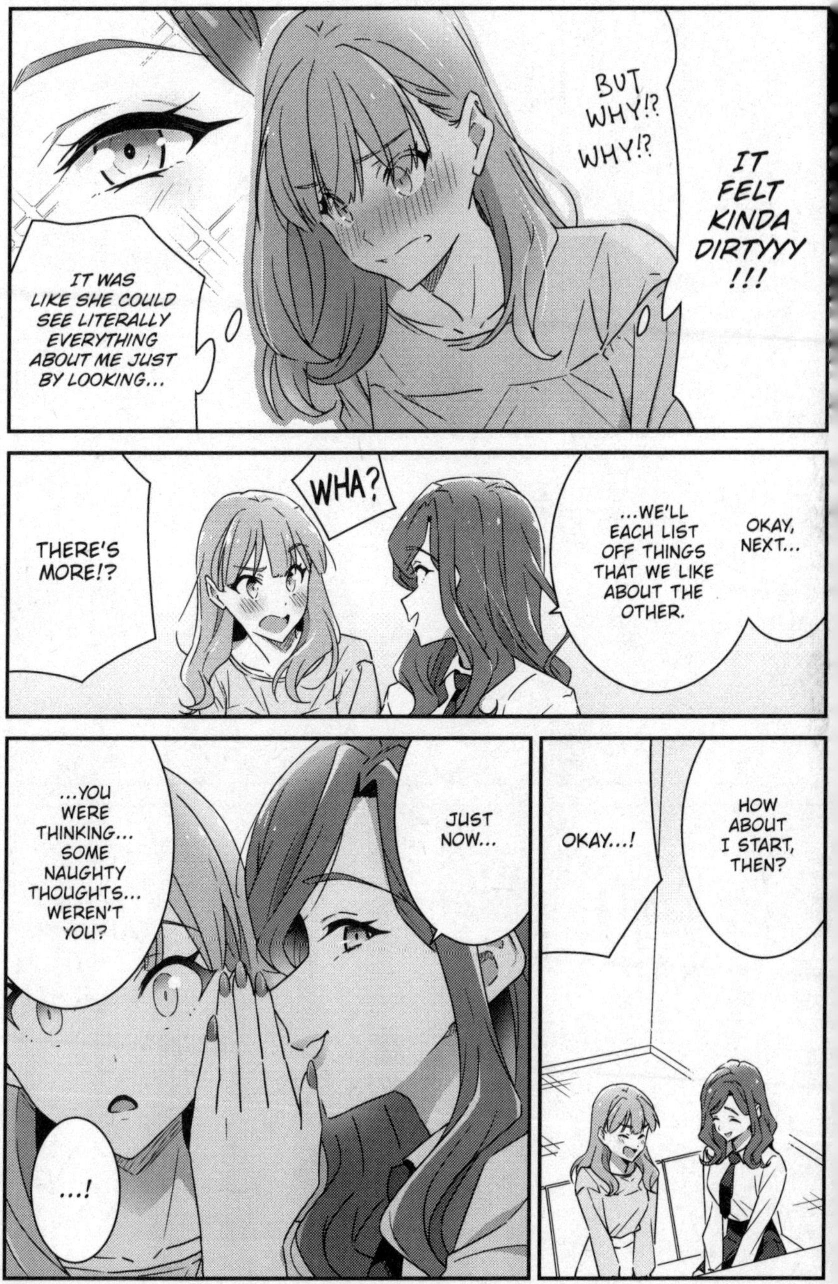
IT FELT KINDA DIRTYYY!!!
BUT WHY!? WHY!?
IT WAS LIKE SHE COULD SEE LITERALLY EVERYTHING ABOUT ME JUST BY LOOKING...
OKAY, NEXT...
...WE'LL EACH LIST OFF THINGS THAT WE LIKE ABOUT THE OTHER.
WHA?
THERE'S MORE!?
HOW ABOUT I START, THEN?
OKAY...!
JUST NOW...
...YOU WERE THINKING... SOME NAUGHTY THOUGHTS... WEREN'T YOU?
...!

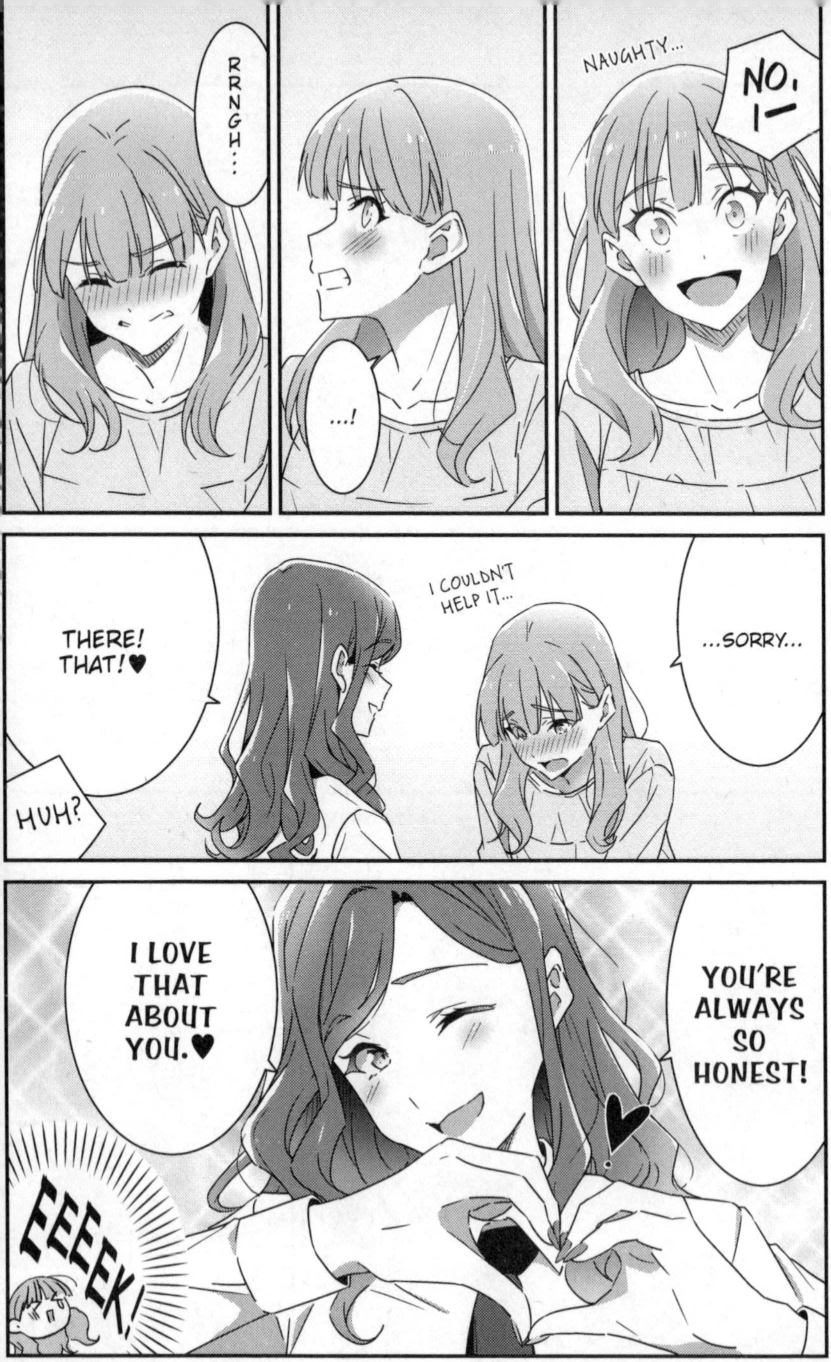
NO, I—
NAUGHTY...
...!
RRNGH...
...SORRY...
I COULDN'T HELP IT...
THERE! THAT!♥
HUH?
YOU'RE ALWAYS SO HONEST!
I LOVE THAT ABOUT YOU.♥
EEEEK!

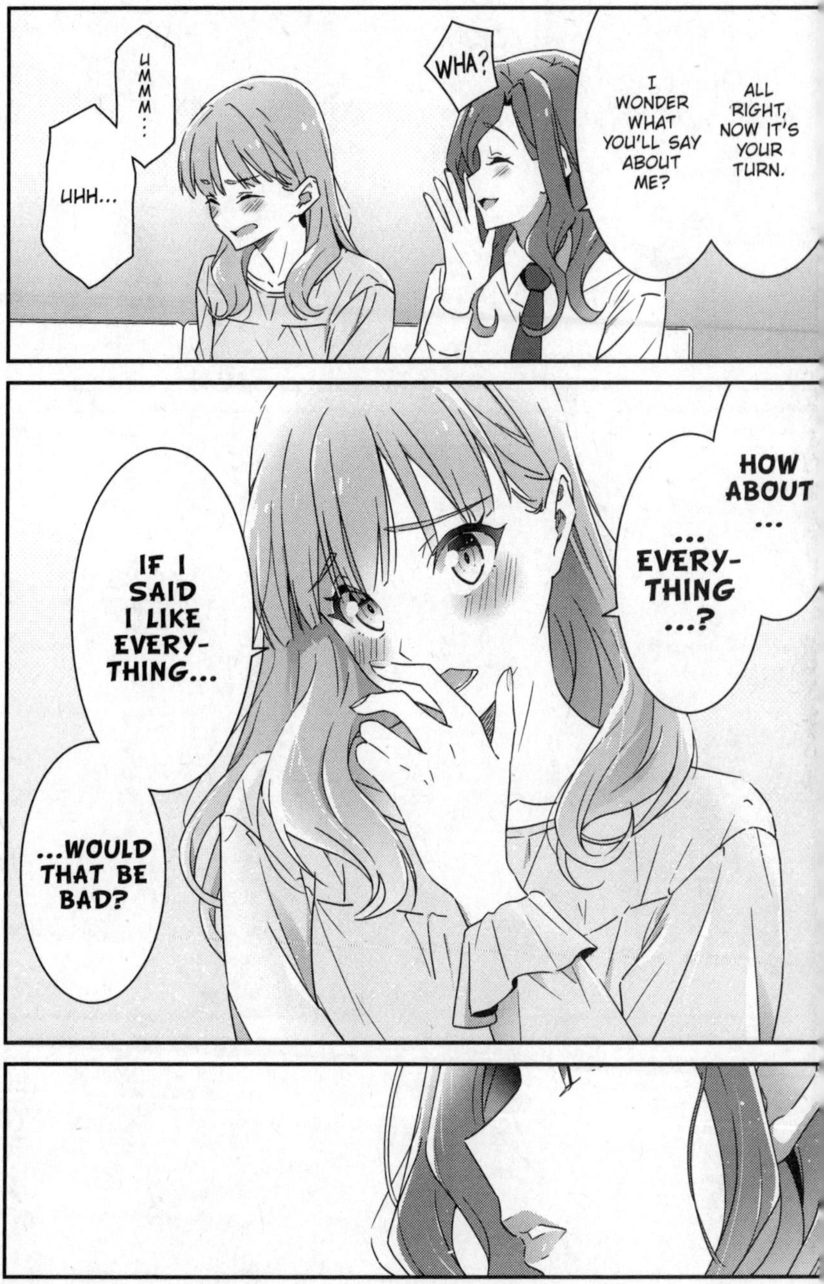
ALL RIGHT, NOW IT'S YOUR TURN.
I WONDER WHAT YOU'LL SAY ABOUT ME?
WHA?
UMMM...
UHH...
HOW ABOUT ...
... EVERY-THING ...?
IF I SAID I LIKE EVERY-THING...
...WOULD THAT BE BAD?

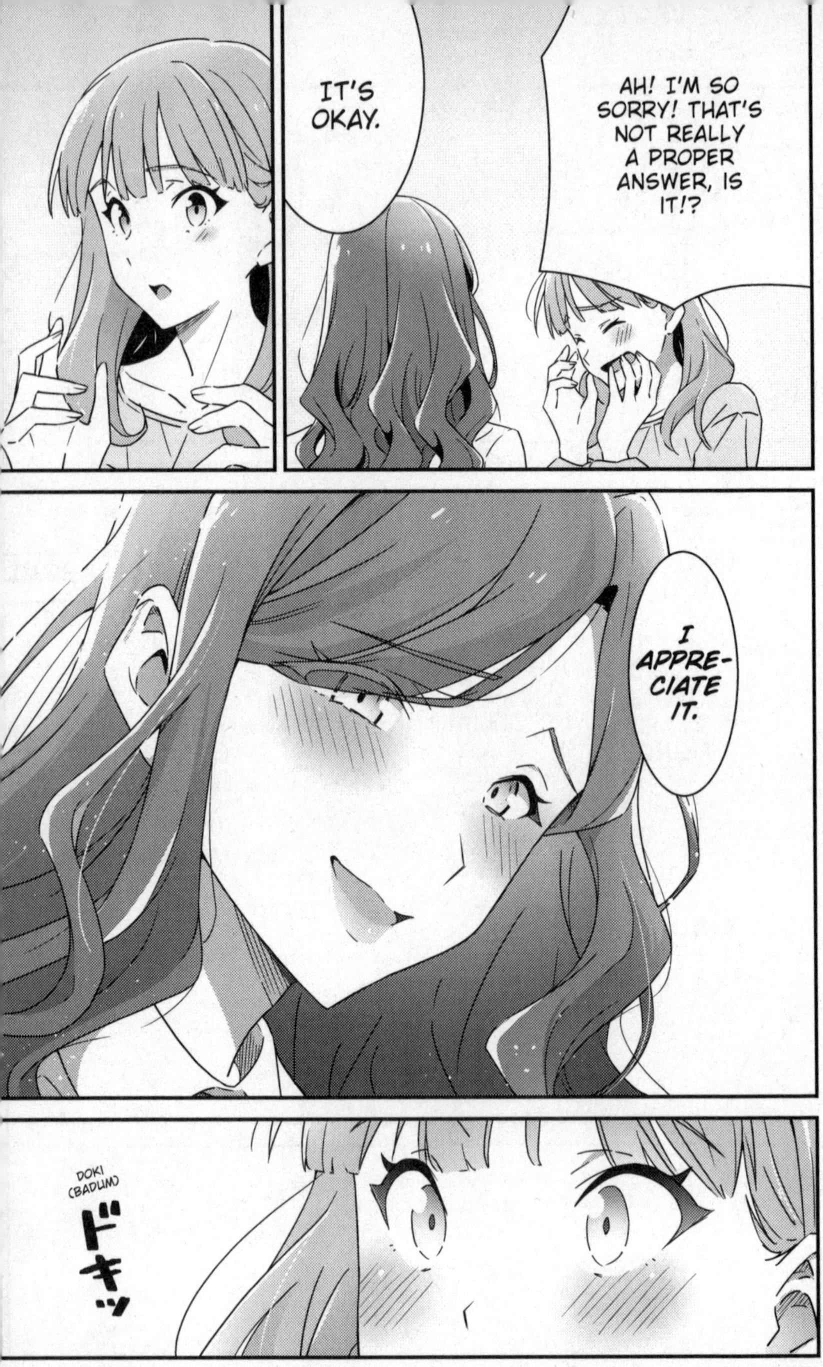
AH! I'M SO SORRY! THAT'S NOT REALLY A PROPER ANSWER, IS IT!?
IT'S OKAY.
I APPRE-CIATE IT.
DOKI (BADUM)
ドキッ

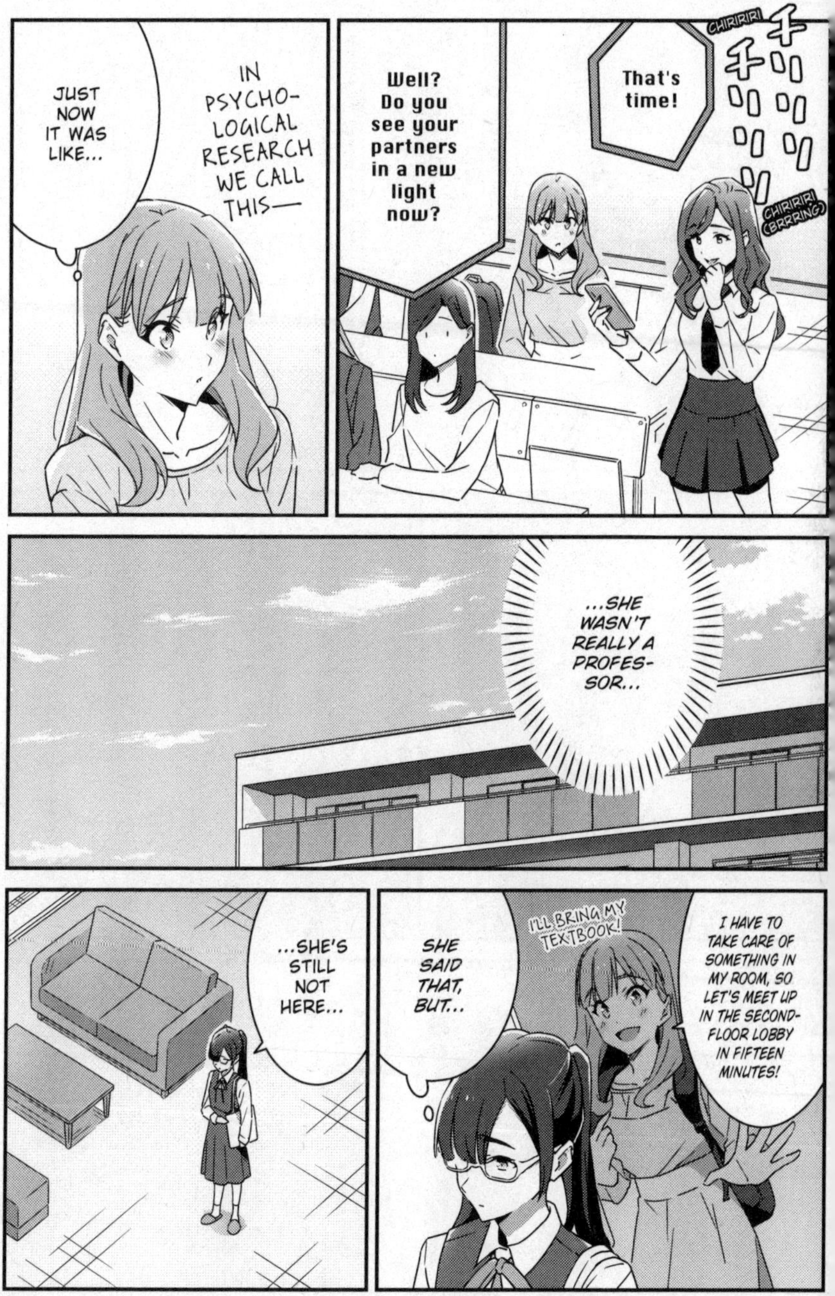
That's time!
CHIRIRIRI
CHIRIRIRI (BRRRING)
Well? Do you see your partners in a new light now?
IN PSYCHO-LOGICAL RESEARCH WE CALL THIS—
JUST NOW IT WAS LIKE...
...SHE WASN'T REALLY A PROFES-SOR...
I HAVE TO TAKE CARE OF SOMETHING IN MY ROOM, SO LET'S MEET UP IN THE SECOND-FLOOR LOBBY IN FIFTEEN MINUTES!
I'LL BRING MY TEXTBOOK!
SHE SAID THAT, BUT...
...SHE'S STILL NOT HERE...

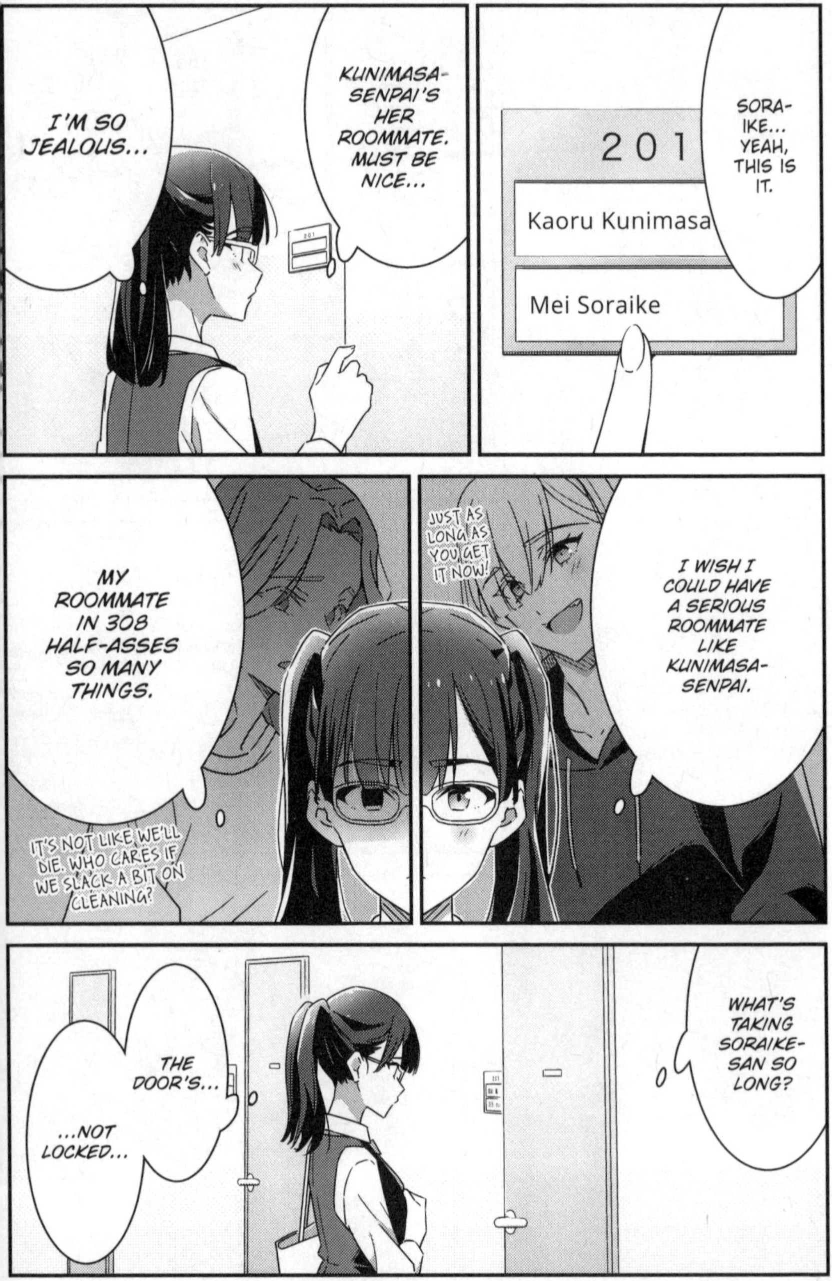
201
Kaoru Kunimasa
Mei Soraike
SORA-IKE... YEAH, THIS IS IT.
KUNIMASA-SENPAI'S HER ROOMMATE. MUST BE NICE...
I'M SO JEALOUS...
I WISH I COULD HAVE A SERIOUS ROOMMATE LIKE KUNIMASA-SENPAI.
JUST AS LONG AS YOU GET IT NOW!
MY ROOMMATE IN 308 HALF-ASSES SO MANY THINGS.
IT'S NOT LIKE WE'LL DIE. WHO CARES IF WE SLACK A BIT ON CLEANING?
WHAT'S TAKING SORAIKE-SAN SO LONG?
THE DOOR'S...
...NOT LOCKED...

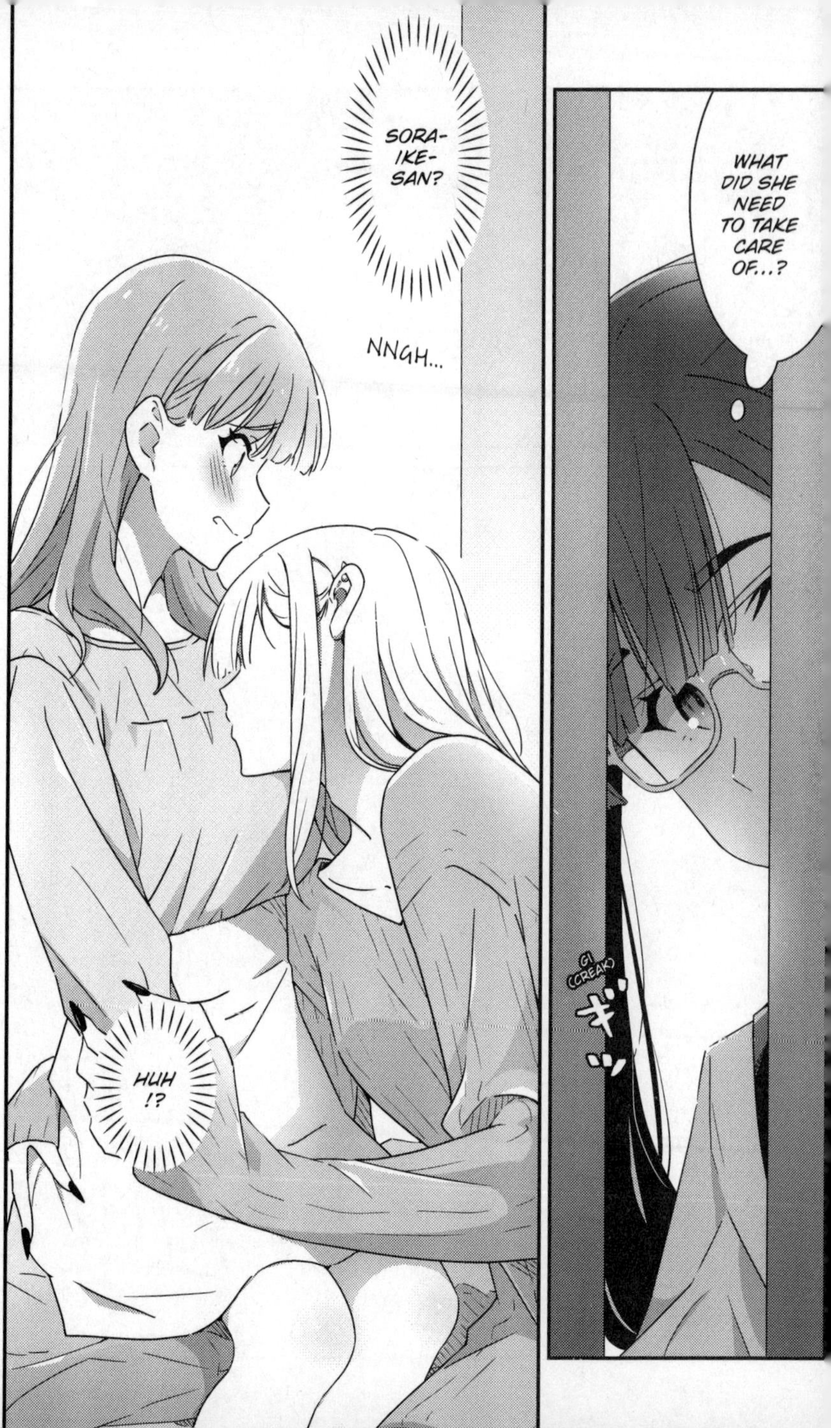
WHAT DID SHE NEED TO TAKE CARE OF...?
GI (CREAK)
ギッ
SORA-IKE-SAN?
NNGH...
HUH!?

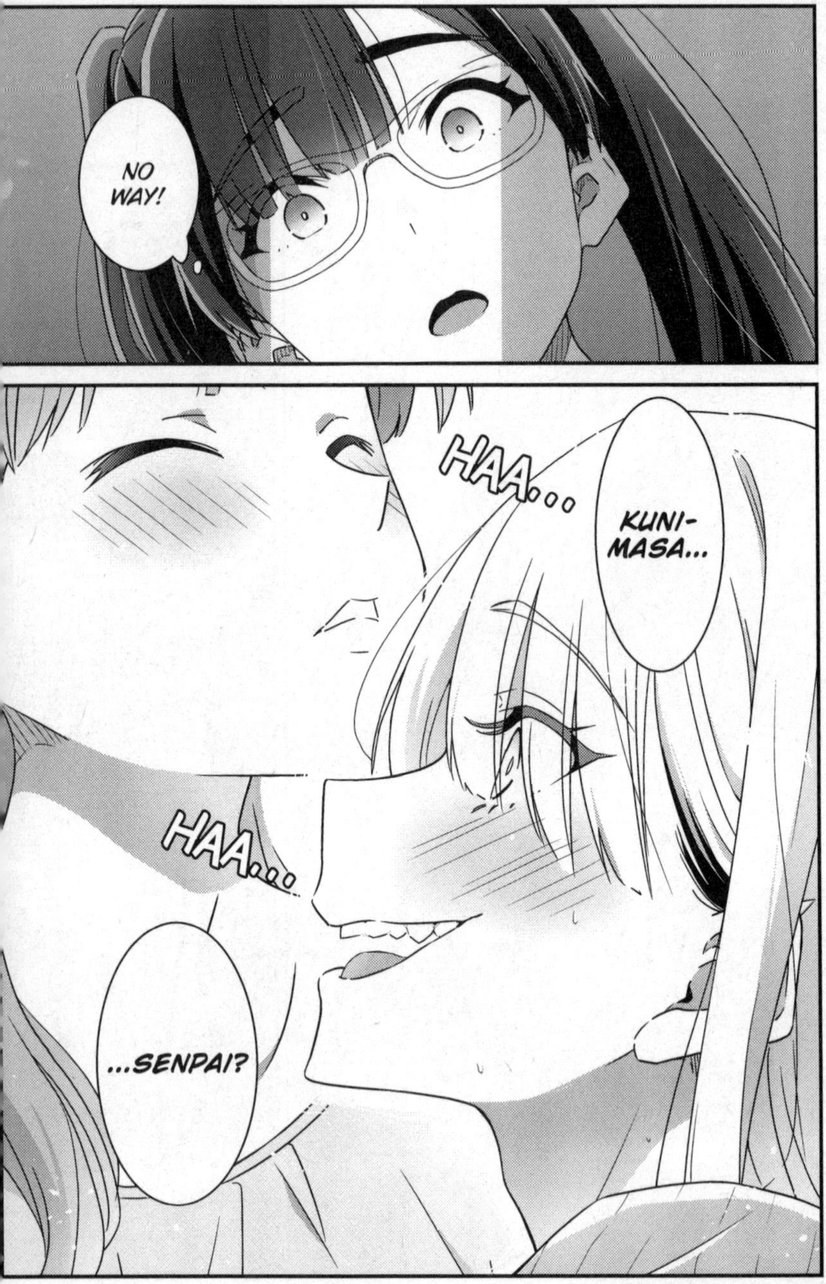
NO WAY!
KUNI-MASA...
HAA...
HAA...
...SENPAI?

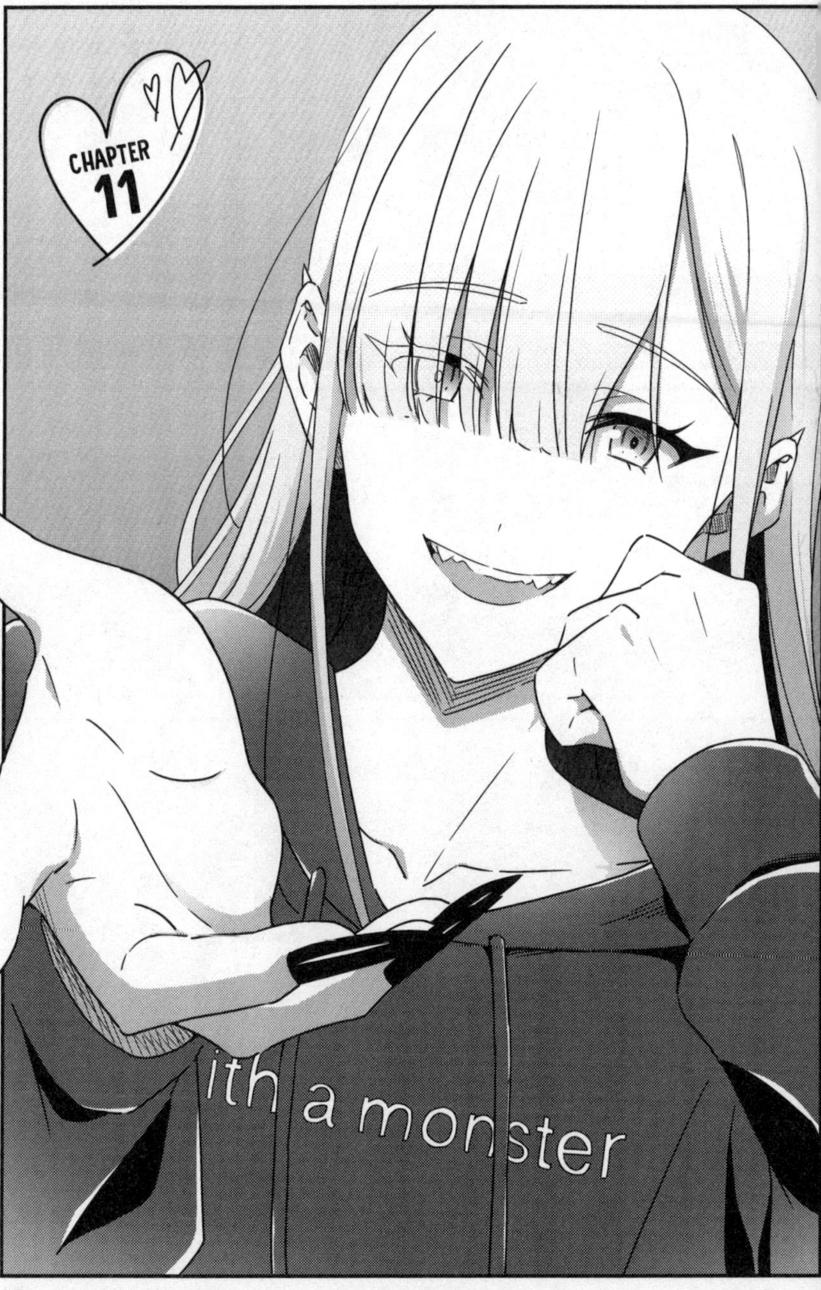
CHAPTER
11
ith a monster

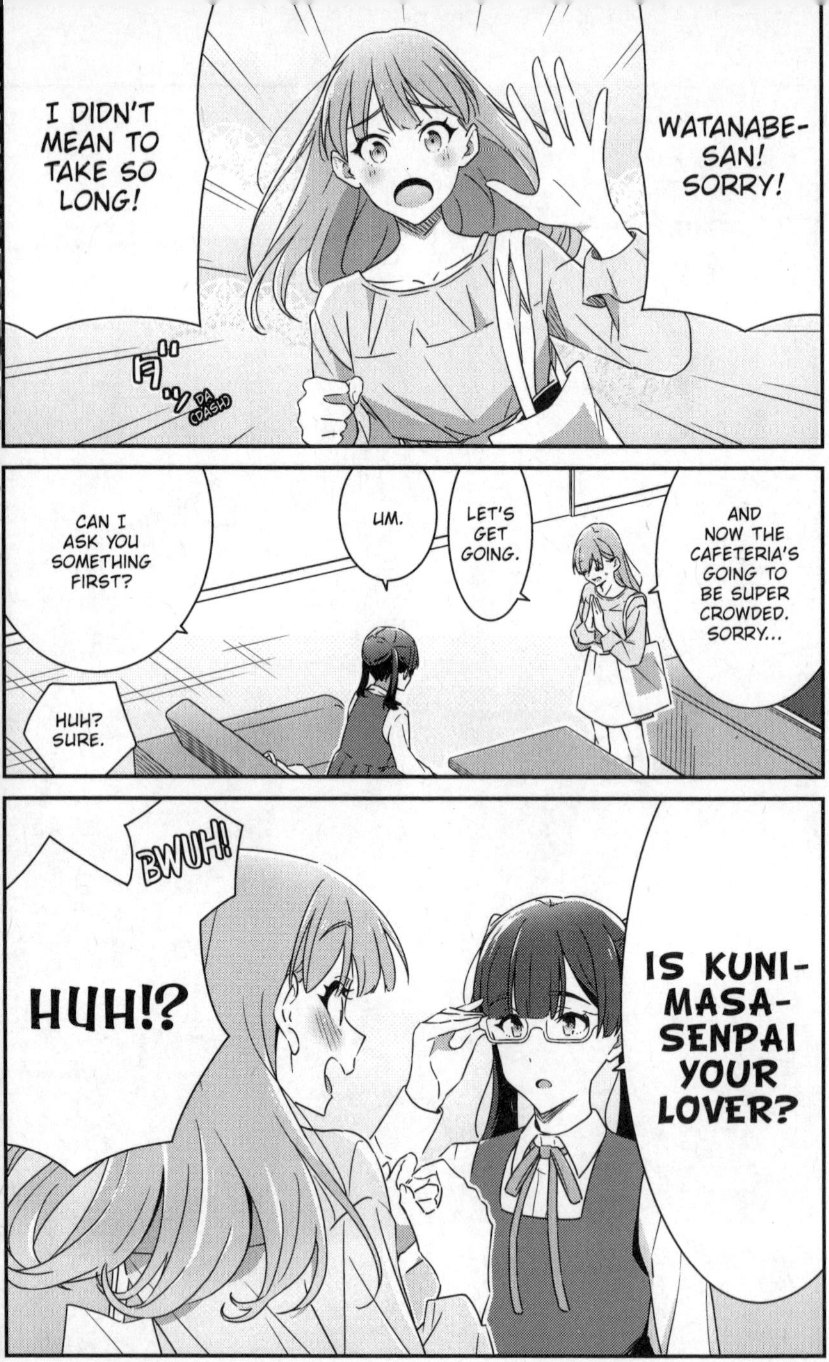
WATANABE-SAN! SORRY!
I DIDN'T MEAN TO TAKE SO LONG!
ダッ
DA (DASH)
AND NOW THE CAFETERIA'S GOING TO BE SUPER CROWDED. SORRY...
LET'S GET GOING.
UM.
CAN I ASK YOU SOMETHING FIRST?
HUH? SURE.
IS KUNI-MASA-SENPAI YOUR LOVER?
BWUH!
HUH!?

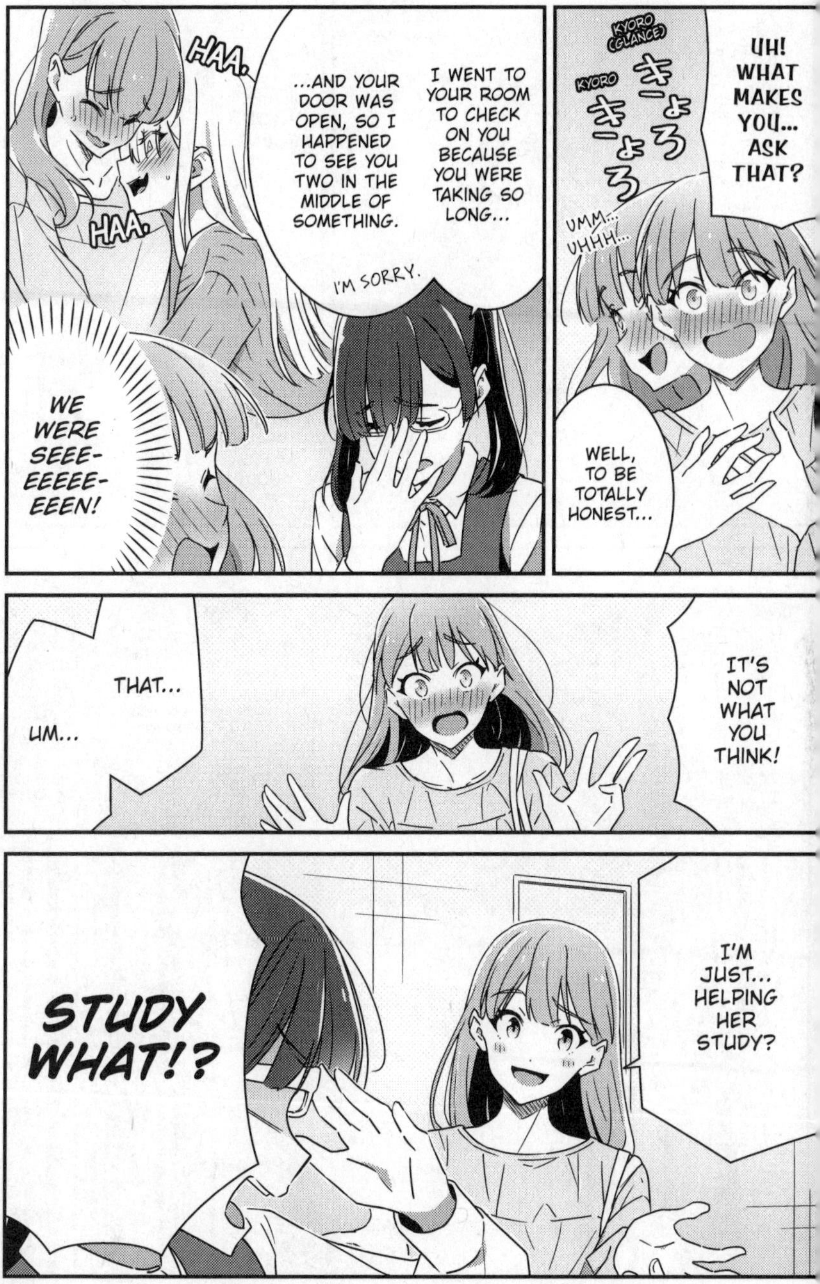
UH! WHAT MAKES YOU... ASK THAT?
KYORO (GLANCE)
きょろ
KYORO
きょろ
UMM... UHHH...
WELL, TO BE TOTALLY HONEST...
I WENT TO YOUR ROOM TO CHECK ON YOU BECAUSE YOU WERE TAKING SO LONG...
...AND YOUR DOOR WAS OPEN, SO I HAPPENED TO SEE YOU TWO IN THE MIDDLE OF SOMETHING.
I'M SORRY.
HAA.
HAA.
WE WERE SEEE-EEEEE-EEEN!
IT'S NOT WHAT YOU THINK!
THAT...
UM...
I'M JUST... HELPING HER STUDY?
STUDY WHAT!?

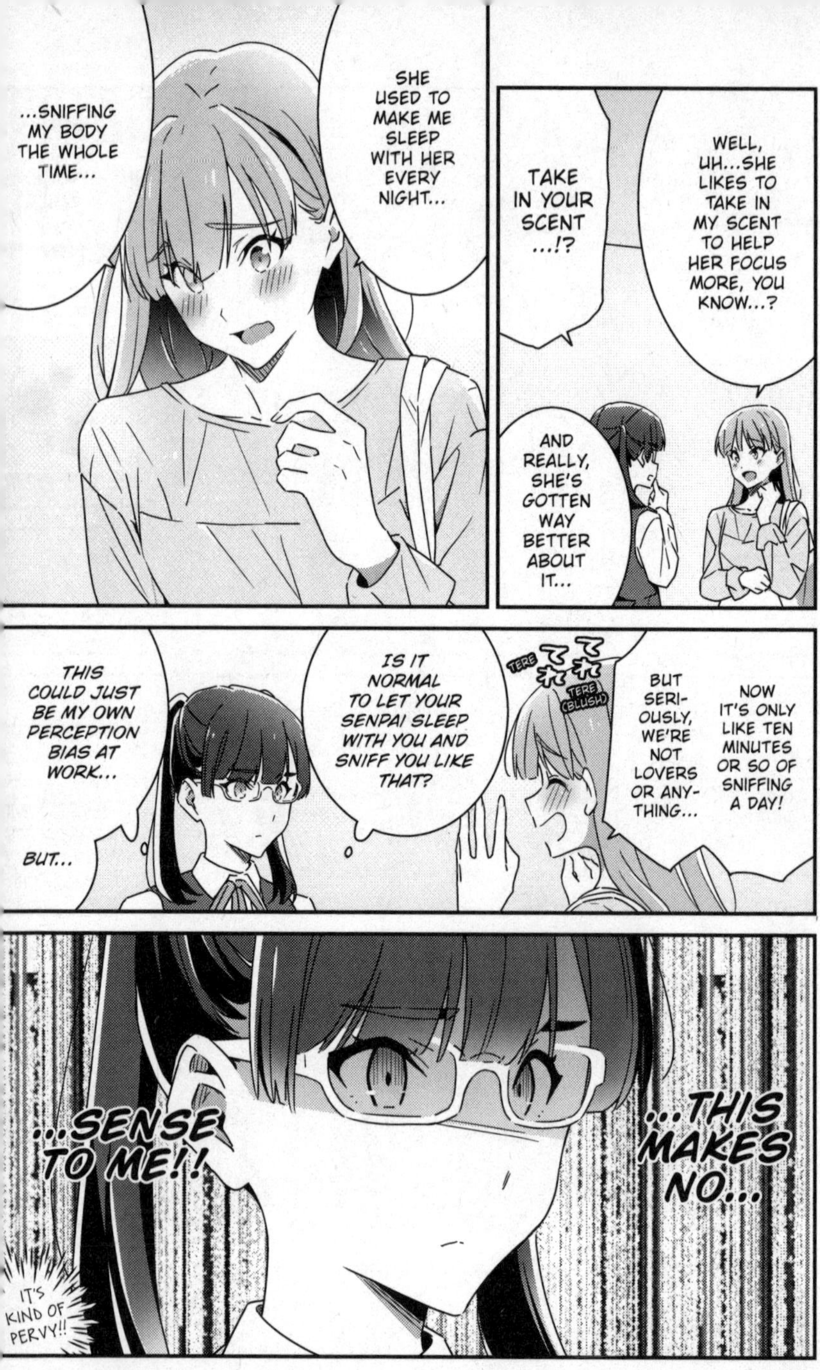
WELL, UH...SHE LIKES TO TAKE IN MY SCENT TO HELP HER FOCUS MORE, YOU KNOW...?
TAKE IN YOUR SCENT ...!?
AND REALLY, SHE'S GOTTEN WAY BETTER ABOUT IT...
SHE USED TO MAKE ME SLEEP WITH HER EVERY NIGHT...
...SNIFFING MY BODY THE WHOLE TIME...
NOW IT'S ONLY LIKE TEN MINUTES OR SO OF SNIFFING A DAY!
BUT SERI-OUSLY, WE'RE NOT LOVERS OR ANY-THING...
TERE TERE (BLUSH)
IS IT NORMAL TO LET YOUR SENPAI SLEEP WITH YOU AND SNIFF YOU LIKE THAT?
THIS COULD JUST BE MY OWN PERCEPTION BIAS AT WORK...
BUT...
...THIS MAKES NO...
...SENSE TO ME!!
IT'S KIND OF PERVY!!

...SENSE TO ME!!

THIS MAKES NO...

EVERYONE ELSE CAN READ THIS JUST FINE...

I PICKED THE EASIEST CLASS I COULD FIND TO FILL MY ENGLISH REQUIREMENT...

ALL RIGHT. <ONCE UPON A TIME...>

OKAY, TIME TO READ THE LAST ONE. NEXT PERSON.

...TO UNDER-STAND THIIIIS!

I'M NEVER GOING...

THERE'S... NO JAPA-NESE...

...BUT I CAN'T...

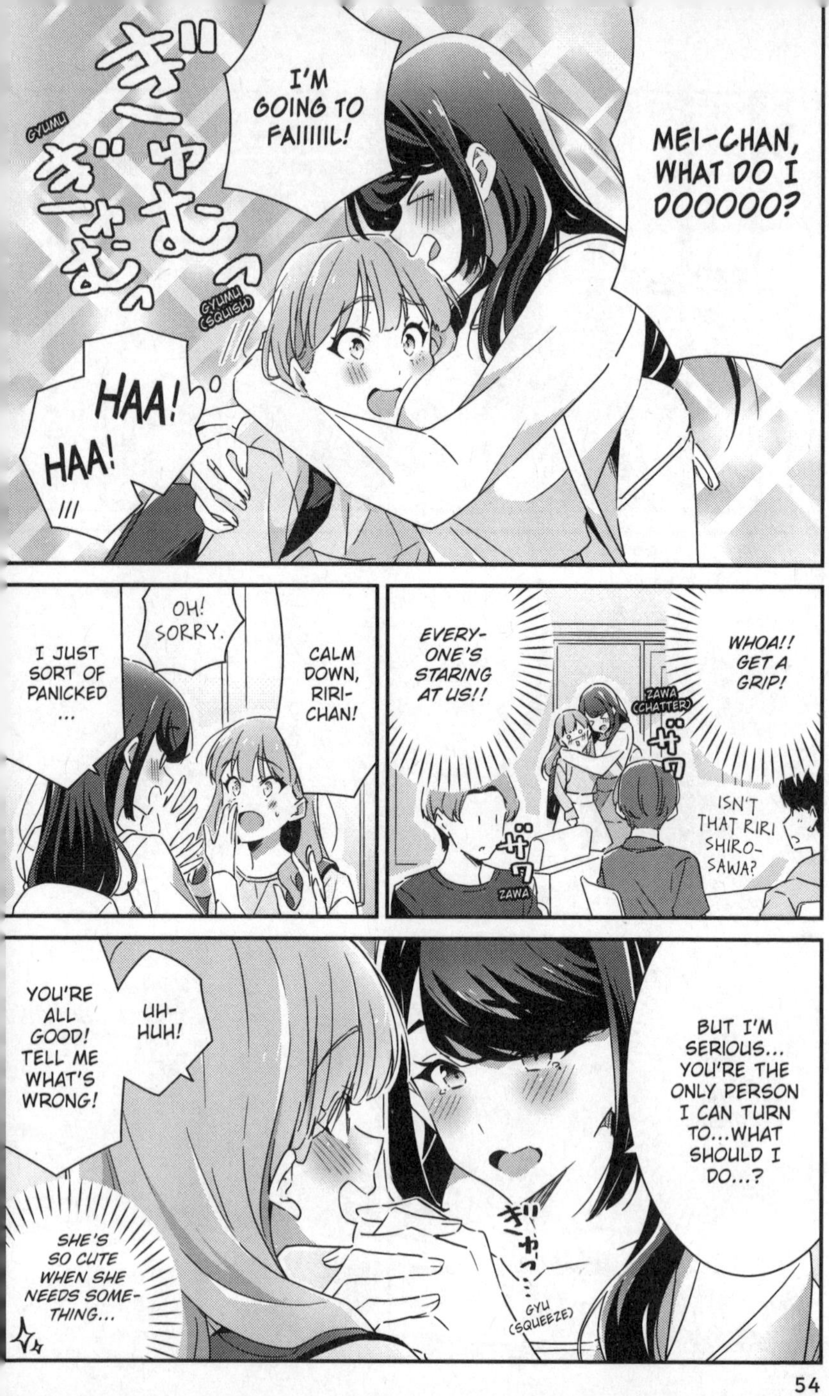
MEI-CHAN, WHAT DO I DOOOOOO?
I'M GOING TO FAIIIIIL!
GYUMU
GYUMU (SQUISH)
HAA! HAA!
WHOA!! GET A GRIP!
EVERY-ONE'S STARING AT US!!
ZAWA (CHATTER)
ISN'T THAT RIRI SHIRO-SAWA?
ZAWA
CALM DOWN, RIRI-CHAN!
OH! SORRY.
I JUST SORT OF PANICKED ...
BUT I'M SERIOUS... YOU'RE THE ONLY PERSON I CAN TURN TO...WHAT SHOULD I DO...?
UH-HUH!
YOU'RE ALL GOOD! TELL ME WHAT'S WRONG!
GYU (SQUEEZE)
SHE'S SO CUTE WHEN SHE NEEDS SOME-THING...

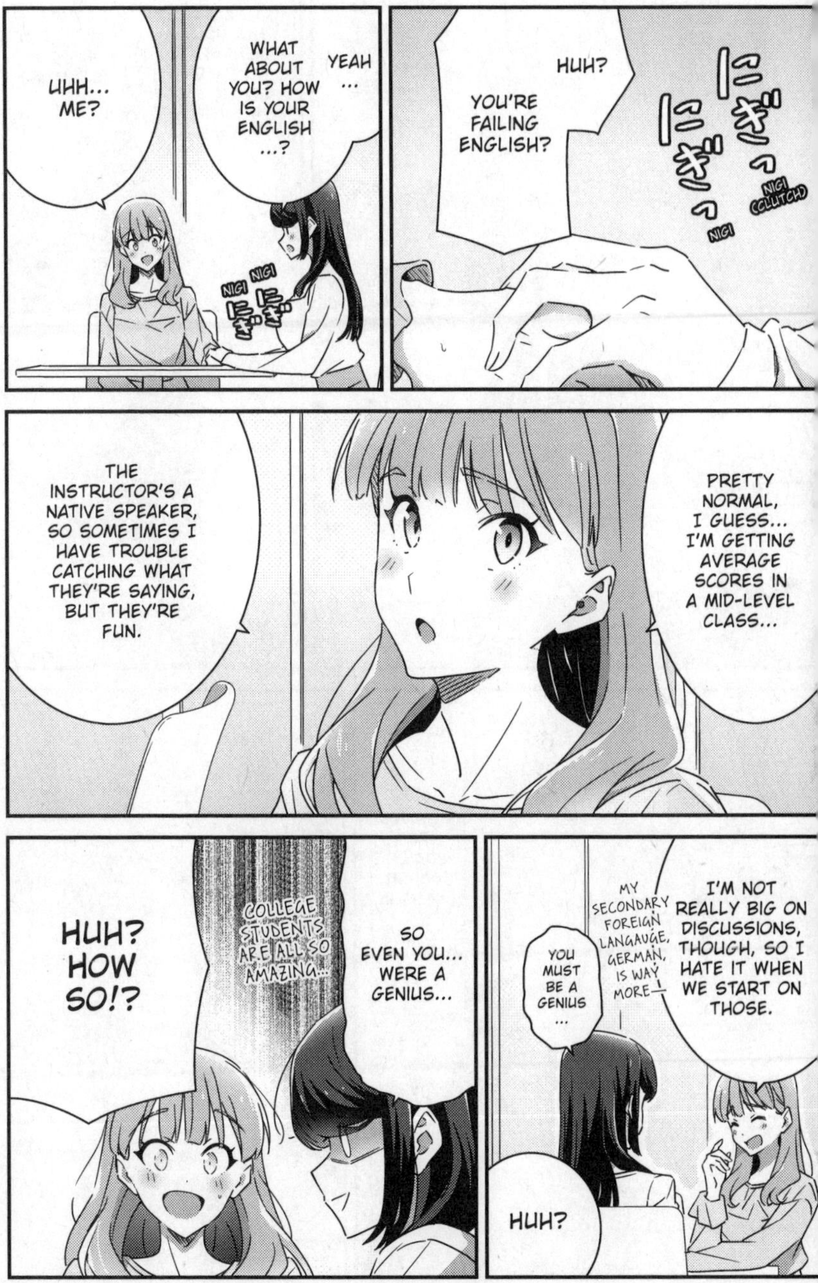
HUH?
YOU'RE FAILING ENGLISH?
にぎっ
にぎっ
NIGI (CLUTCH)
NIGI
YEAH ...
WHAT ABOUT YOU? HOW IS YOUR ENGLISH ...?
UHH... ME?
NIGI
NIGI
にぎ
にぎ
PRETTY NORMAL, I GUESS... I'M GETTING AVERAGE SCORES IN A MID-LEVEL CLASS...
THE INSTRUCTOR'S A NATIVE SPEAKER, SO SOMETIMES I HAVE TROUBLE CATCHING WHAT THEY'RE SAYING, BUT THEY'RE FUN.
I'M NOT REALLY BIG ON DISCUSSIONS, THOUGH, SO I HATE IT WHEN WE START ON THOSE.
MY SECONDARY FOREIGN LANGAUGE, GERMAN, IS WAY MORE—
YOU MUST BE A GENIUS ...
HUH?
SO EVEN YOU... WERE A GENIUS...
COLLEGE STUDENTS ARE ALL SO AMAZING...
HUH? HOW SO!?

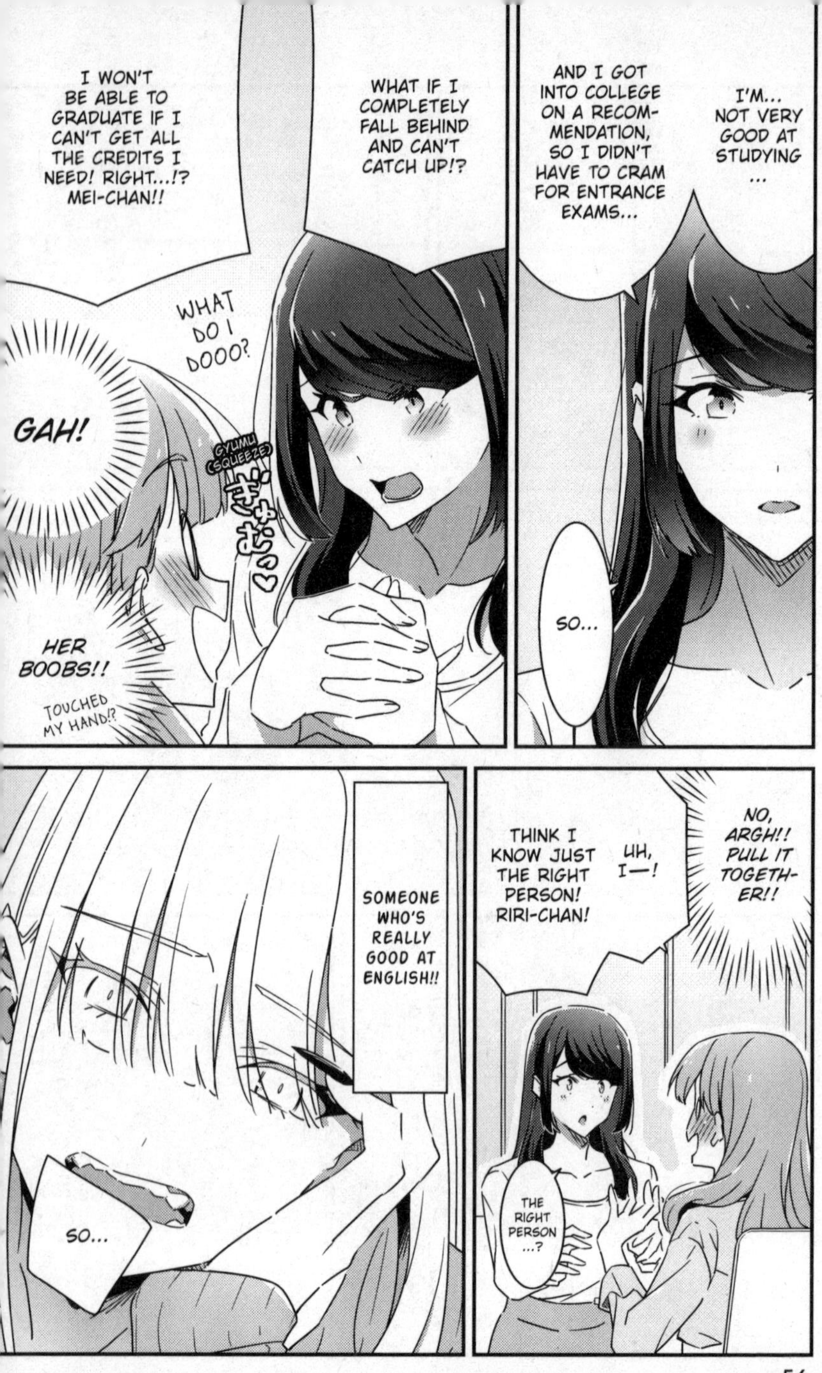
I'M... NOT VERY GOOD AT STUDYING...
AND I GOT INTO COLLEGE ON A RECOMMENDATION, SO I DIDN'T HAVE TO CRAM FOR ENTRANCE EXAMS...
SO...
WHAT IF I COMPLETELY FALL BEHIND AND CAN'T CATCH UP!?
I WON'T BE ABLE TO GRADUATE IF I CAN'T GET ALL THE CREDITS I NEED! RIGHT...!? MEI-CHAN!!
WHAT DO I DOOO?
GAH!
GYUMU (SQUEEZE)
ぎゅむっ♥
HER BOOBS!!
TOUCHED MY HAND!?
NO, ARGH!! PULL IT TOGETHER!!
UH, I—!
THINK I KNOW JUST THE RIGHT PERSON! RIRI-CHAN!
THE RIGHT PERSON...?
SOMEONE WHO'S REALLY GOOD AT ENGLISH!!
SO...

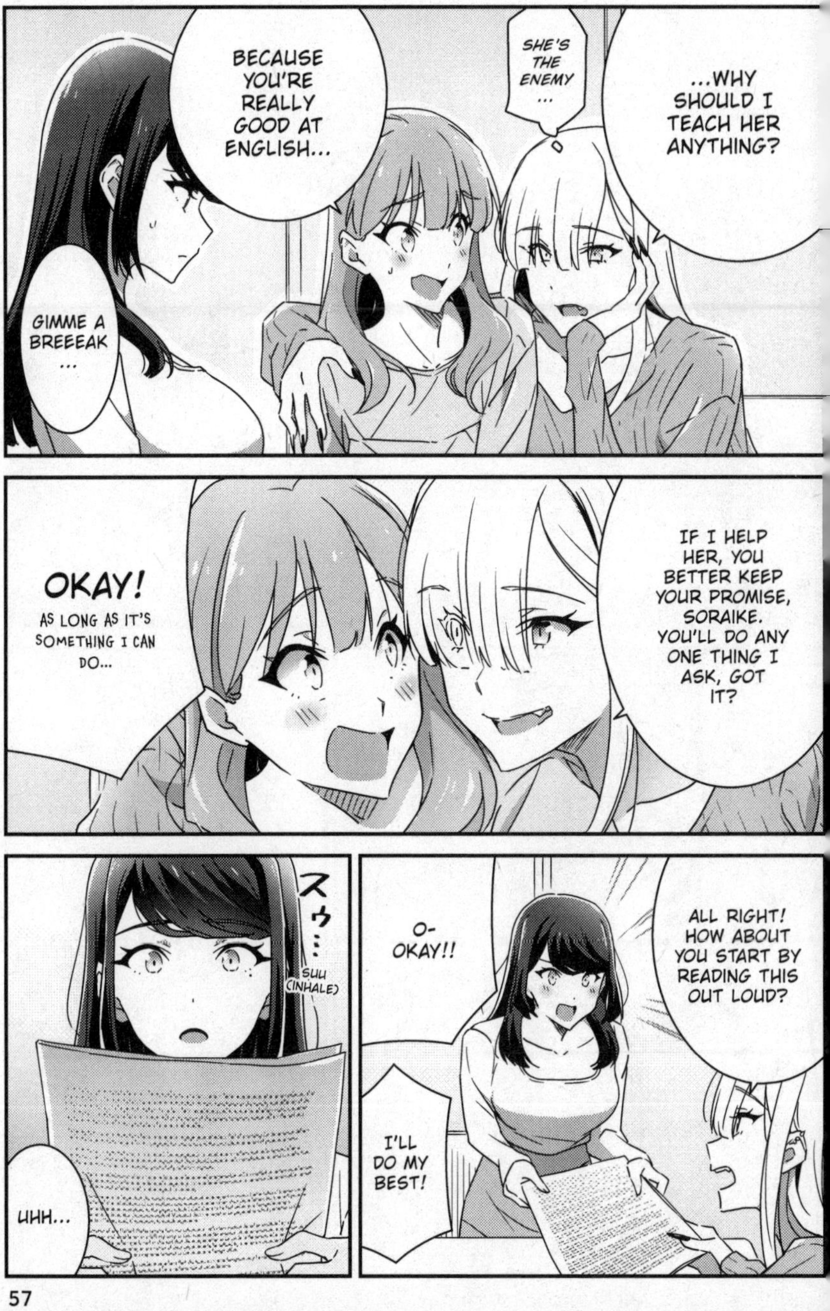
...WHY SHOULD I TEACH HER ANYTHING?
SHE'S THE ENEMY...
BECAUSE YOU'RE REALLY GOOD AT ENGLISH...
GIMME A BREEEAK...
IF I HELP HER, YOU BETTER KEEP YOUR PROMISE, SORAIKE. YOU'LL DO ANY ONE THING I ASK, GOT IT?
OKAY!
AS LONG AS IT'S SOMETHING I CAN DO...
ALL RIGHT! HOW ABOUT YOU START BY READING THIS OUT LOUD?
O-OKAY!!
I'LL DO MY BEST!
スゥ…
SUU (INHALE)
UHH...

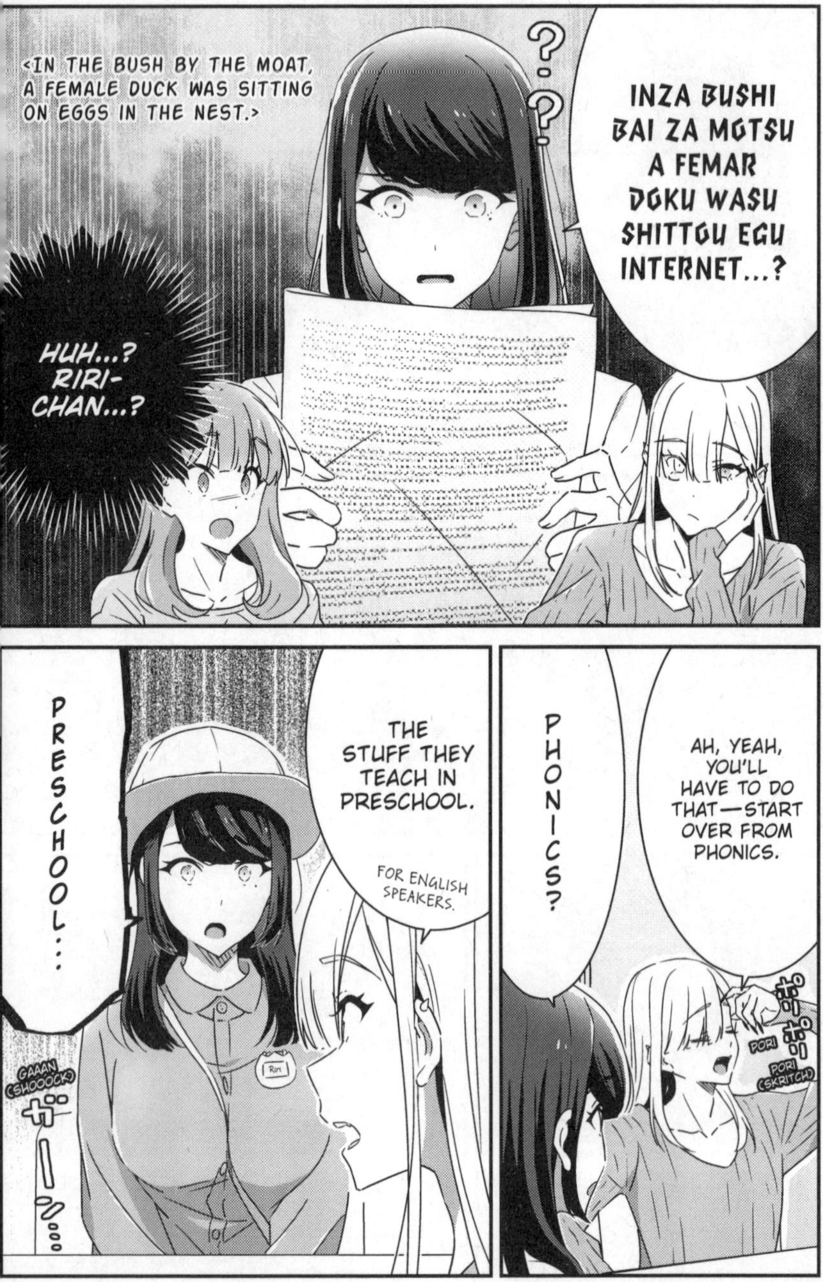

??
INZA BUSHI BAI ZA MOTSU A FEMAR DOKU WASU SHITTOU EGU INTERNET...?
<IN THE BUSH BY THE MOAT, A FEMALE DUCK WAS SITTING ON EGGS IN THE NEST.>
HUH...? RIRI-CHAN...?
AH, YEAH, YOU'LL HAVE TO DO THAT—START OVER FROM PHONICS.
PHONICS?
ポリポリ
PORI PORI (SKRITCH)
THE STUFF THEY TEACH IN PRESCHOOL.
FOR ENGLISH SPEAKERS.
PRESCHOOL...
RIRI
GAAAN (SHOOOCK)
ガーン…

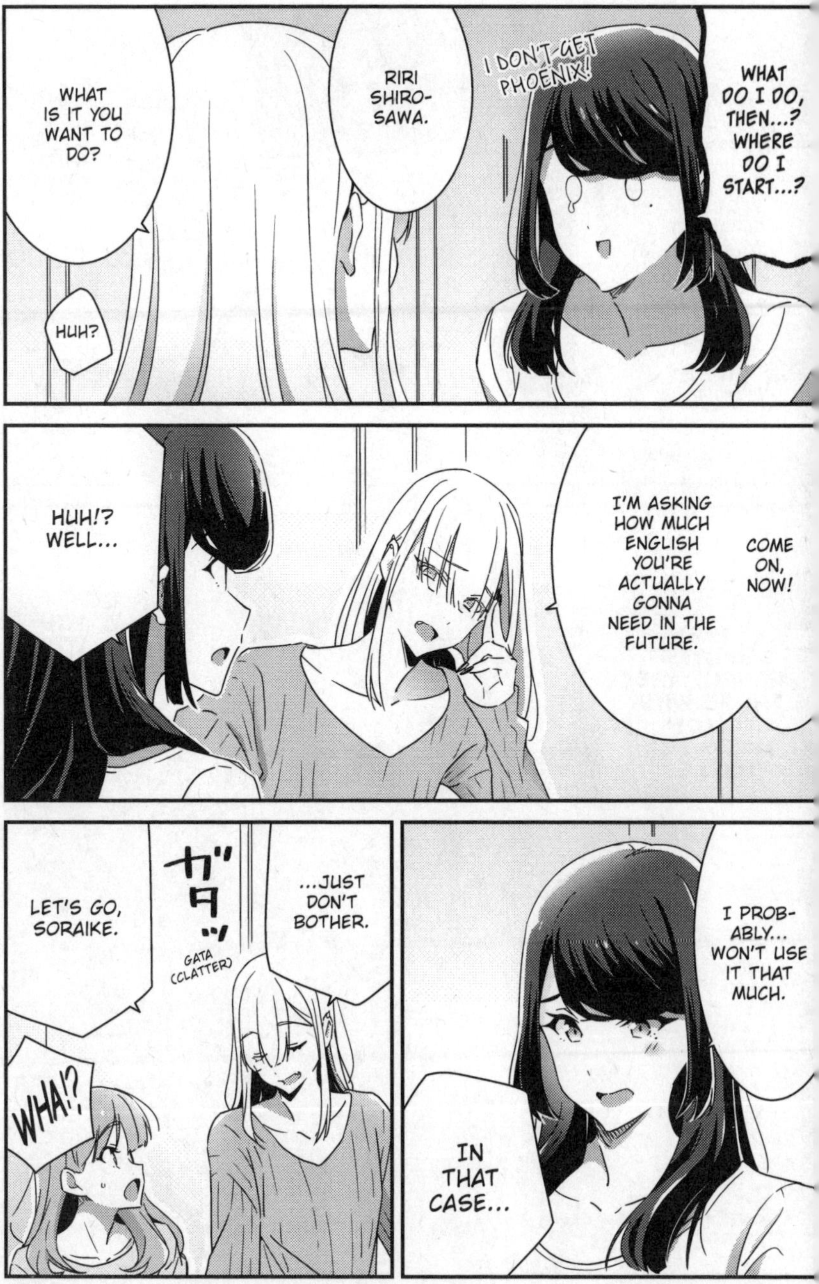
WHAT DO I DO, THEN...? WHERE DO I START...?
I DON'T GET PHOENIX!
RIRI SHIRO-SAWA.
WHAT IS IT YOU WANT TO DO?
HUH?
COME ON, NOW!
I'M ASKING HOW MUCH ENGLISH YOU'RE ACTUALLY GONNA NEED IN THE FUTURE.
HUH!? WELL...
I PROB-ABLY... WON'T USE IT THAT MUCH.
IN THAT CASE...
...JUST DON'T BOTHER.
ガタッ
GATA (CLATTER)
LET'S GO, SORAIKE.
WHA!?

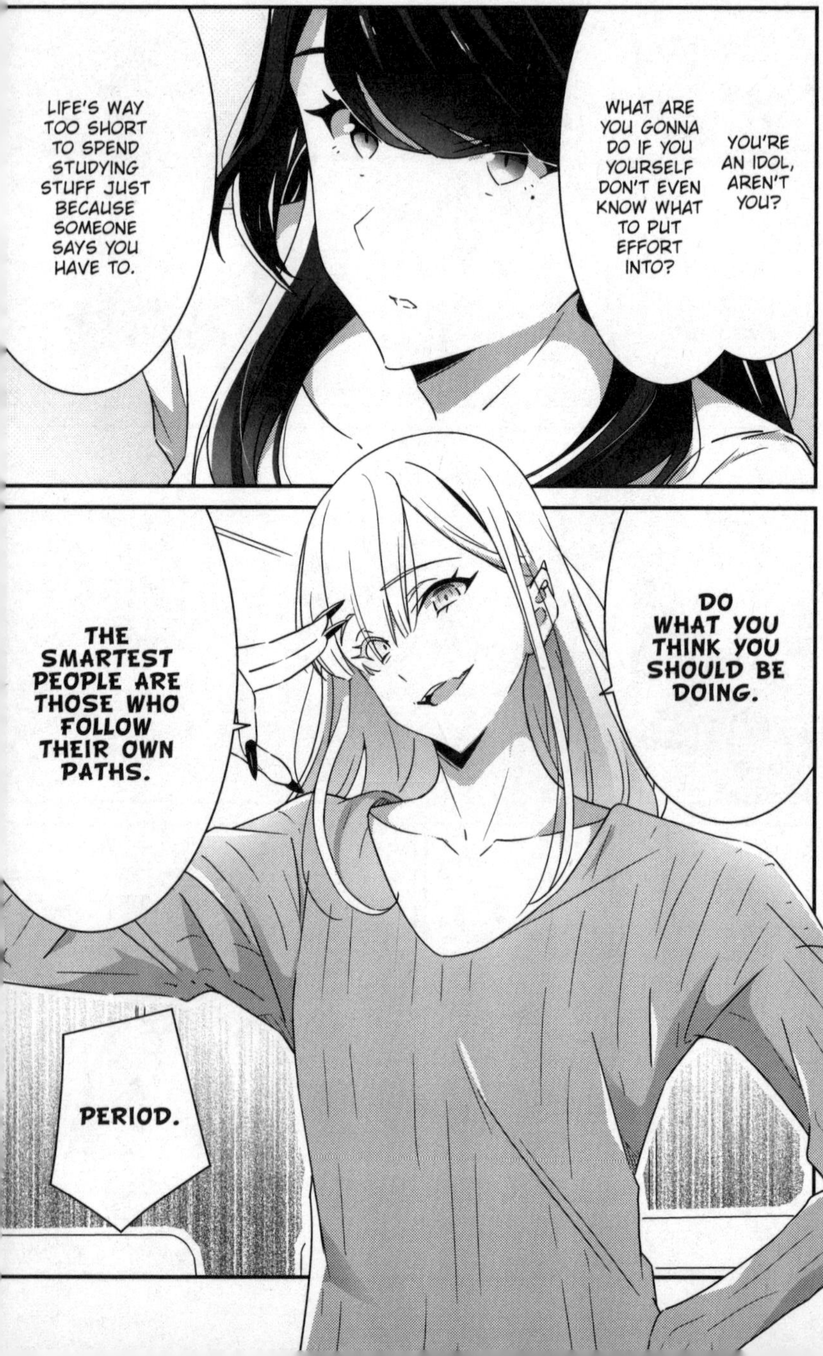
YOU'RE AN IDOL, AREN'T YOU?
WHAT ARE YOU GONNA DO IF YOU YOURSELF DON'T EVEN KNOW WHAT TO PUT EFFORT INTO?
LIFE'S WAY TOO SHORT TO SPEND STUDYING STUFF JUST BECAUSE SOMEONE SAYS YOU HAVE TO.
DO WHAT YOU THINK YOU SHOULD BE DOING.
THE SMARTEST PEOPLE ARE THOSE WHO FOLLOW THEIR OWN PATHS.
PERIOD.

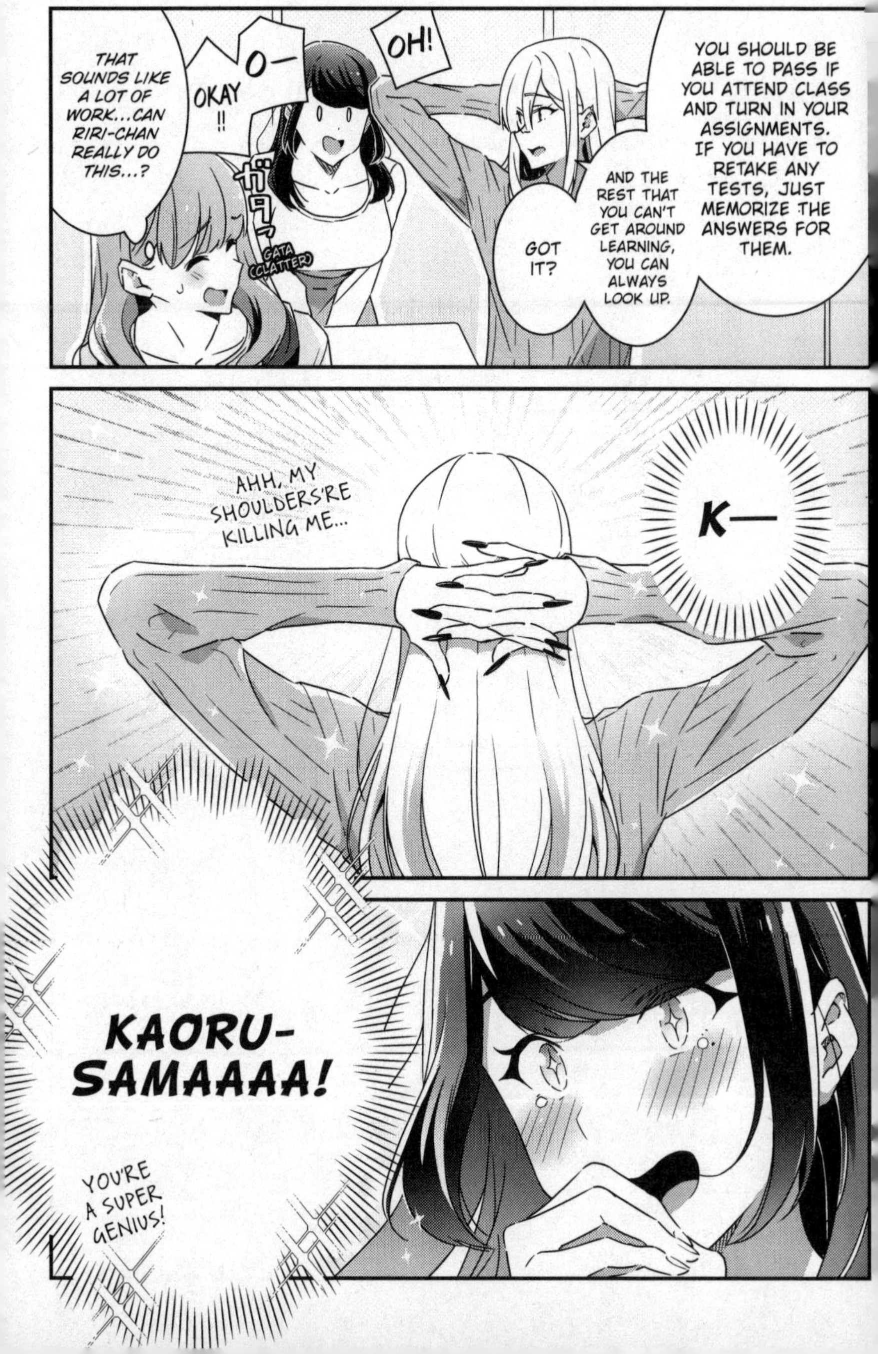
YOU SHOULD BE ABLE TO PASS IF YOU ATTEND CLASS AND TURN IN YOUR ASSIGNMENTS. IF YOU HAVE TO RETAKE ANY TESTS, JUST MEMORIZE THE ANSWERS FOR THEM.
AND THE REST THAT YOU CAN'T GET AROUND LEARNING, YOU CAN ALWAYS LOOK UP.
GOT IT?
OH!
O— OKAY !!
ガタッ
GATA (CLATTER)
THAT SOUNDS LIKE A LOT OF WORK...CAN RIRI-CHAN REALLY DO THIS...?
K—
AHH, MY SHOULDERS'RE KILLING ME...
KAORU-SAMAAAA!
YOU'RE A SUPER GENIUS!

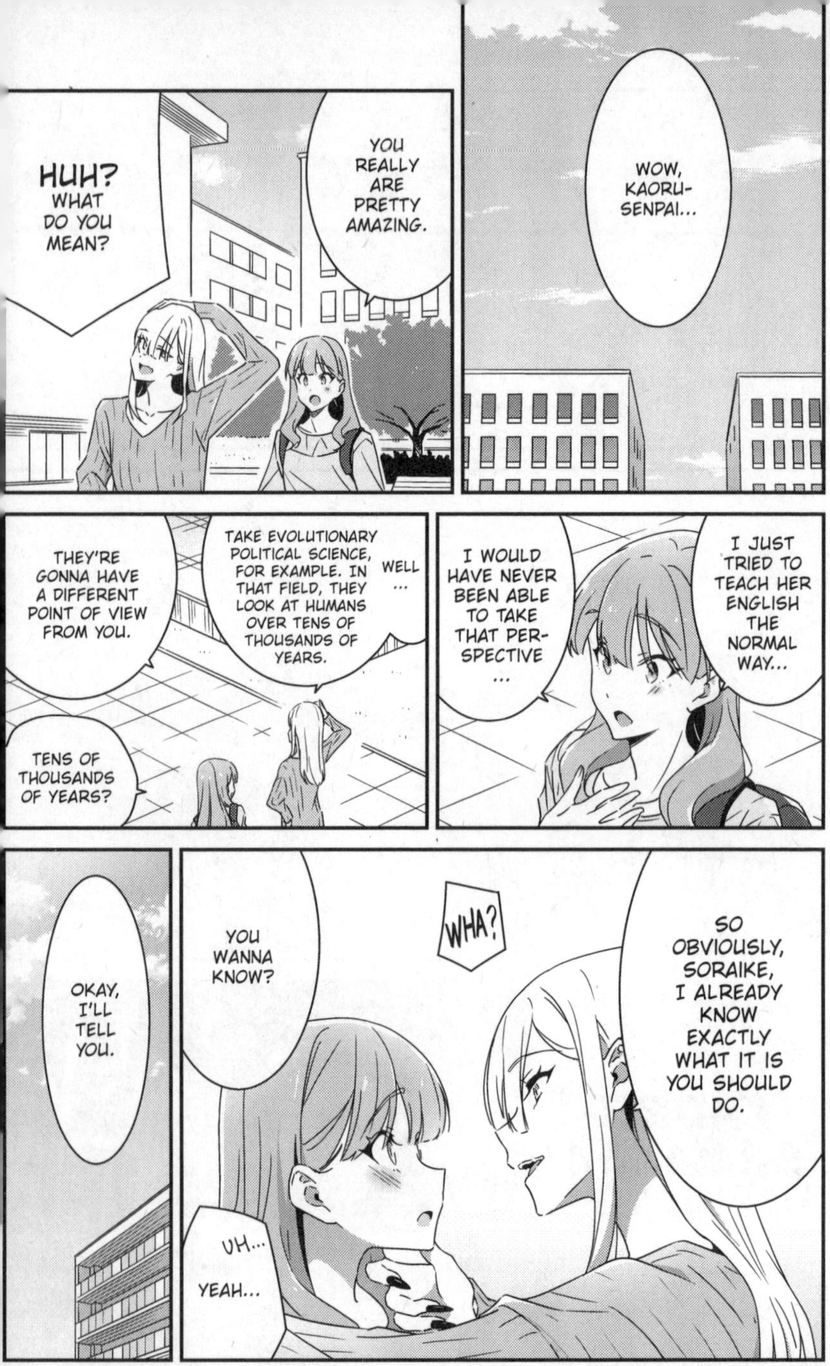
WOW, KAORU-SENPAI...
YOU REALLY ARE PRETTY AMAZING.
HUH? WHAT DO YOU MEAN?
I JUST TRIED TO TEACH HER ENGLISH THE NORMAL WAY...
I WOULD HAVE NEVER BEEN ABLE TO TAKE THAT PERSPECTIVE ...
WELL ...
TAKE EVOLUTIONARY POLITICAL SCIENCE, FOR EXAMPLE. IN THAT FIELD, THEY LOOK AT HUMANS OVER TENS OF THOUSANDS OF YEARS.
THEY'RE GONNA HAVE A DIFFERENT POINT OF VIEW FROM YOU.
TENS OF THOUSANDS OF YEARS?
SO OBVIOUSLY, SORAIKE, I ALREADY KNOW EXACTLY WHAT IT IS YOU SHOULD DO.
WHA?
YOU WANNA KNOW?
UH...
YEAH...
OKAY, I'LL TELL YOU.

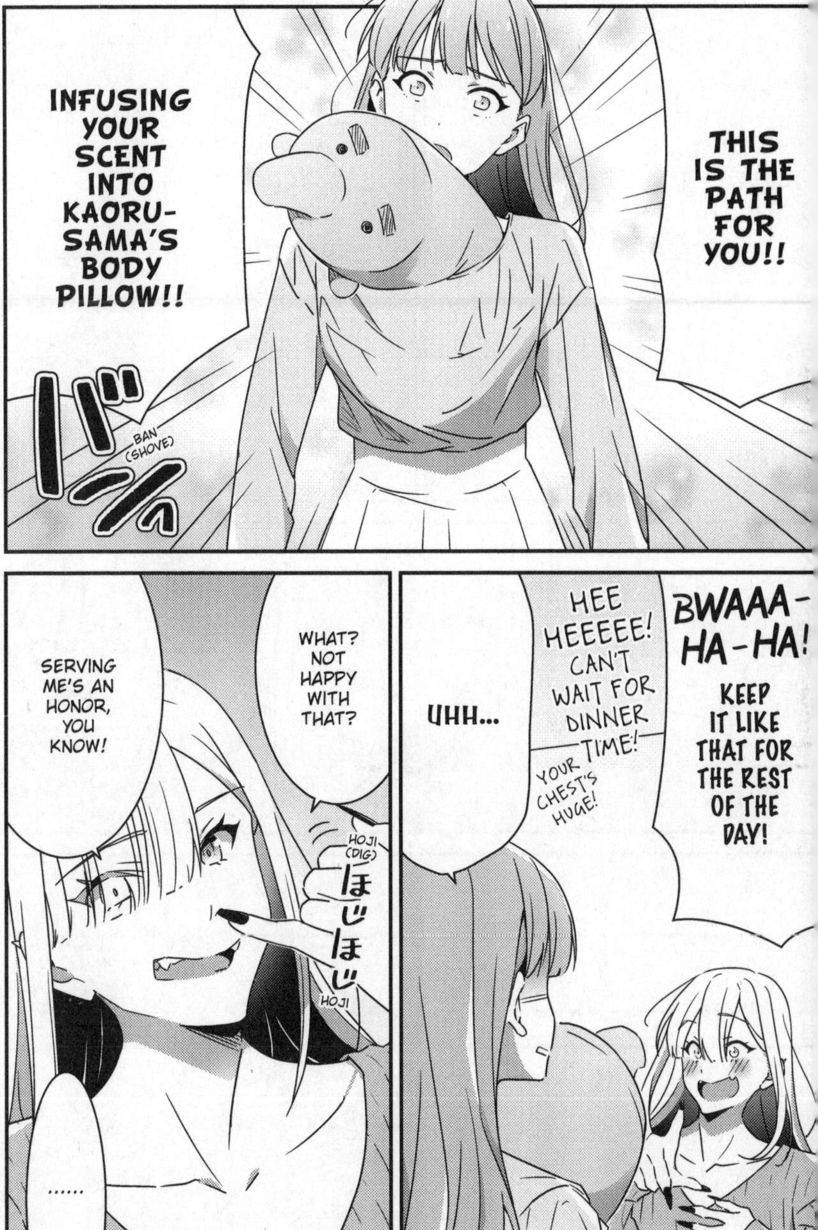
THIS IS THE PATH FOR YOU!!
INFUSING YOUR SCENT INTO KAORU-SAMA'S BODY PILLOW!!
BAN (SHOVE)
BWAAA-HA-HA!
KEEP IT LIKE THAT FOR THE REST OF THE DAY!
HEE HEEEEE! CAN'T WAIT FOR DINNER TIME!
YOUR CHEST'S HUGE!
UHH...
WHAT? NOT HAPPY WITH THAT?
SERVING ME'S AN HONOR, YOU KNOW!
HOJI (DIG)
ほじほじ
HOJI
......

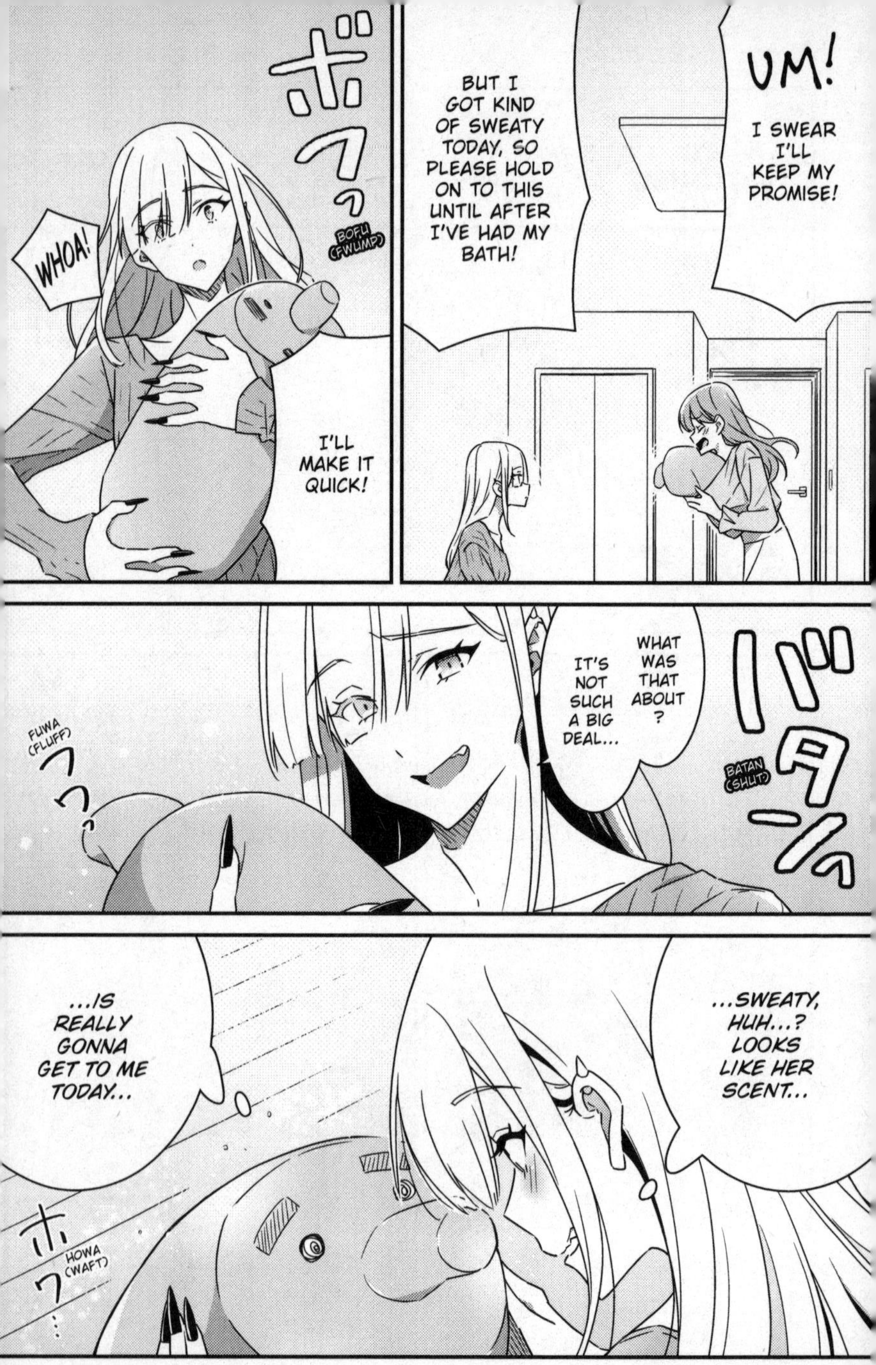
UM!
I SWEAR I'LL KEEP MY PROMISE!
BUT I GOT KIND OF SWEATY TODAY, SO PLEASE HOLD ON TO THIS UNTIL AFTER I'VE HAD MY BATH!
ボフッ
BOFU (FWUMP)
WHOA!
I'LL MAKE IT QUICK!
バタン
BATAN (SHUT)
WHAT WAS THAT ABOUT?
IT'S NOT SUCH A BIG DEAL...
フワッ
FUWA (FLUFF)
...SWEATY, HUH...? LOOKS LIKE HER SCENT...
...IS REALLY GONNA GET TO ME TODAY...
ホワ…
HOWA (WAFT)

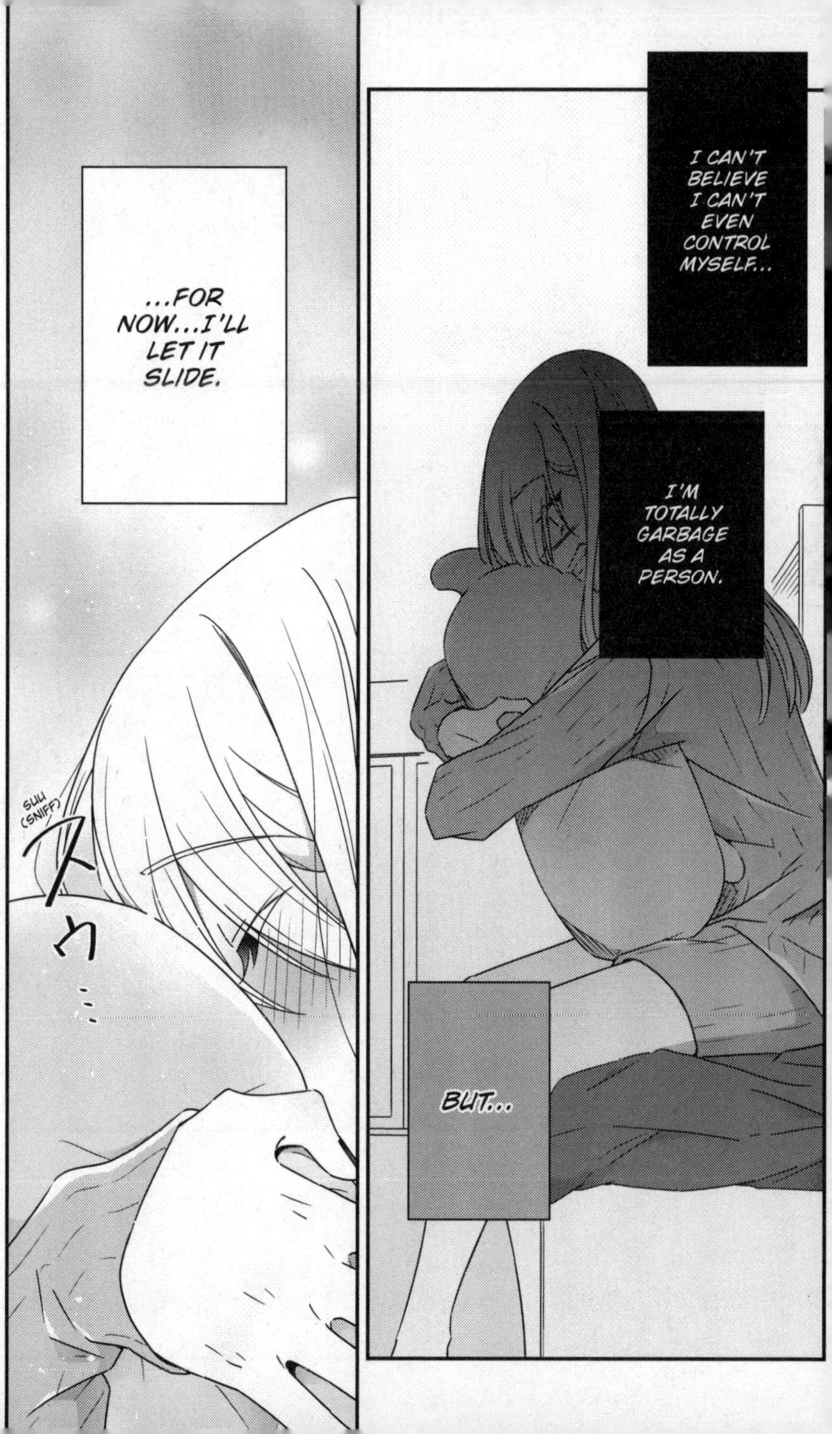
I CAN'T BELIEVE I CAN'T EVEN CONTROL MYSELF...
I'M TOTALLY GARBAGE AS A PERSON.
BUT...
...FOR NOW...I'LL LET IT SLIDE.
SUU (SNIFF)
スゥ…

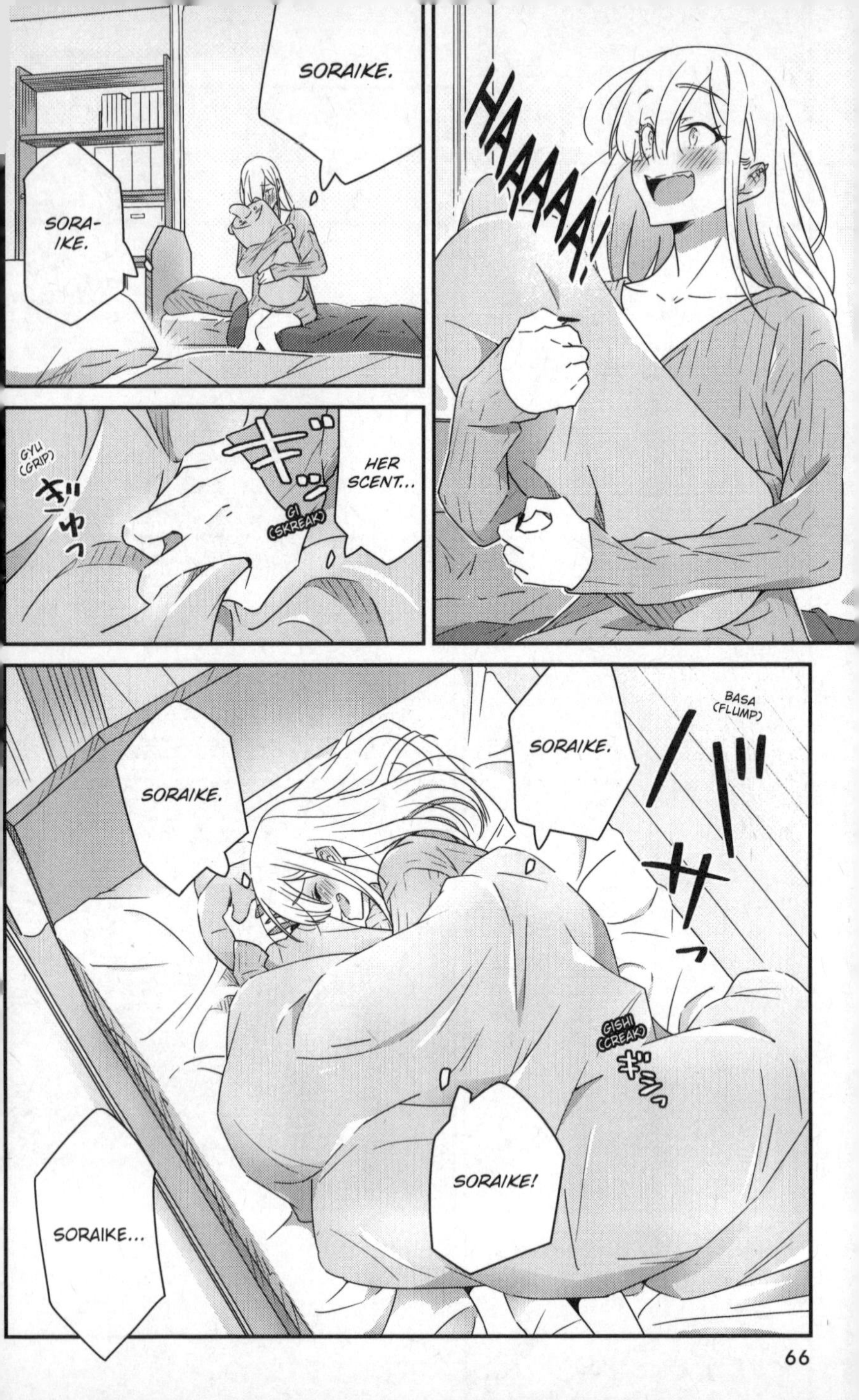

HAAAAA!
SORAIKE.
SORA-IKE.
HER SCENT...
ギッ
GI (SKREAK)
ぎゅっ
GYU (GRIP)
BASA (FLUMP)
バサッ
SORAIKE.
SORAIKE.
GISHI (CREAK)
ギシッ
SORAIKE!
SORAIKE...

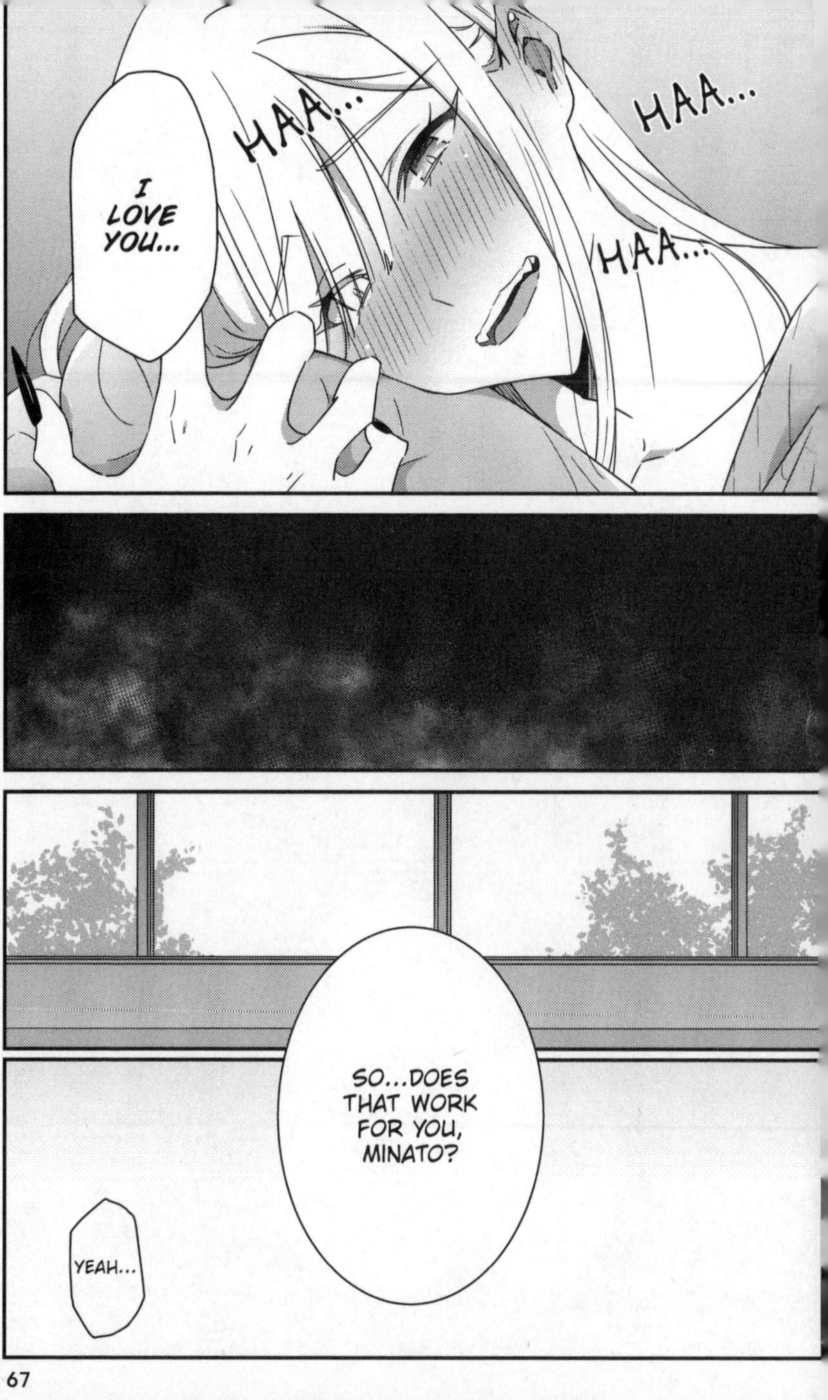
HAA...
HAA...
HAA...
I LOVE YOU...
SO...DOES THAT WORK FOR YOU, MINATO?
YEAH...

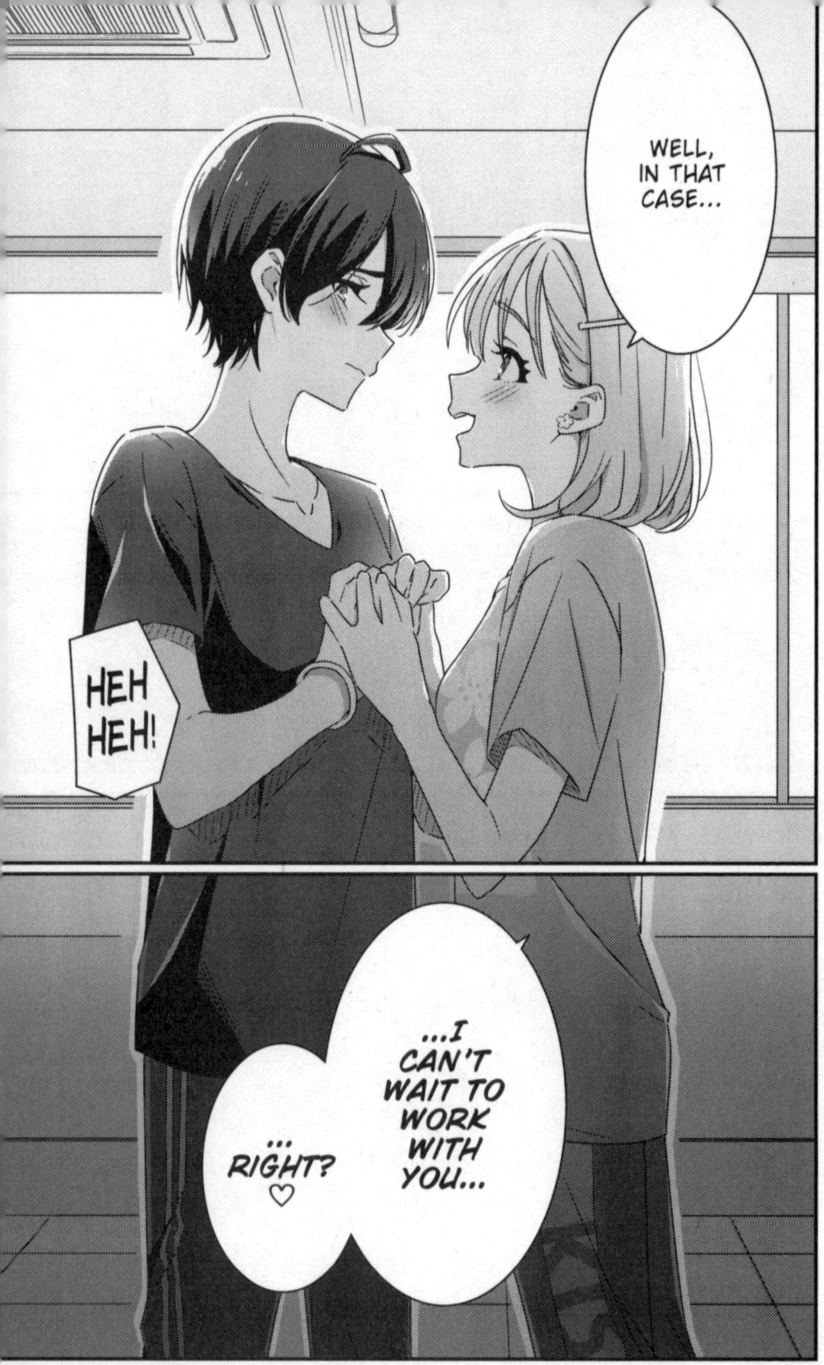
WELL, IN THAT CASE...
HEH HEH!
...I CAN'T WAIT TO WORK WITH YOU...
... RIGHT? ♡

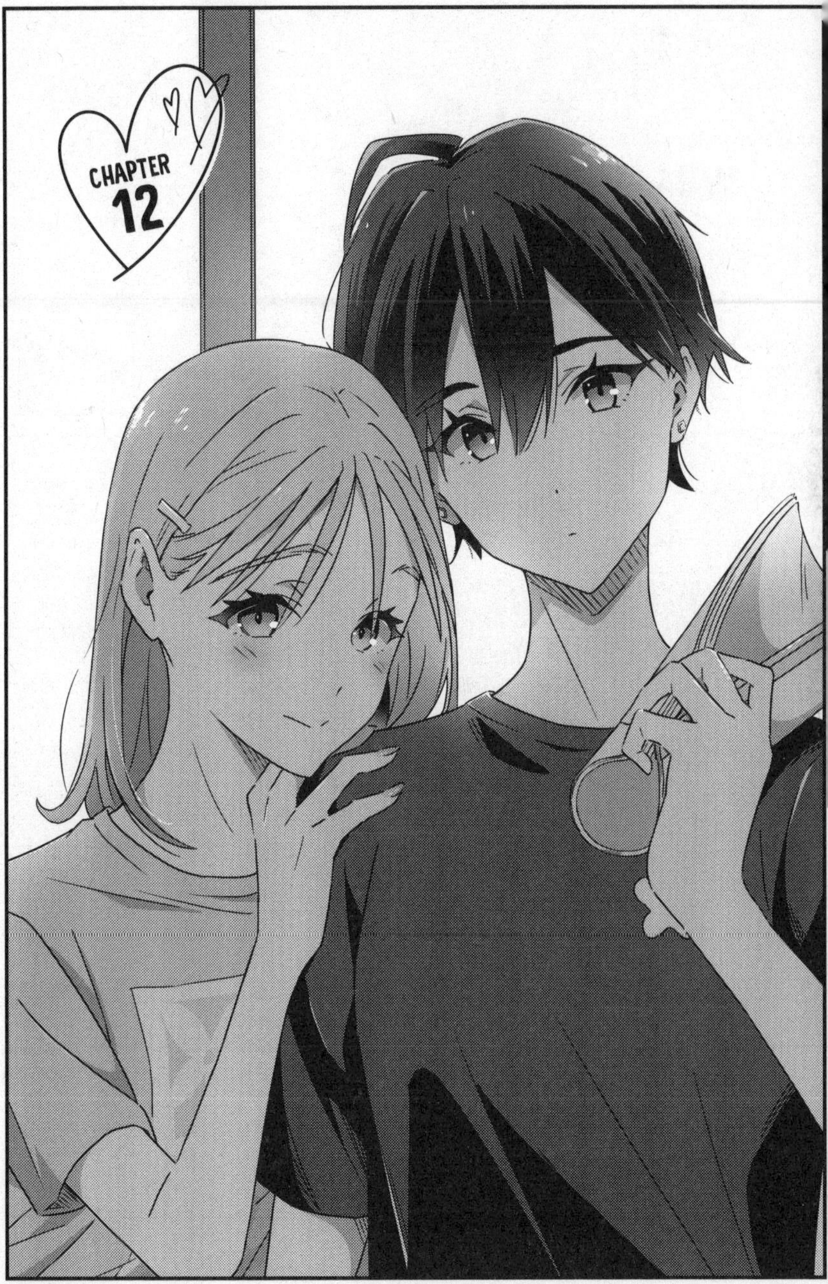
CHAPTER 12

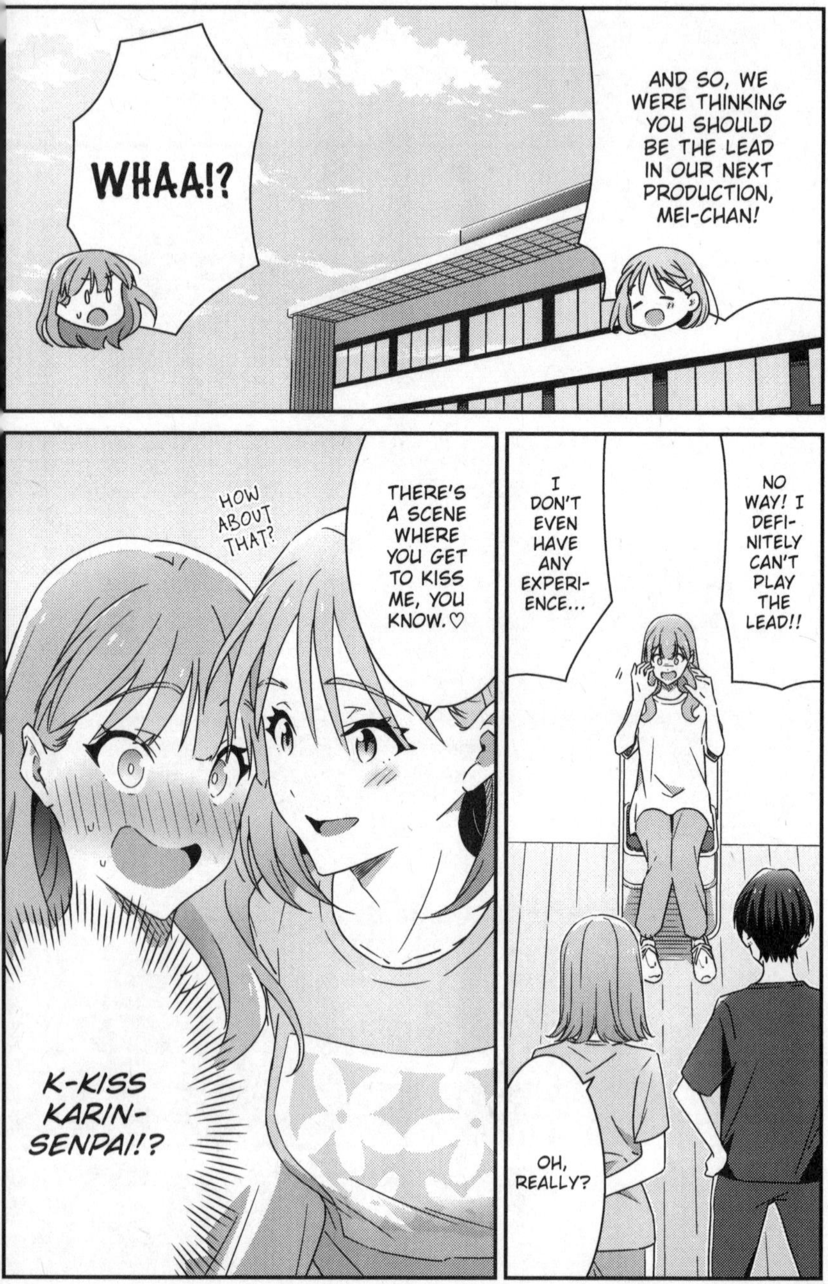
AND SO, WE WERE THINKING YOU SHOULD BE THE LEAD IN OUR NEXT PRODUCTION, MEI-CHAN!
WHAA!?
NO WAY! I DEFINITELY CAN'T PLAY THE LEAD!!
I DON'T EVEN HAVE ANY EXPERIENCE...
OH, REALLY?
THERE'S A SCENE WHERE YOU GET TO KISS ME, YOU KNOW.♡
HOW ABOUT THAT?
K-KISS KARIN-SENPAI!?

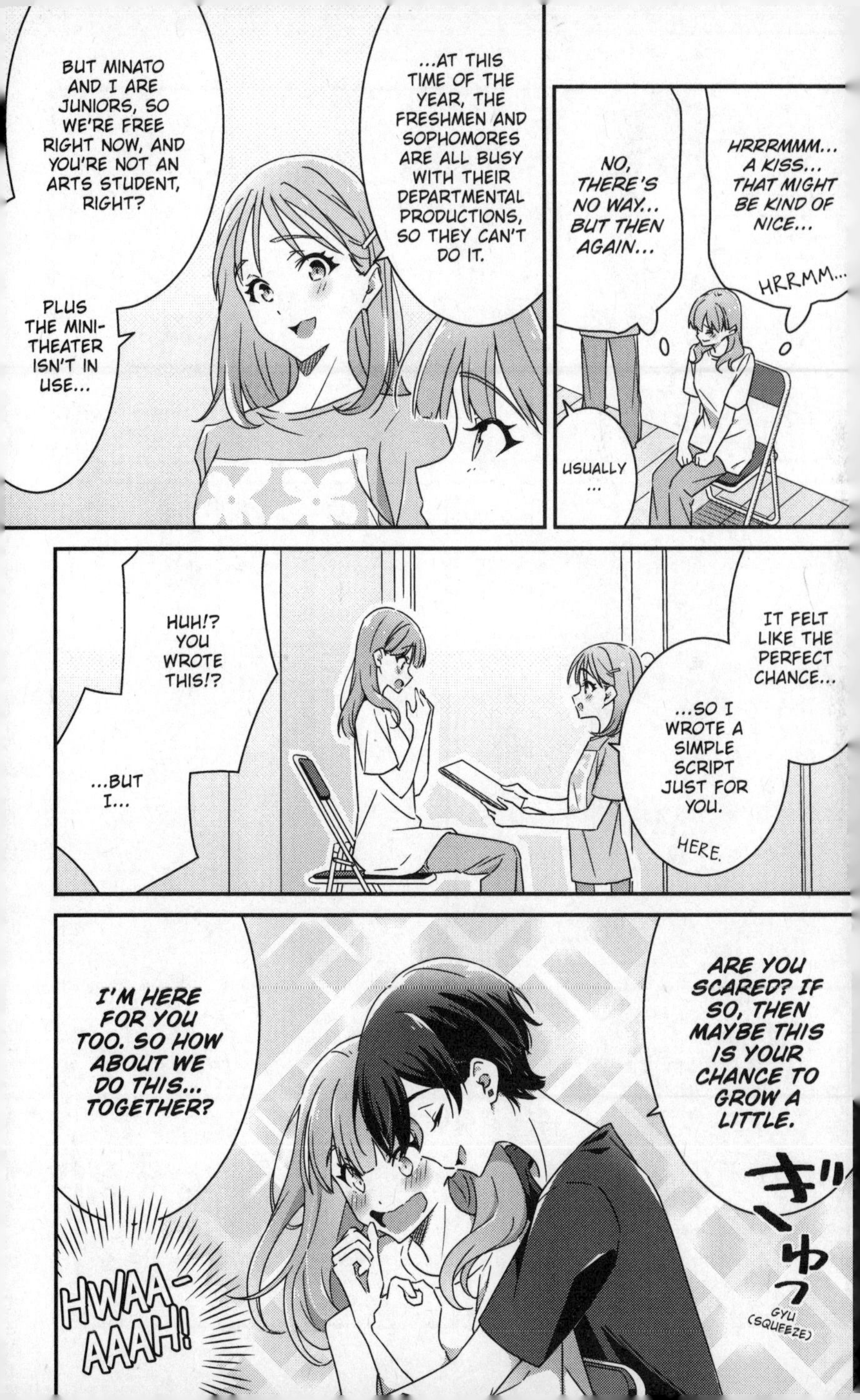
HRRRMMM... A KISS... THAT MIGHT BE KIND OF NICE...
HRRMM...
NO, THERE'S NO WAY... BUT THEN AGAIN...
USUALLY...
...AT THIS TIME OF THE YEAR, THE FRESHMEN AND SOPHOMORES ARE ALL BUSY WITH THEIR DEPARTMENTAL PRODUCTIONS, SO THEY CAN'T DO IT.
BUT MINATO AND I ARE JUNIORS, SO WE'RE FREE RIGHT NOW, AND YOU'RE NOT AN ARTS STUDENT, RIGHT?
PLUS THE MINI-THEATER ISN'T IN USE...
IT FELT LIKE THE PERFECT CHANCE...
...SO I WROTE A SIMPLE SCRIPT JUST FOR YOU.
HERE.
HUH!? YOU WROTE THIS!?
...BUT I...
ARE YOU SCARED? IF SO, THEN MAYBE THIS IS YOUR CHANCE TO GROW A LITTLE.
ギュッ
GYU (SQUEEZE)
I'M HERE FOR YOU TOO. SO HOW ABOUT WE DO THIS... TOGETHER?
HWAA-AAAH!

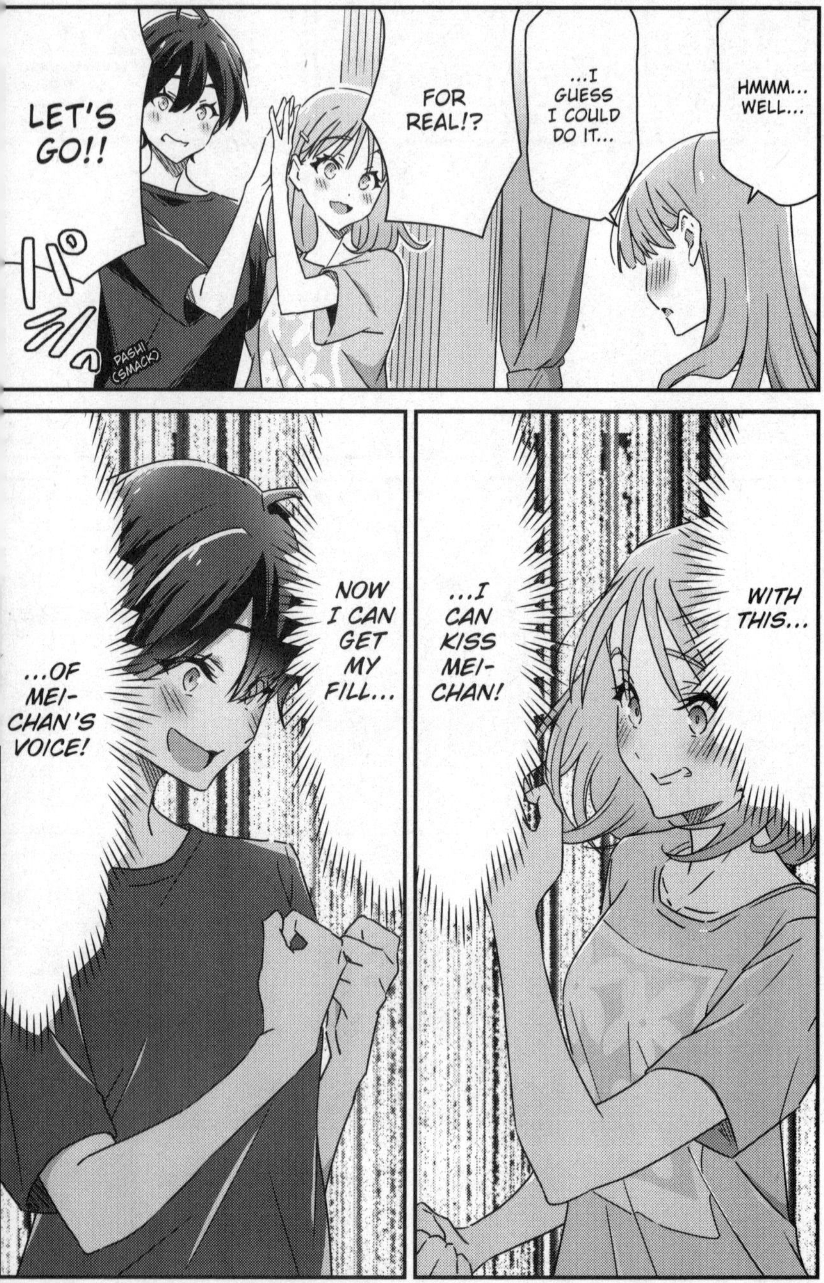
HMMM... WELL...
...I GUESS I COULD DO IT...
FOR REAL!?
LET'S GO!!
PASHI (SMACK)
WITH THIS...
...I CAN KISS MEI-CHAN!
NOW I CAN GET MY FILL...
...OF MEI-CHAN'S VOICE!

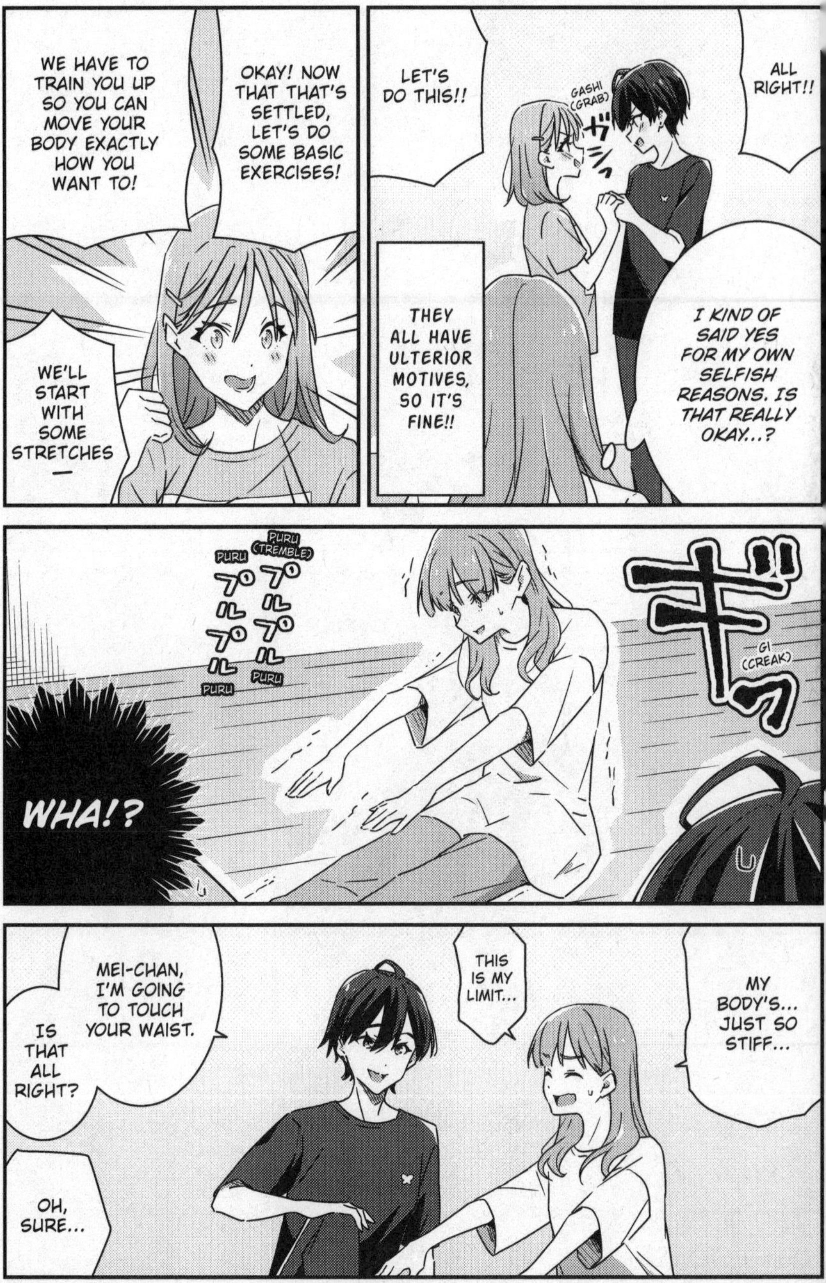
ALL RIGHT!!
GASHI (GRAB)
ガシ
LET'S DO THIS!!
I KIND OF SAID YES FOR MY OWN SELFISH REASONS. IS THAT REALLY OKAY...?
THEY ALL HAVE ULTERIOR MOTIVES, SO IT'S FINE!!
OKAY! NOW THAT THAT'S SETTLED, LET'S DO SOME BASIC EXERCISES!
WE HAVE TO TRAIN YOU UP SO YOU CAN MOVE YOUR BODY EXACTLY HOW YOU WANT TO!
WE'LL START WITH SOME STRETCHES—
ギッ
GI (CREAK)
PURU (TREMBLE)
プルプル
PURU
PURU
プルプル
PURU
WHA!?
MY BODY'S... JUST SO STIFF...
THIS IS MY LIMIT...
MEI-CHAN, I'M GOING TO TOUCH YOUR WAIST.
IS THAT ALL RIGHT?
OH, SURE...

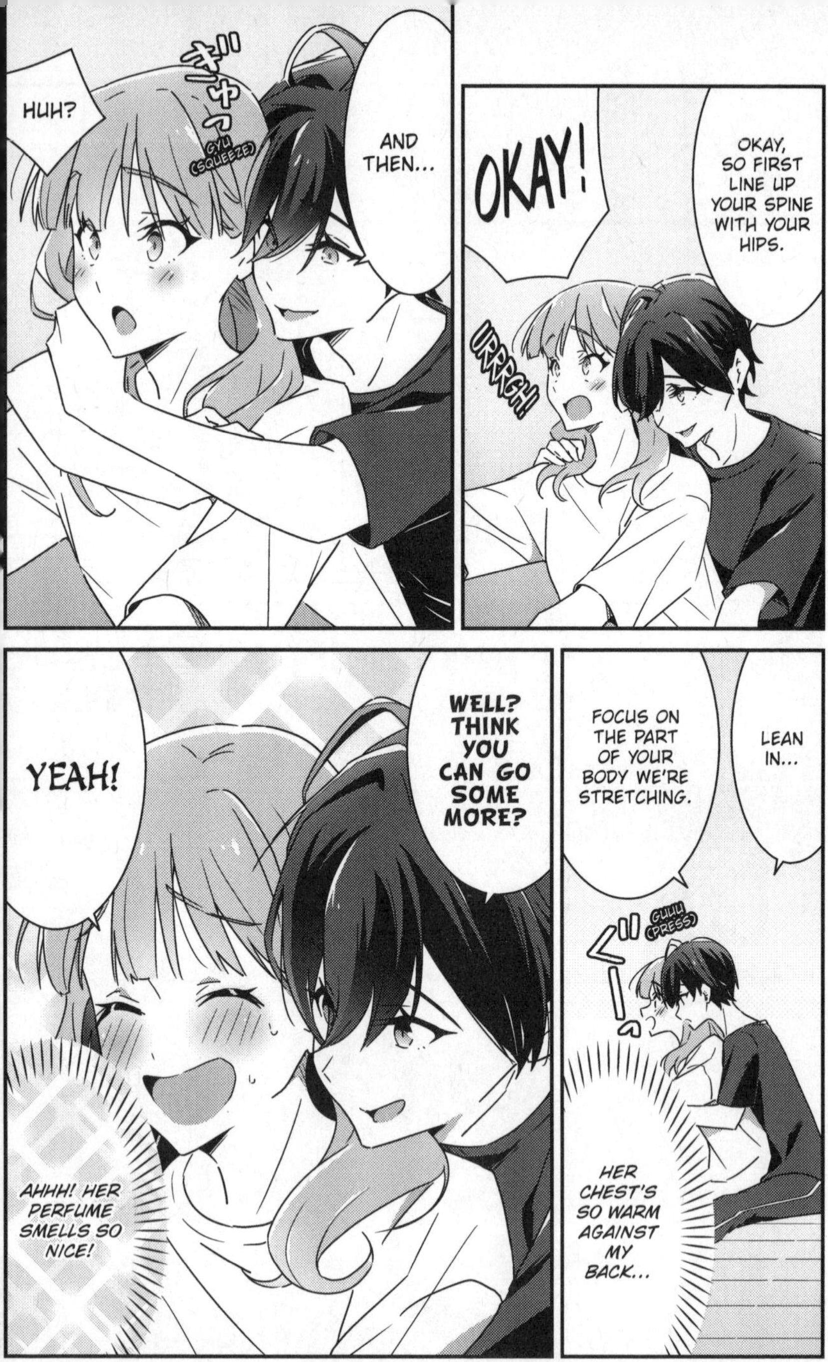
OKAY, SO FIRST LINE UP YOUR SPINE WITH YOUR HIPS.
OKAY!
URRRGH!
AND THEN...
ぎゅっ
GYU (SQUEEZE)
HUH?
LEAN IN...
FOCUS ON THE PART OF YOUR BODY WE'RE STRETCHING.
GUUU (PRESS)
HER CHEST'S SO WARM AGAINST MY BACK...
WELL? THINK YOU CAN GO SOME MORE?
YEAH!
AHHH! HER PERFUME SMELLS SO NICE!

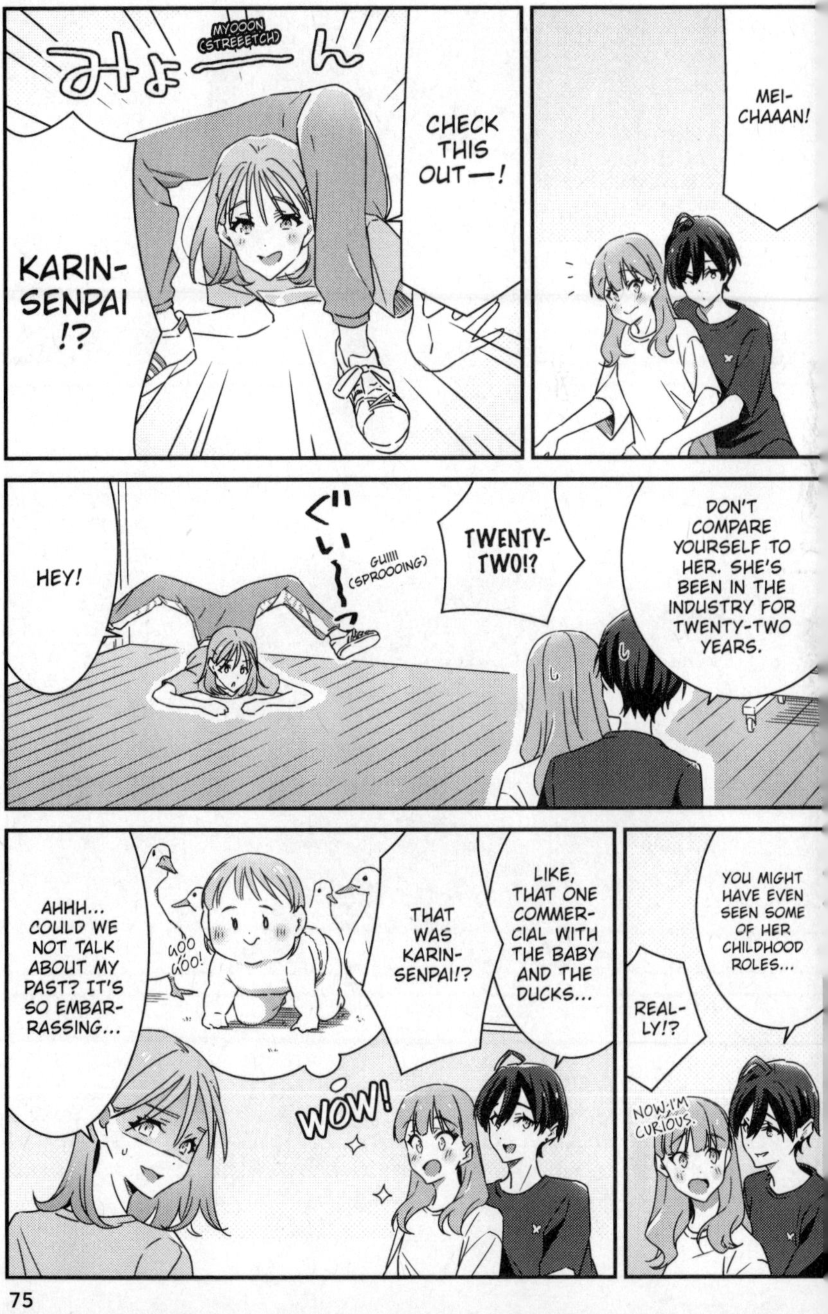
MEI-CHAAAN!
CHECK THIS OUT—!
みょーーん
MYOOON (STREEETCH)
KARIN-SENPAI!?
DON'T COMPARE YOURSELF TO HER. SHE'S BEEN IN THE INDUSTRY FOR TWENTY-TWO YEARS.
TWENTY-TWO!?
ぐいーっ
GUIIII (SPROOOING)
HEY!
YOU MIGHT HAVE EVEN SEEN SOME OF HER CHILDHOOD ROLES...
REAL-LY!?
NOW I'M CURIOUS.
LIKE, THAT ONE COMMER-CIAL WITH THE BABY AND THE DUCKS...
THAT WAS KARIN-SENPAI!?
WOW!
GOO GOO!
AHHH... COULD WE NOT TALK ABOUT MY PAST? IT'S SO EMBAR-RASSING...

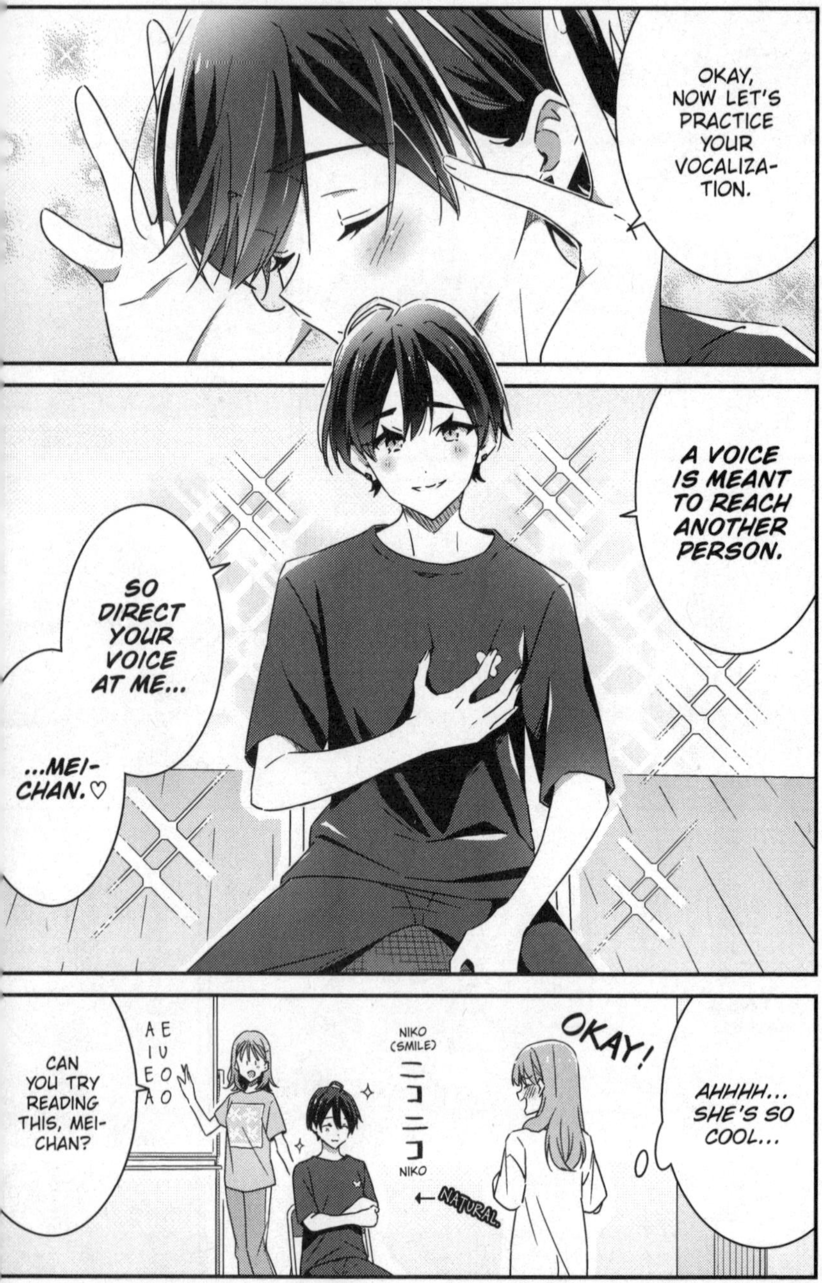
OKAY, NOW LET'S PRACTICE YOUR VOCALIZATION.
A VOICE IS MEANT TO REACH ANOTHER PERSON.
SO DIRECT YOUR VOICE AT ME...
...MEI-CHAN. ♡
AHHHH... SHE'S SO COOL...
OKAY!
NIKO (SMILE)
ニコニコ
NIKO
NATURAL
CAN YOU TRY READING THIS, MEI-CHAN?
A E
I U
E O
A O

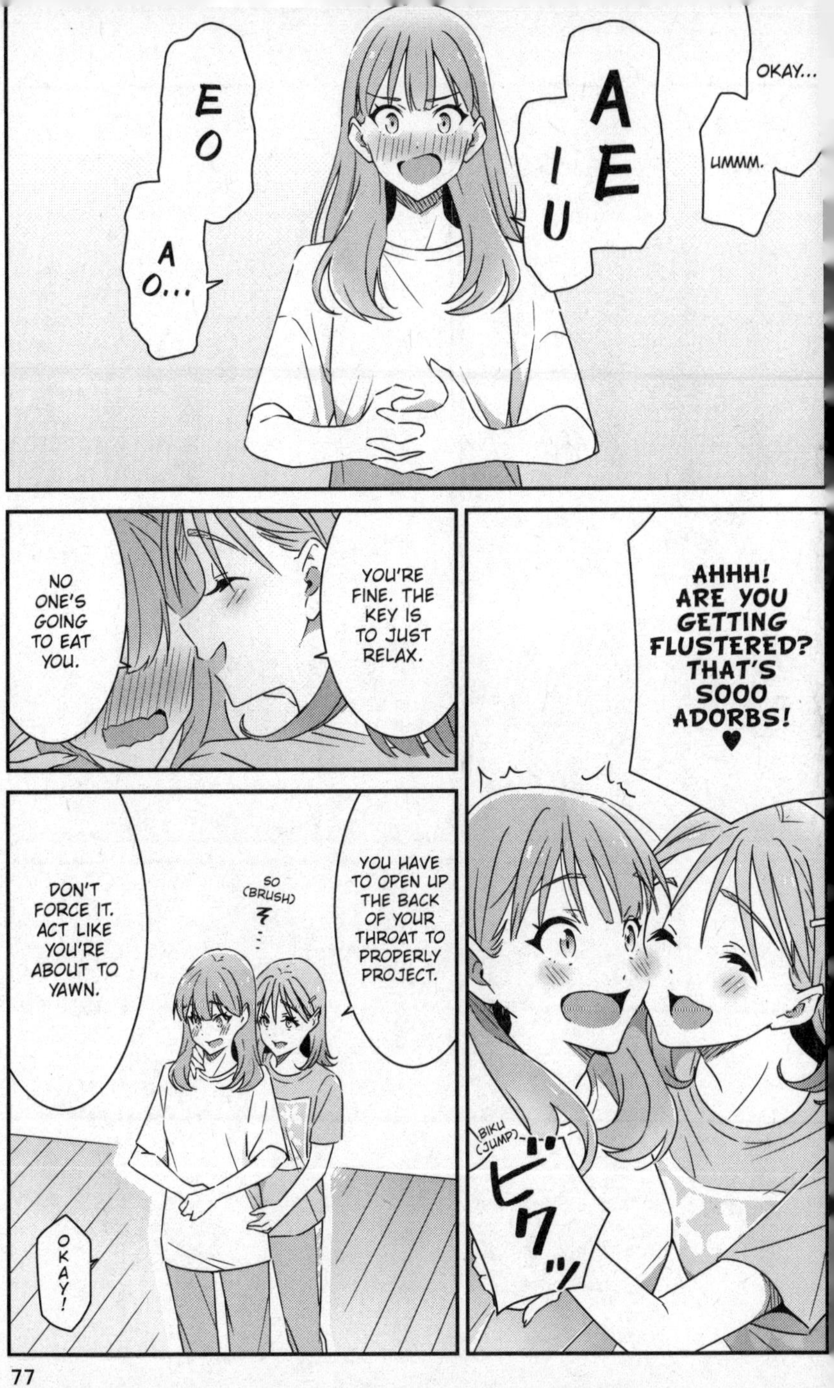
OKAY...
UMMM.
A E I U
E O A O...
AHHH! ARE YOU GETTING FLUSTERED? THAT'S SOOO ADORBS! ♥
BIKU (JUMP)
YOU'RE FINE. THE KEY IS TO JUST RELAX.
NO ONE'S GOING TO EAT YOU.
YOU HAVE TO OPEN UP THE BACK OF YOUR THROAT TO PROPERLY PROJECT.
SO (BRUSH)
DON'T FORCE IT. ACT LIKE YOU'RE ABOUT TO YAWN.
OKAY!

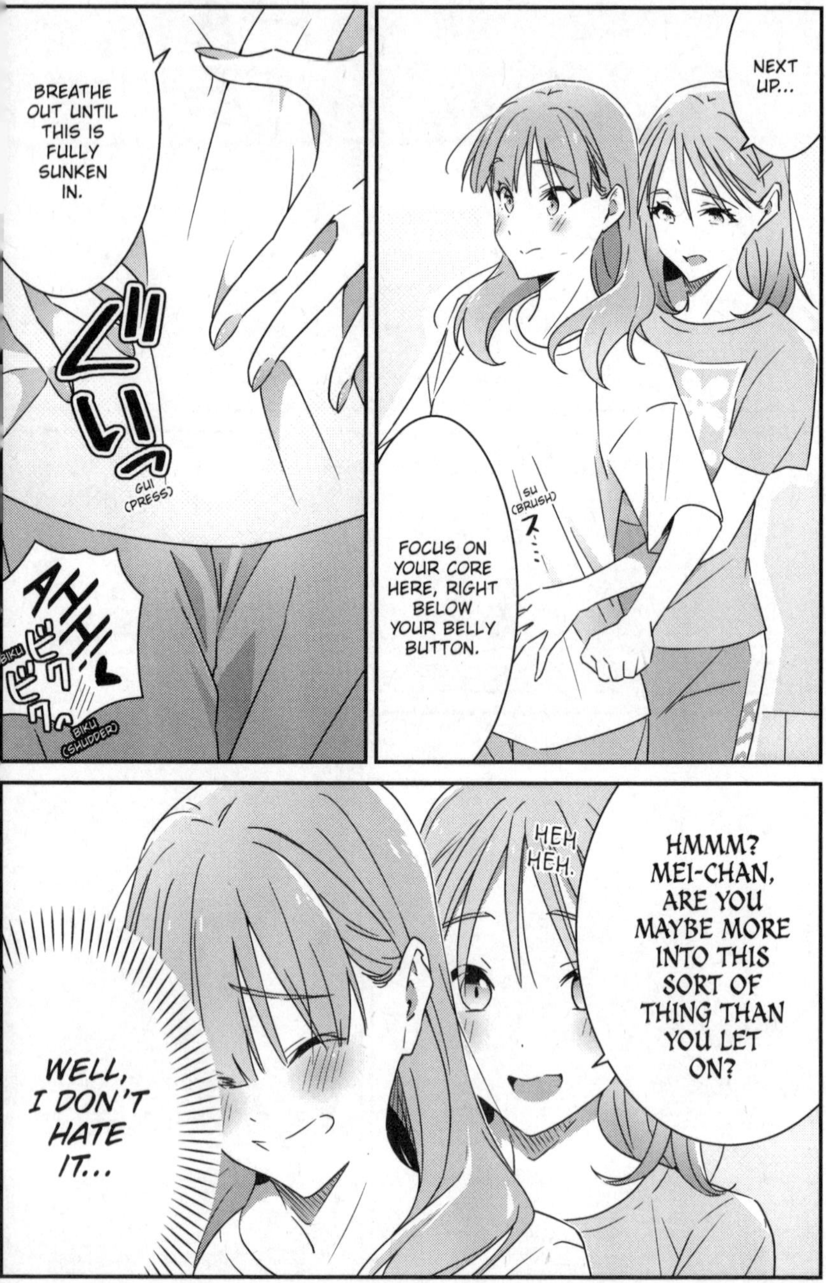
NEXT UP...
SU (BRUSH)
FOCUS ON YOUR CORE HERE, RIGHT BELOW YOUR BELLY BUTTON.
BREATHE OUT UNTIL THIS IS FULLY SUNKEN IN.
GUI (PRESS)
AHH!
BIKU
BIKU (SHUDDER)
HMMM? MEI-CHAN, ARE YOU MAYBE MORE INTO THIS SORT OF THING THAN YOU LET ON?
HEH HEH.
WELL, I DON'T HATE IT...

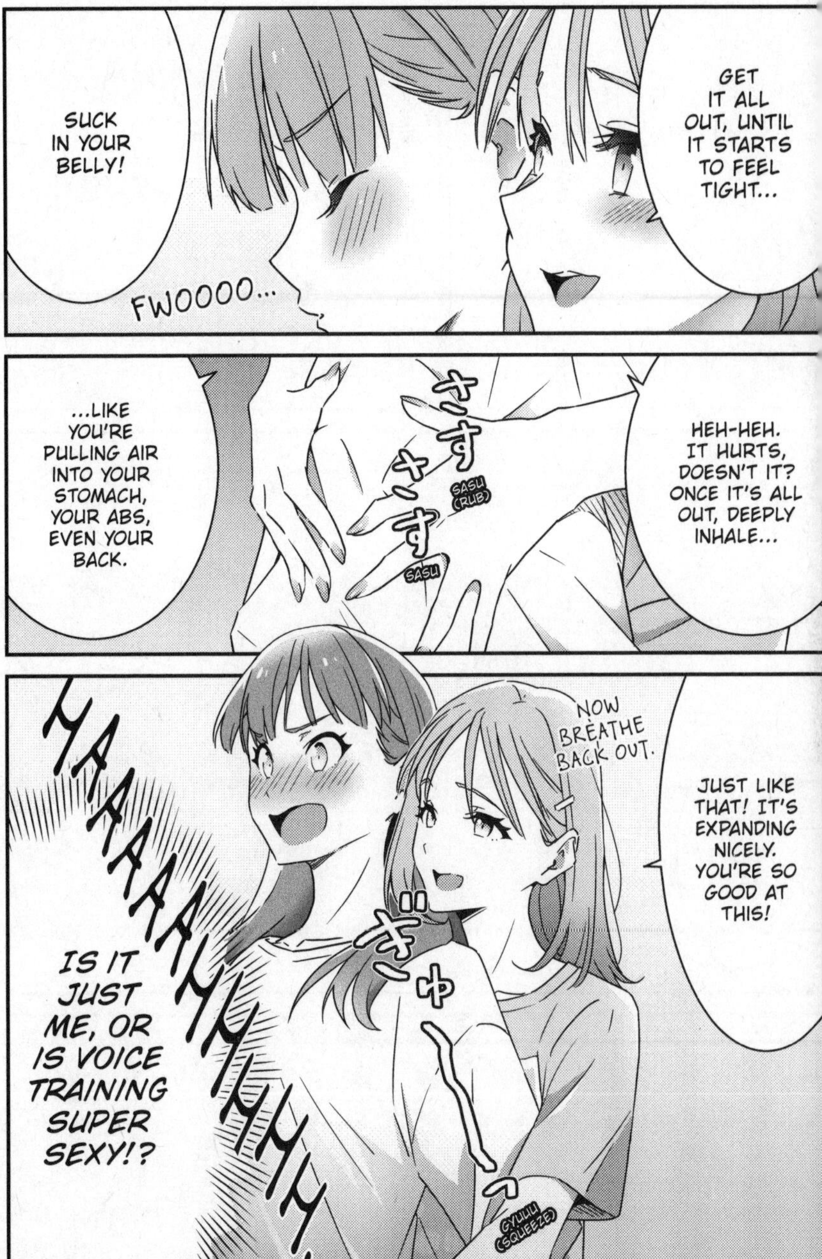
GET IT ALL OUT, UNTIL IT STARTS TO FEEL TIGHT...
SUCK IN YOUR BELLY!
FWOOOO...
HEH-HEH. IT HURTS, DOESN'T IT? ONCE IT'S ALL OUT, DEEPLY INHALE...
さすさす
SASU (RUB)
SASU
...LIKE YOU'RE PULLING AIR INTO YOUR STOMACH, YOUR ABS, EVEN YOUR BACK.
JUST LIKE THAT! IT'S EXPANDING NICELY. YOU'RE SO GOOD AT THIS!
NOW BREATHE BACK OUT.
ぎゅ〜っ
GYUUU (SQUEEZE)
HAAAAAHHHHHH...
IS IT JUST ME, OR IS VOICE TRAINING SUPER SEXY!?

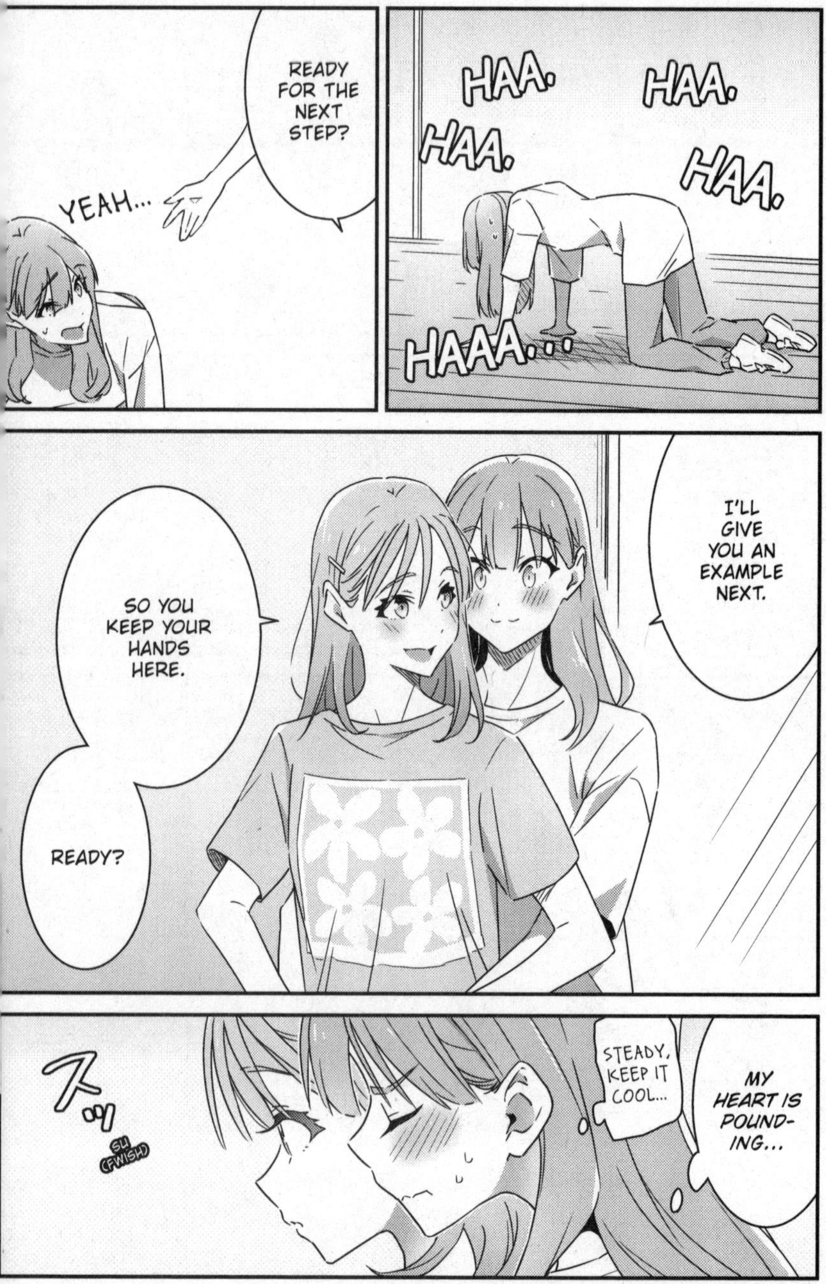
HAA.
HAA.
HAA.
HAA.
HAAA...
READY FOR THE NEXT STEP?
YEAH...
I'LL GIVE YOU AN EXAMPLE NEXT.
SO YOU KEEP YOUR HANDS HERE.
READY?
MY HEART IS POUNDING...
STEADY, KEEP IT COOL...
スッ
SU (FWISH)

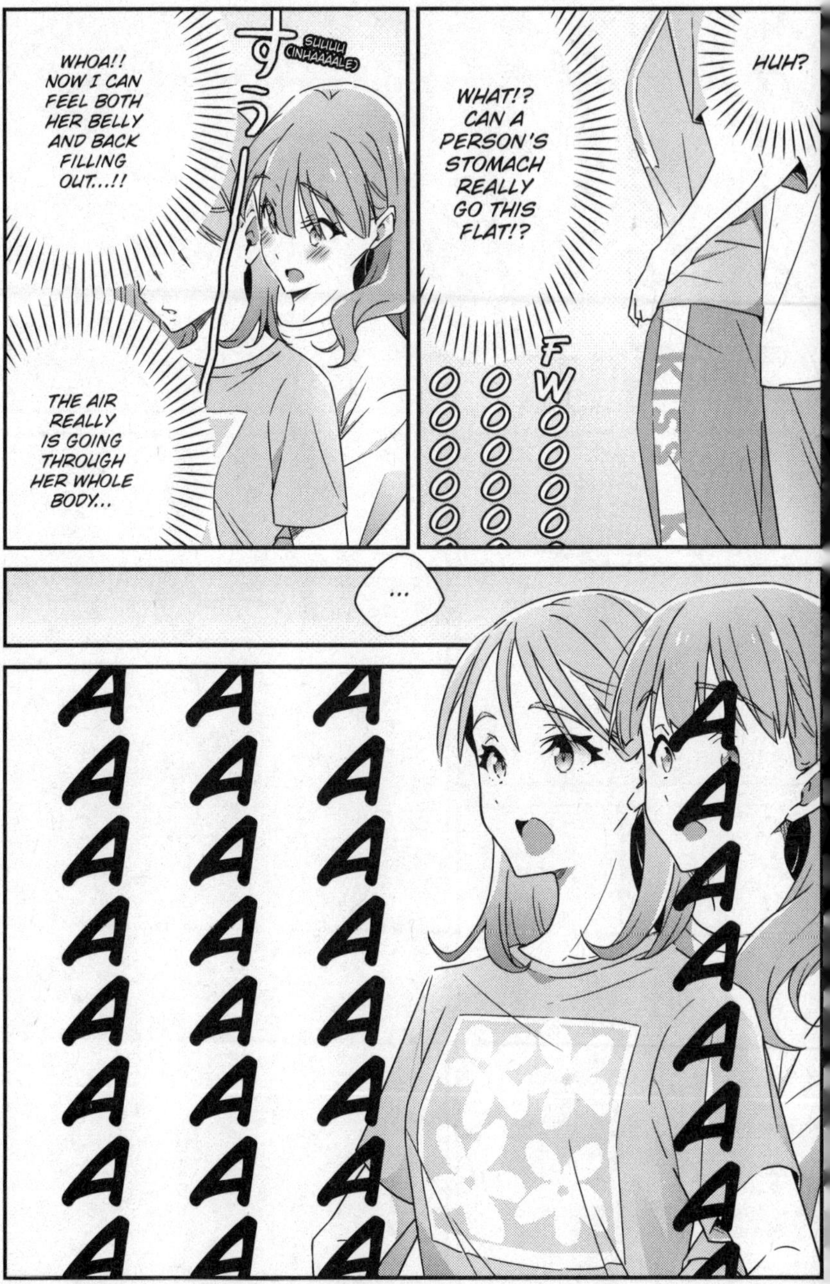
HUH?
WHAT!? CAN A PERSON'S STOMACH REALLY GO THIS FLAT!?
FWOOOOOO
OOOOOO
OOOOOO
すう
SUUUU (INHAAAALE)
WHOA!! NOW I CAN FEEL BOTH HER BELLY AND BACK FILLING OUT...!!
THE AIR REALLY IS GOING THROUGH HER WHOLE BODY...
...
AAAAAAAAA
AAAAAAAAA
AAAAAAAAA
AAAAAAAAA

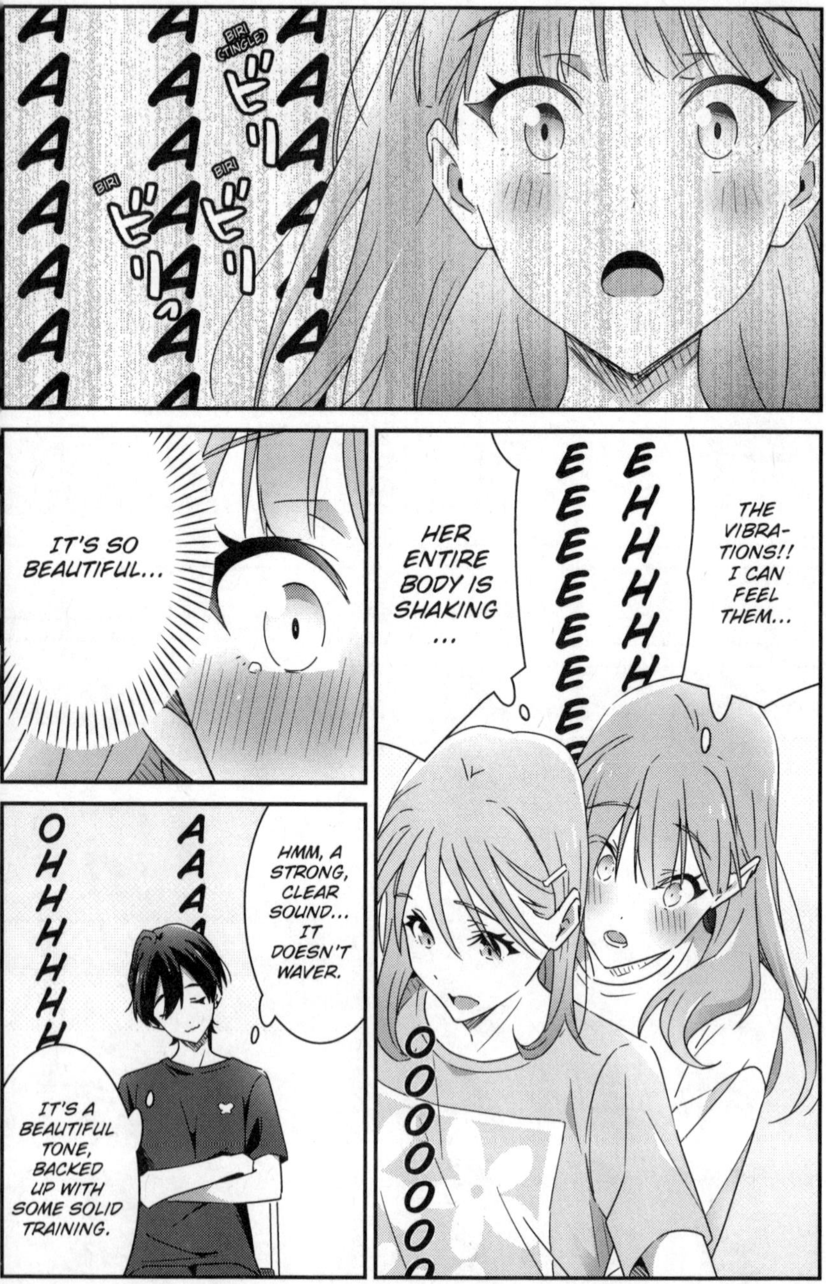
AAAAAAA
BIRI (TINGLE)
ビリ
AAAAAAA
BIRI
ビリ
BIRI
ビリッ
AAAAAAA
THE VIBRATIONS!! I CAN FEEL THEM...
EHHHHHH
EEEEEEEEE
HER ENTIRE BODY IS SHAKING...
OOOOOOOO
IT'S SO BEAUTIFUL...
AAAA
HMM, A STRONG, CLEAR SOUND... IT DOESN'T WAVER.
OHHHHHH
IT'S A BEAUTIFUL TONE, BACKED UP WITH SOME SOLID TRAINING.

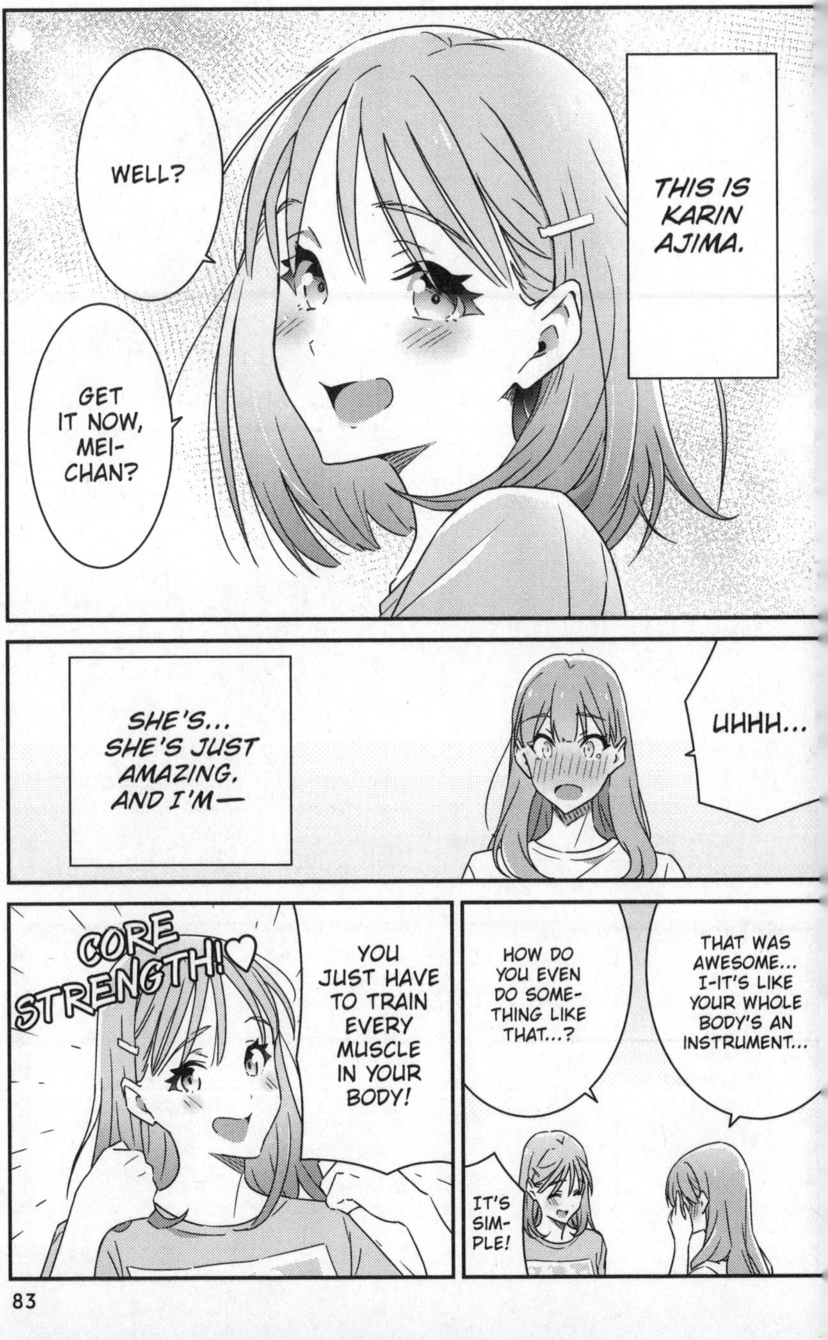
THIS IS KARIN AJIMA.
WELL?
GET IT NOW, MEI-CHAN?
UHHH...
SHE'S... SHE'S JUST AMAZING. AND I'M—
THAT WAS AWESOME... I-IT'S LIKE YOUR WHOLE BODY'S AN INSTRUMENT...
HOW DO YOU EVEN DO SOME-THING LIKE THAT...?
IT'S SIM-PLE!
YOU JUST HAVE TO TRAIN EVERY MUSCLE IN YOUR BODY!
CORE STRENGTH!♥

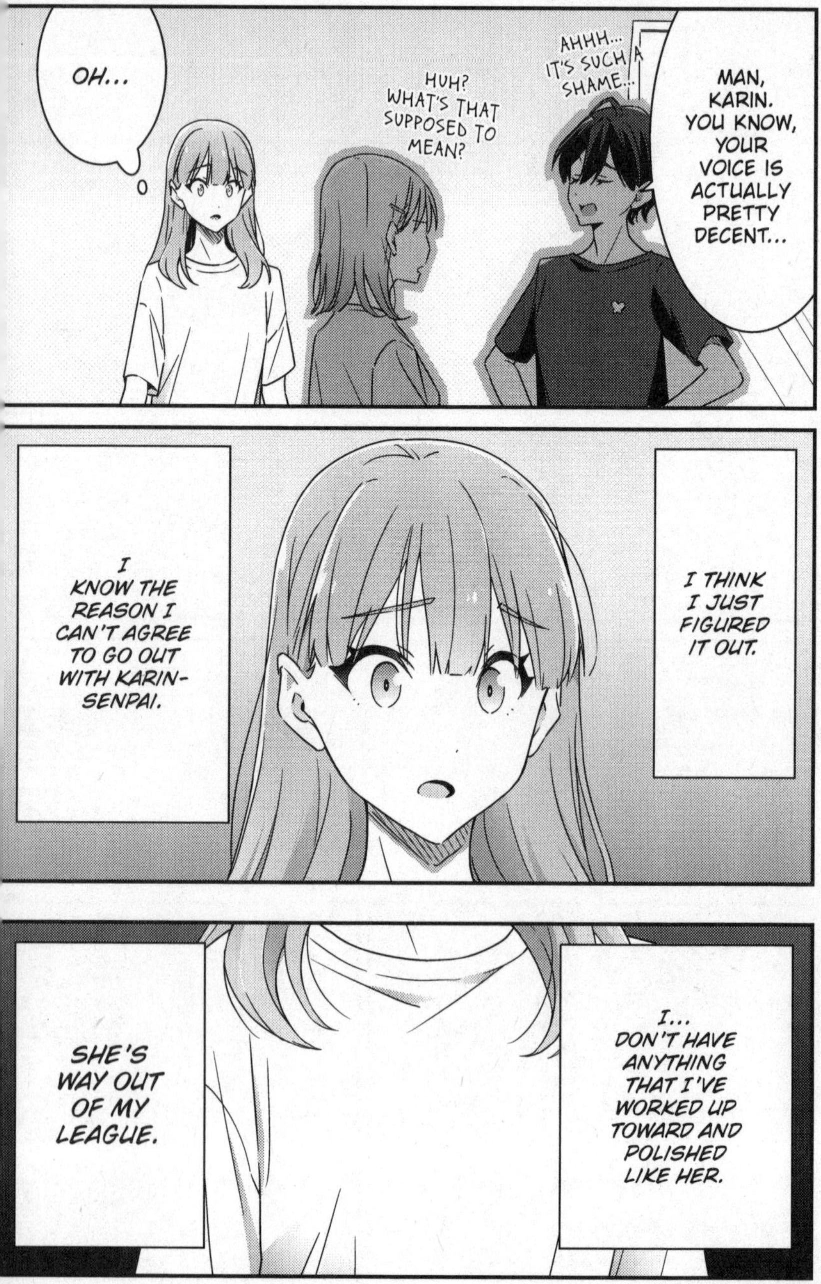
MAN, KARIN. YOU KNOW, YOUR VOICE IS ACTUALLY PRETTY DECENT...
AHHH... IT'S SUCH A SHAME...
HUH? WHAT'S THAT SUPPOSED TO MEAN?
OH...
I THINK I JUST FIGURED IT OUT.
I KNOW THE REASON I CAN'T AGREE TO GO OUT WITH KARIN-SENPAI.
I... DON'T HAVE ANYTHING THAT I'VE WORKED UP TOWARD AND POLISHED LIKE HER.
SHE'S WAY OUT OF MY LEAGUE.

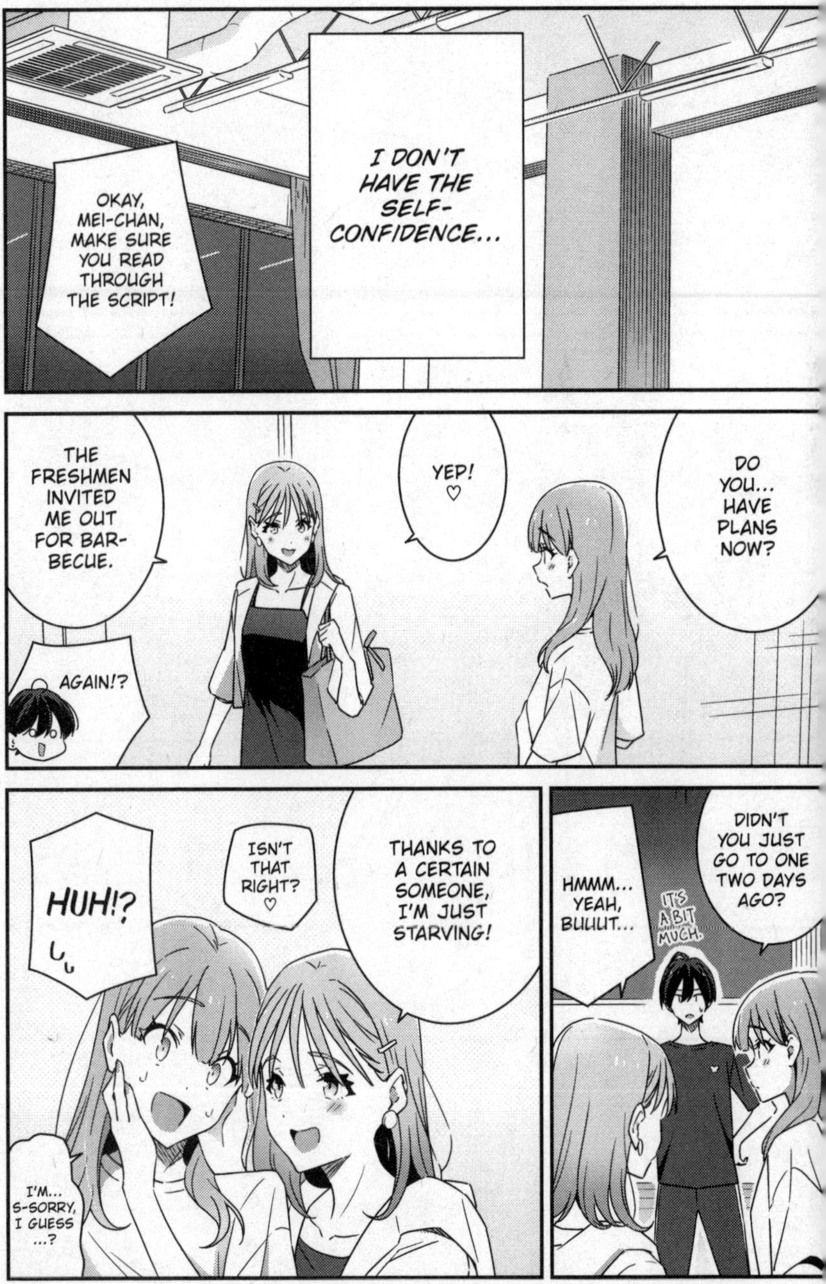
I DON'T HAVE THE SELF-CONFIDENCE...
OKAY, MEI-CHAN, MAKE SURE YOU READ THROUGH THE SCRIPT!
DO YOU... HAVE PLANS NOW?
YEP! ♡
THE FRESHMEN INVITED ME OUT FOR BAR-BECUE.
AGAIN!?
DIDN'T YOU JUST GO TO ONE TWO DAYS AGO?
IT'S A BIT MUCH.
HMMM... YEAH, BUUUT...
THANKS TO A CERTAIN SOMEONE, I'M JUST STARVING!
ISN'T THAT RIGHT? ♡
HUH!?
I'M... S-SORRY, I GUESS ...?

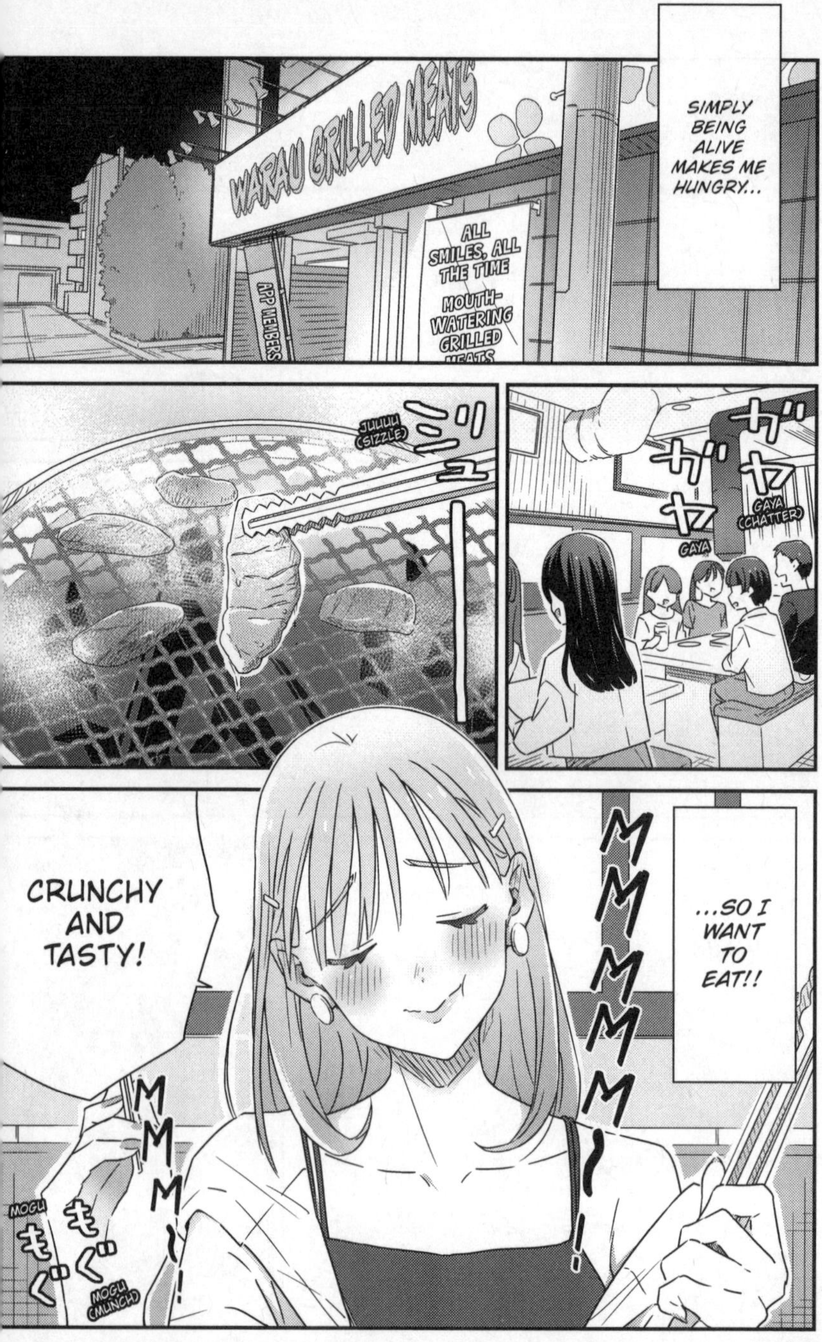
SIMPLY BEING ALIVE MAKES ME HUNGRY...
WARAU GRILLED MEATS
ALL SMILES, ALL THE TIME
MOUTH-WATERING GRILLED MEATS
APP MEMBERS
ガヤガヤ
GAYA GAYA (CHATTER)
ジュ〜ッ
JUUUU (SIZZLE)
...SO I WANT TO EAT!!
MMMMMM~!
CRUNCHY AND TASTY!
MMM~!
もぐもぐ
MOGU MOGU (MUNCH)

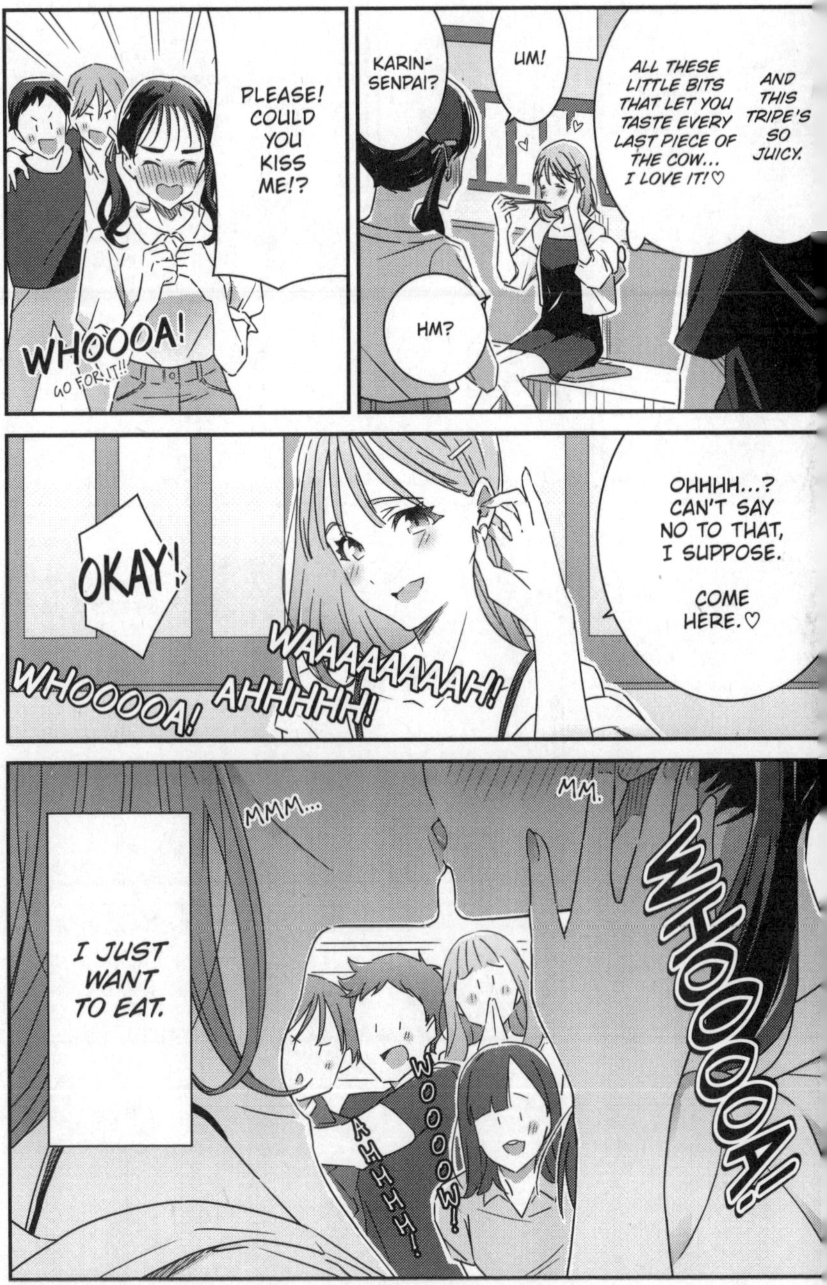
AND THIS TRIPE'S SO JUICY.
ALL THESE LITTLE BITS THAT LET YOU TASTE EVERY LAST PIECE OF THE COW... I LOVE IT!♡
UM!
KARIN-SENPAI?
HM?
PLEASE! COULD YOU KISS ME!?
WHOOOA!
GO FOR IT!!
OHHHH...? CAN'T SAY NO TO THAT, I SUPPOSE.
COME HERE.♡
WAAAAAAAAAH!
AHHHHH!
OKAY!
WHOOOOOA!
WHOOOOA!
MM.
MMM...
WOOOOOW!
AHHHHH!
I JUST WANT TO EAT.

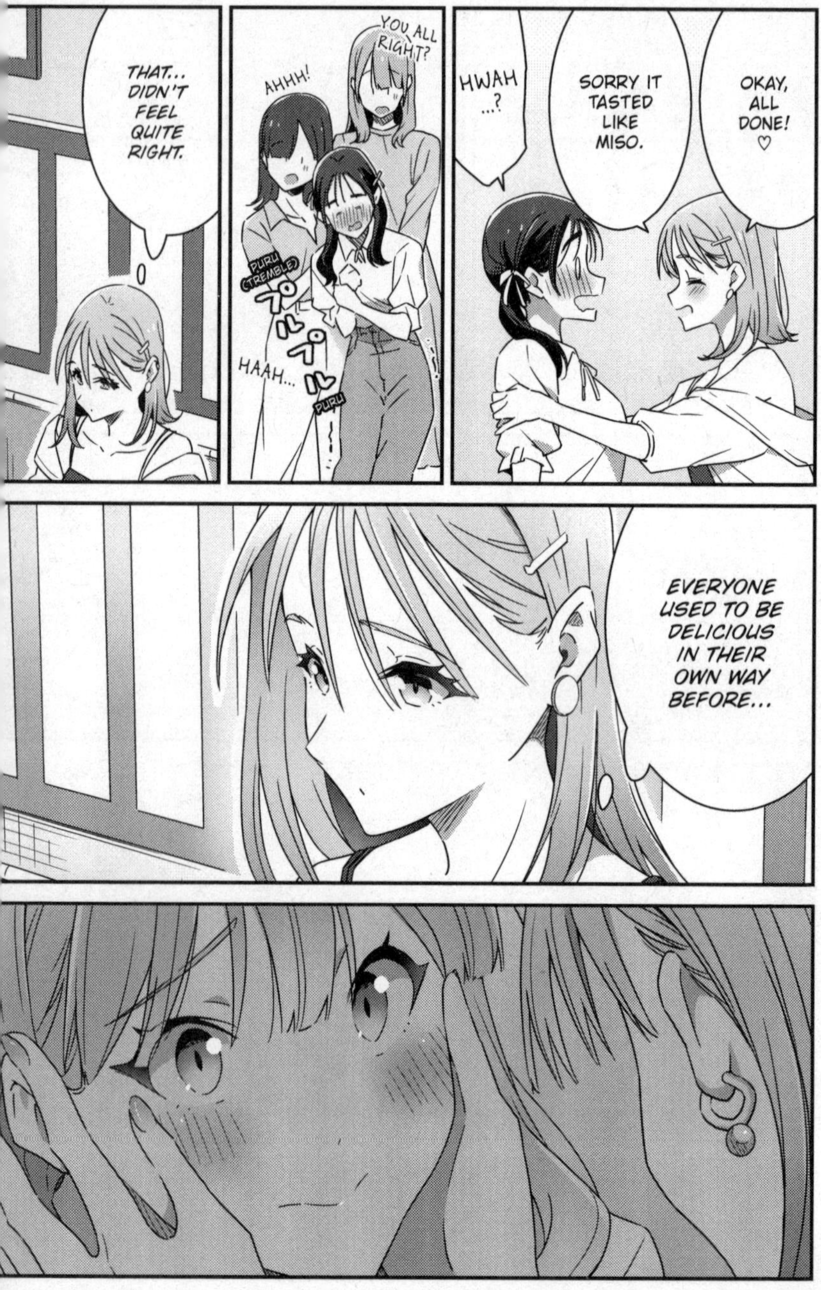
OKAY, ALL DONE! ♡
SORRY IT TASTED LIKE MISO.
HWAH ...?
YOU ALL RIGHT?
AHHH!
PURU (TREMBLE)
HAAH...
PURU
THAT... DIDN'T FEEL QUITE RIGHT.
EVERYONE USED TO BE DELICIOUS IN THEIR OWN WAY BEFORE...

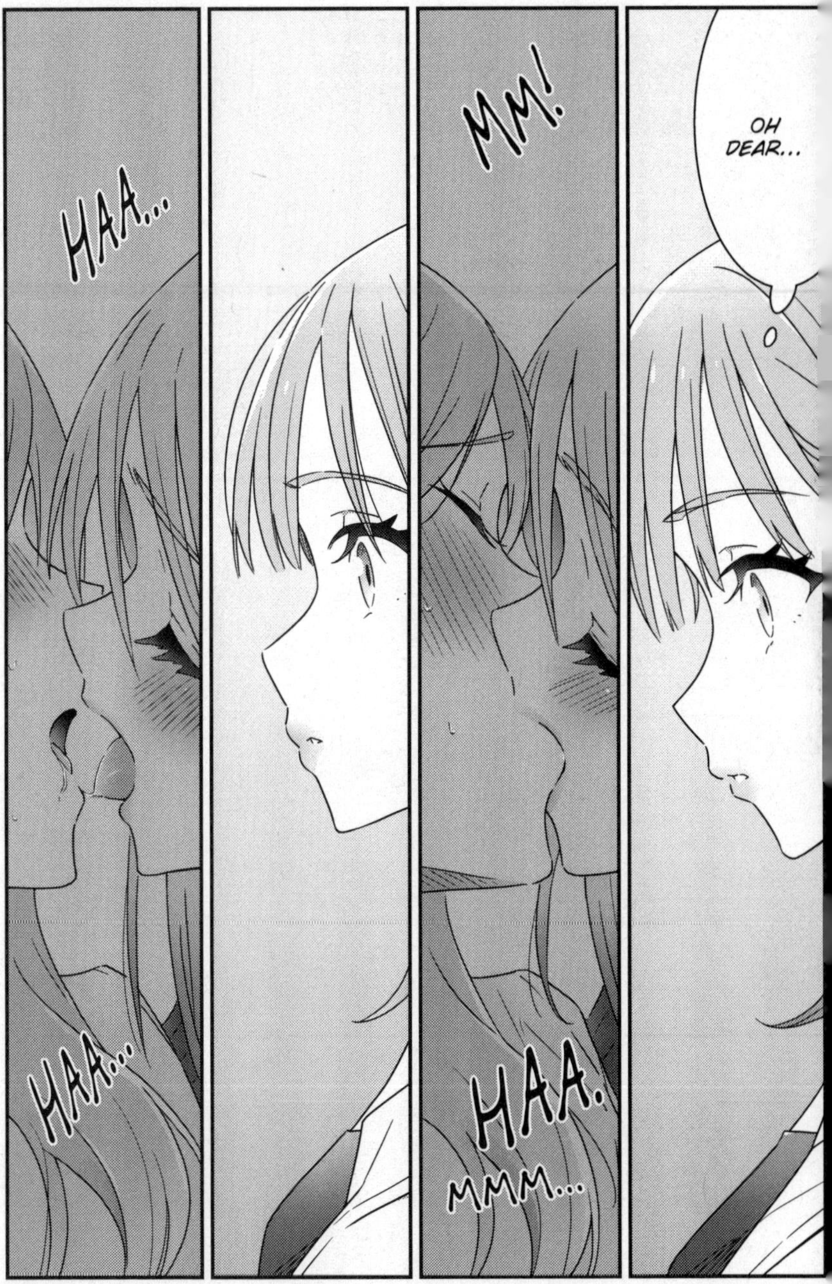
OH DEAR...
MM!
HAA.
MMM...
HAA...
HAA...

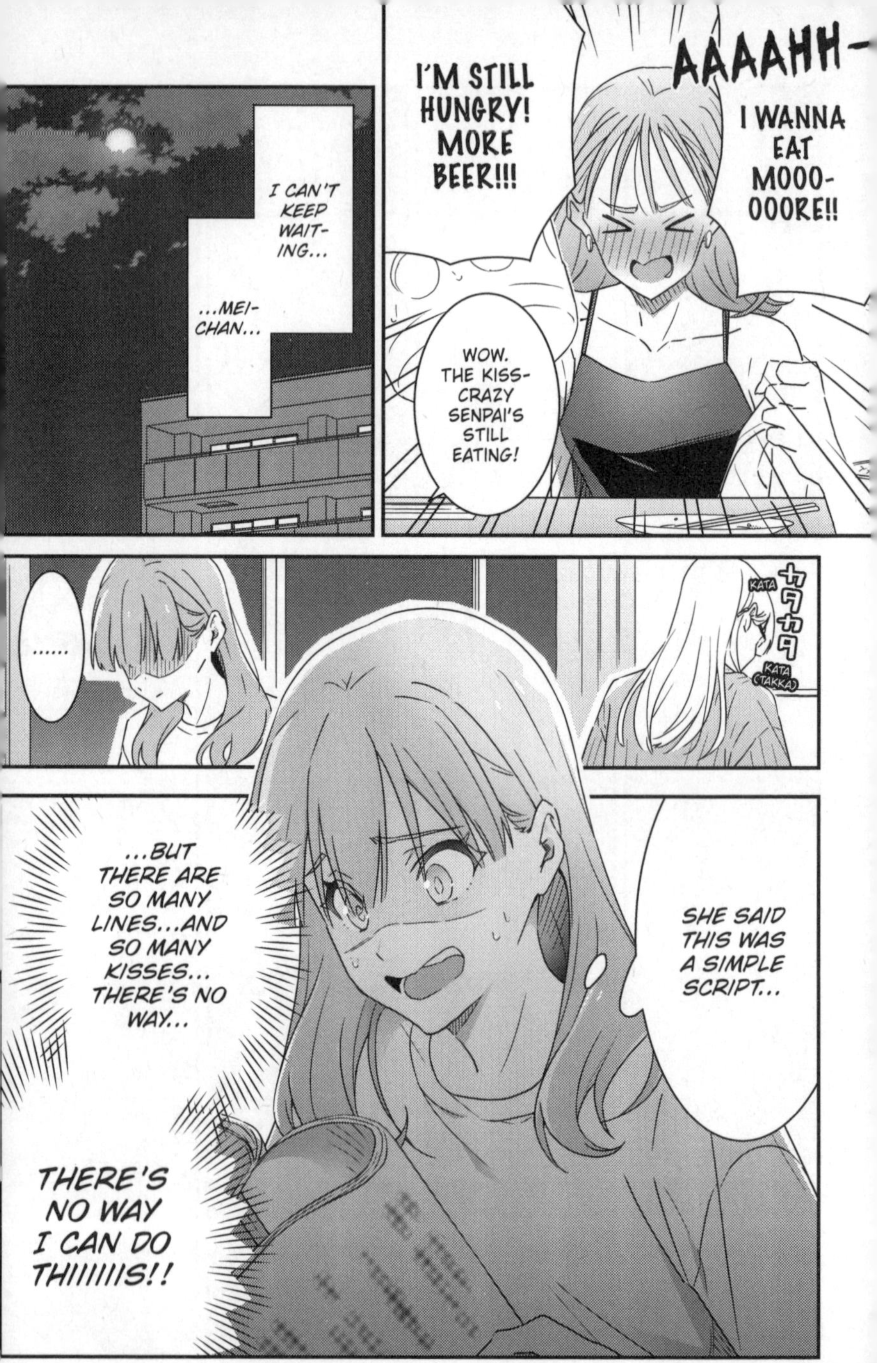

AAAAHH-
I WANNA EAT MOOOO-OOORE!!
I'M STILL HUNGRY! MORE BEER!!!
WOW. THE KISS-CRAZY SENPAI'S STILL EATING!
I CAN'T KEEP WAITING...
...MEI-CHAN...
カタカタ
KATA KATA (TAKKA)
......
SHE SAID THIS WAS A SIMPLE SCRIPT...
...BUT THERE ARE SO MANY LINES...AND SO MANY KISSES... THERE'S NO WAY...
THERE'S NO WAY I CAN DO THIIIIIIS!!

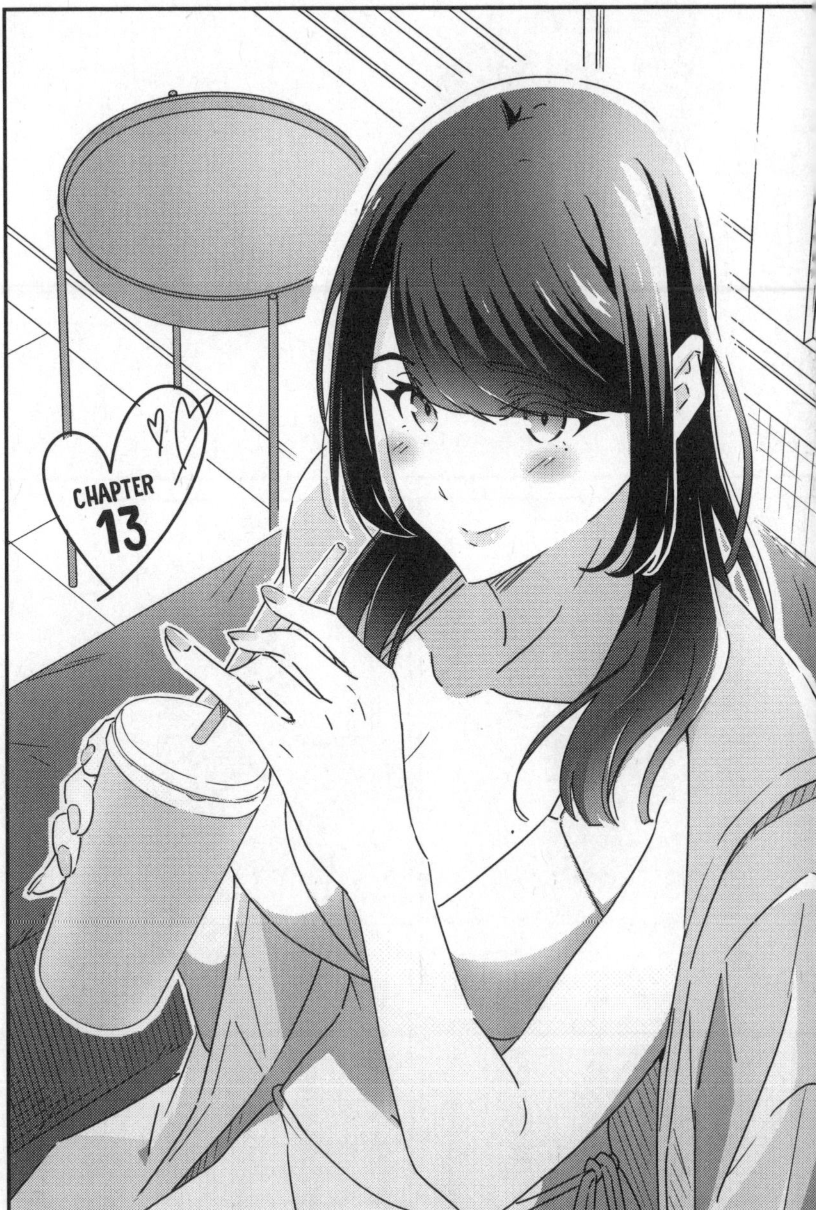
CHAPTER
13

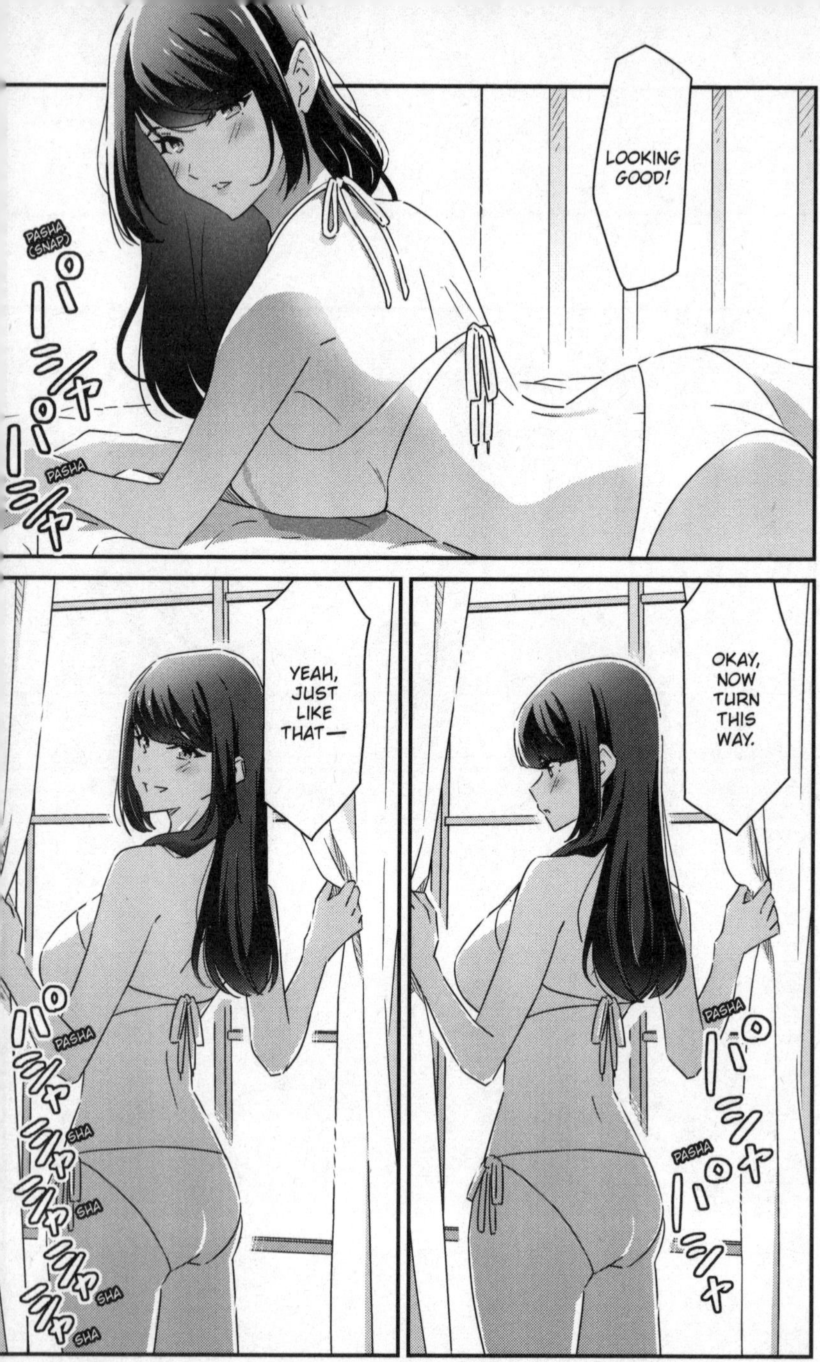
LOOKING GOOD!
PASHA (SNAP)
PASHA
OKAY, NOW TURN THIS WAY.
PASHA
PASHA
YEAH, JUST LIKE THAT—
PASHA
SHA
SHA
SHA
SHA

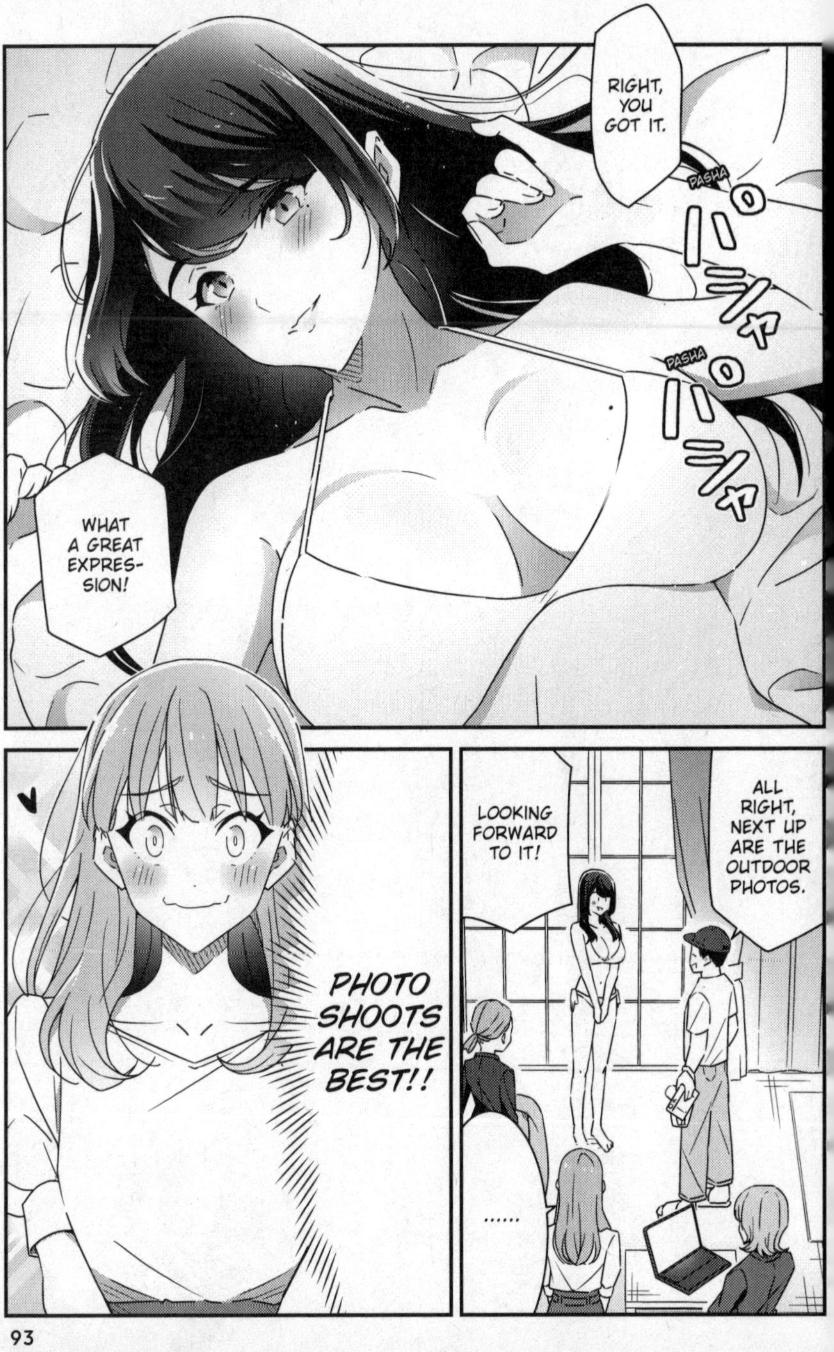
RIGHT, YOU GOT IT.
PASHA
パシャ
PASHA
パシャ
WHAT A GREAT EXPRES-SION!
ALL RIGHT, NEXT UP ARE THE OUTDOOR PHOTOS.
LOOKING FORWARD TO IT!
......
PHOTO SHOOTS ARE THE BEST!!

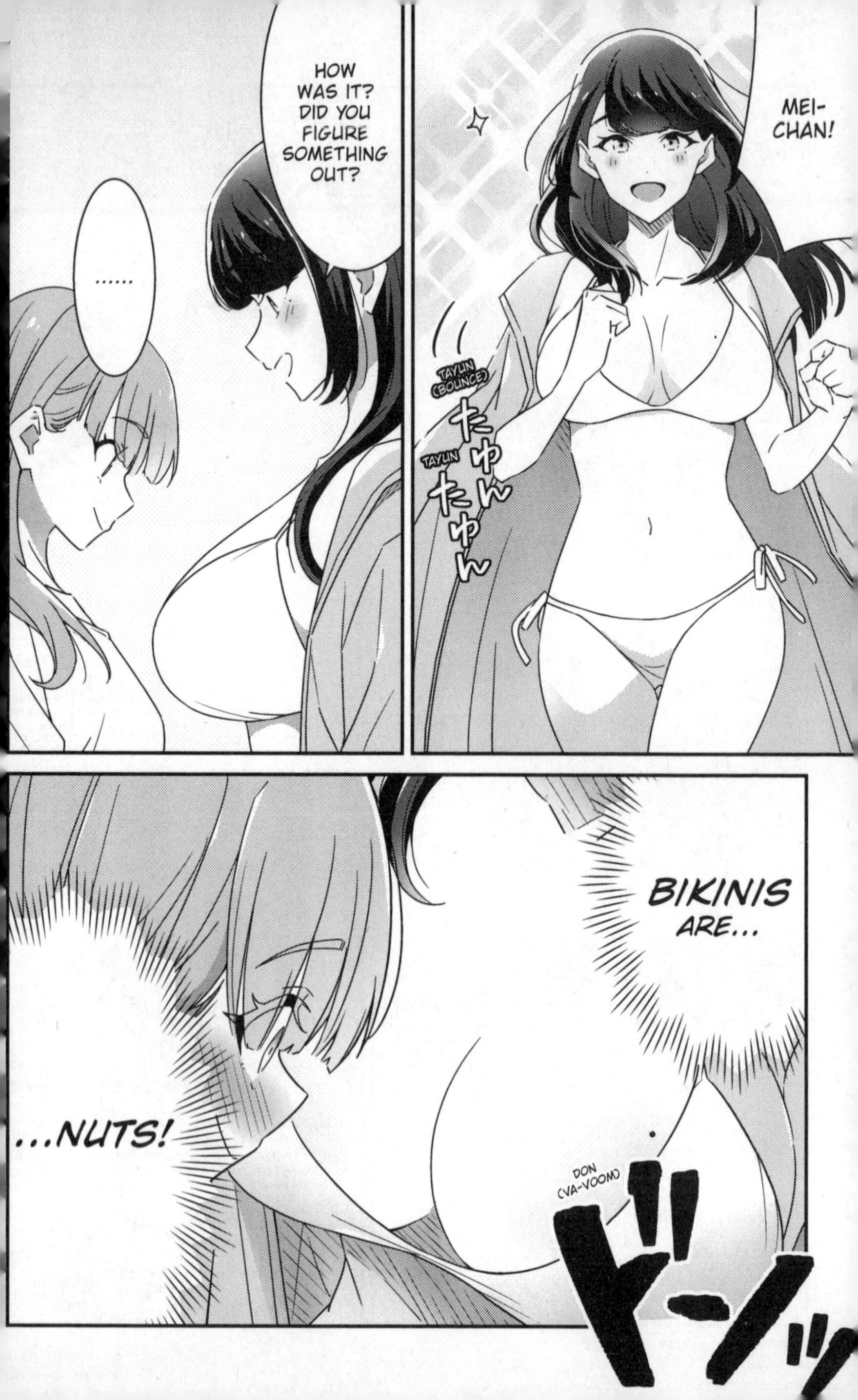
MEI-CHAN!
TAYUN (BOUNCE)
たゆん
TAYUN
たゆん
HOW WAS IT? DID YOU FIGURE SOMETHING OUT?
......
BIKINIS ARE...
...NUTS!
DON (VA-VOOM)
ドーンッ

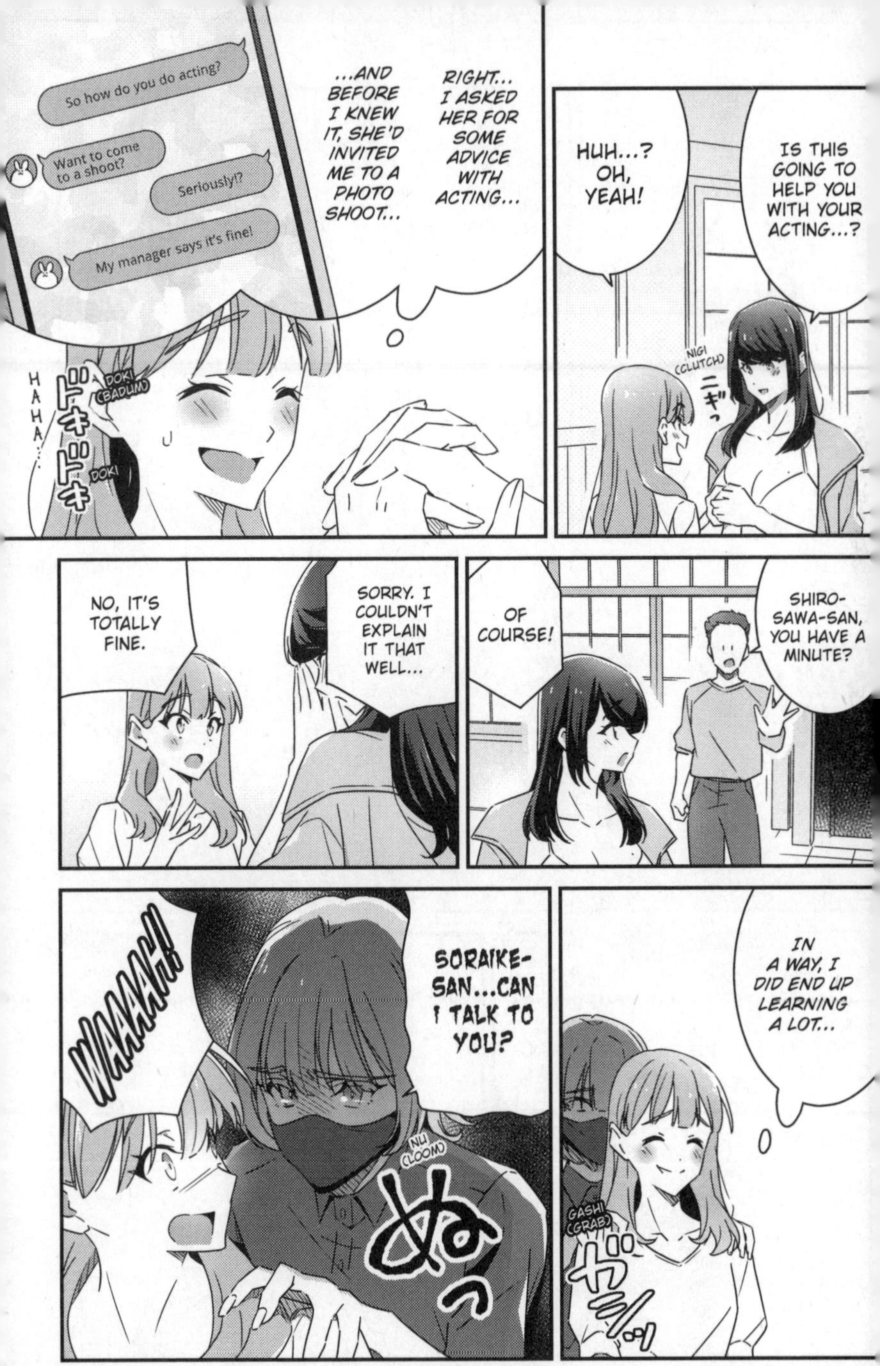
IS THIS GOING TO HELP YOU WITH YOUR ACTING...?
HUH...? OH, YEAH!
NIGI (CLUTCH)
RIGHT... I ASKED HER FOR SOME ADVICE WITH ACTING...
...AND BEFORE I KNEW IT, SHE'D INVITED ME TO A PHOTO SHOOT...
So how do you do acting?
Want to come to a shoot?
Seriously!?
My manager says it's fine!
DOKI (BADUM)
HAHA...
DOKI
SHIRO-SAWA-SAN, YOU HAVE A MINUTE?
OF COURSE!
SORRY. I COULDN'T EXPLAIN IT THAT WELL...
NO, IT'S TOTALLY FINE.
IN A WAY, I DID END UP LEARNING A LOT...
GASHI (GRAB)
SORAIKE-SAN...CAN I TALK TO YOU?
NU (LOOM)
WAAAAAGH!

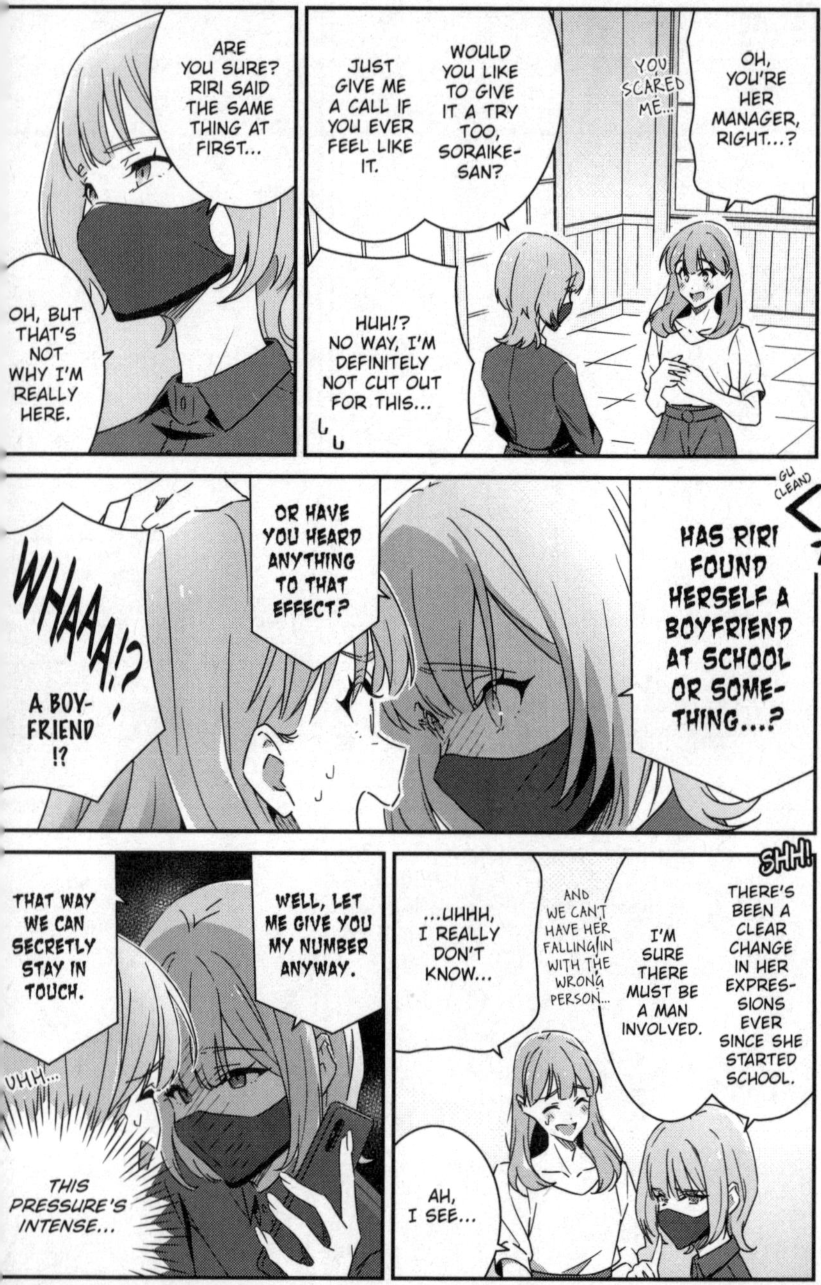
OH, YOU'RE HER MANAGER, RIGHT...?
YOU SCARED ME...
WOULD YOU LIKE TO GIVE IT A TRY TOO, SORAIKE-SAN?
JUST GIVE ME A CALL IF YOU EVER FEEL LIKE IT.
HUH!? NO WAY, I'M DEFINITELY NOT CUT OUT FOR THIS...
ARE YOU SURE? RIRI SAID THE SAME THING AT FIRST...
OH, BUT THAT'S NOT WHY I'M REALLY HERE.
GU CLEAND
ぐっ
HAS RIRI FOUND HERSELF A BOYFRIEND AT SCHOOL OR SOMETHING...?
OR HAVE YOU HEARD ANYTHING TO THAT EFFECT?
WHAAAA!?
A BOY-FRIEND!?
SHH!
THERE'S BEEN A CLEAR CHANGE IN HER EXPRESSIONS EVER SINCE SHE STARTED SCHOOL.
I'M SURE THERE MUST BE A MAN INVOLVED.
AND WE CAN'T HAVE HER FALLING IN WITH THE WRONG PERSON...
...UHHH, I REALLY DON'T KNOW...
AH, I SEE...
WELL, LET ME GIVE YOU MY NUMBER ANYWAY.
THAT WAY WE CAN SECRETLY STAY IN TOUCH.
UHH...
THIS PRESSURE'S INTENSE...

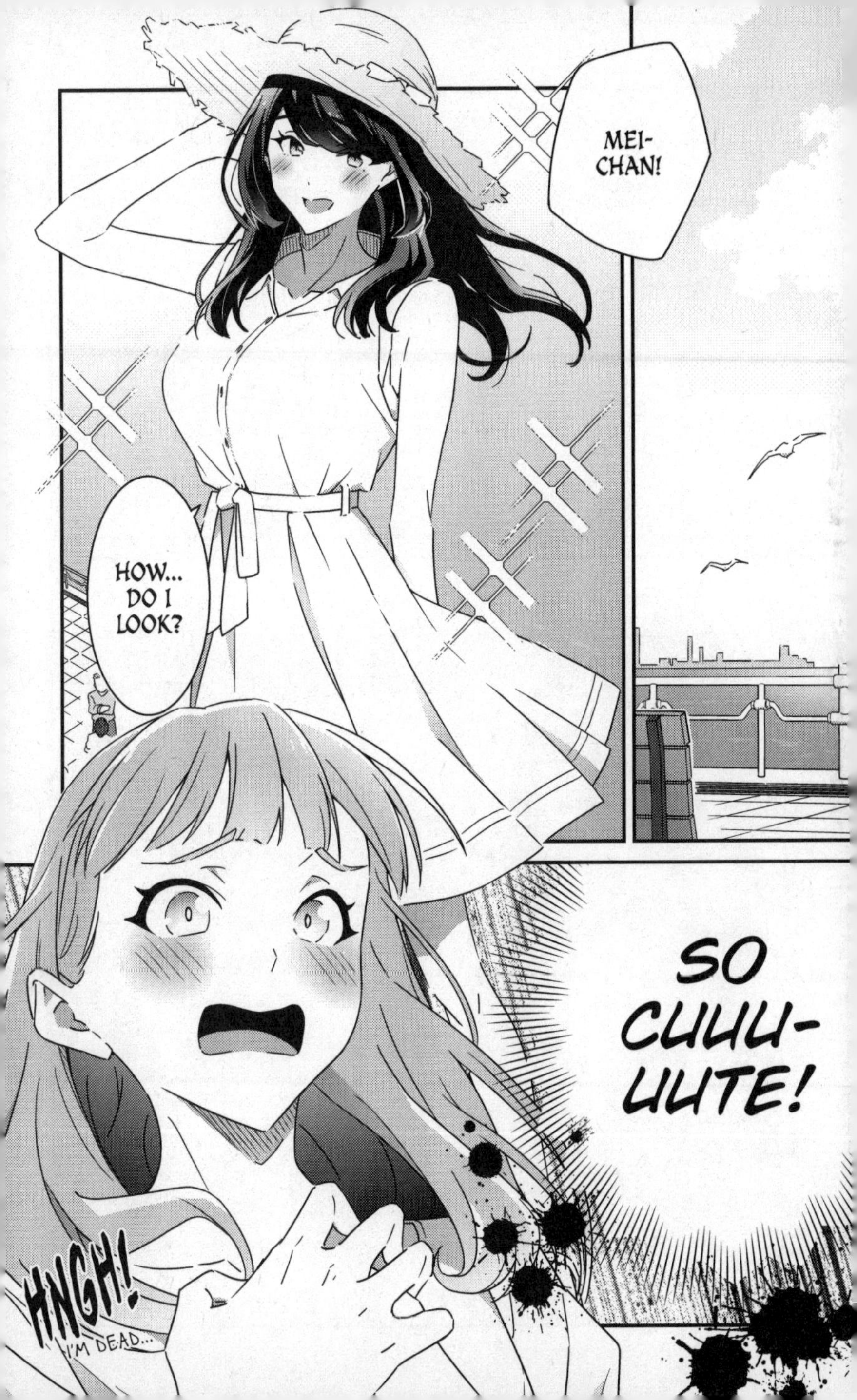
MEI-CHAN!
HOW... DO I LOOK?
SO CUUU-UUTE!
HNGH!
I'M DEAD...

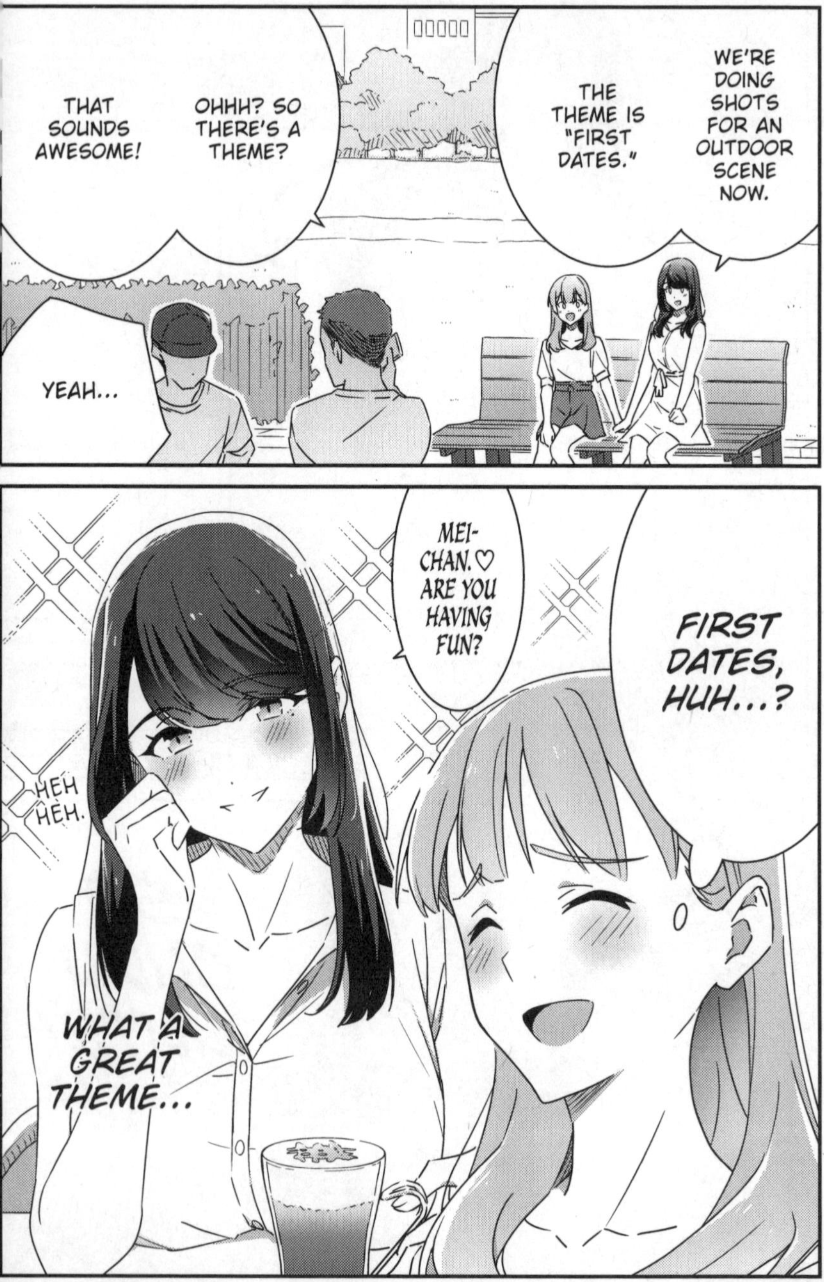
WE'RE DOING SHOTS FOR AN OUTDOOR SCENE NOW.
THE THEME IS "FIRST DATES."
OHHH? SO THERE'S A THEME?
THAT SOUNDS AWESOME!
YEAH...
FIRST DATES, HUH...?
MEI-CHAN.♡ ARE YOU HAVING FUN?
HEH HEH.
WHAT A GREAT THEME...

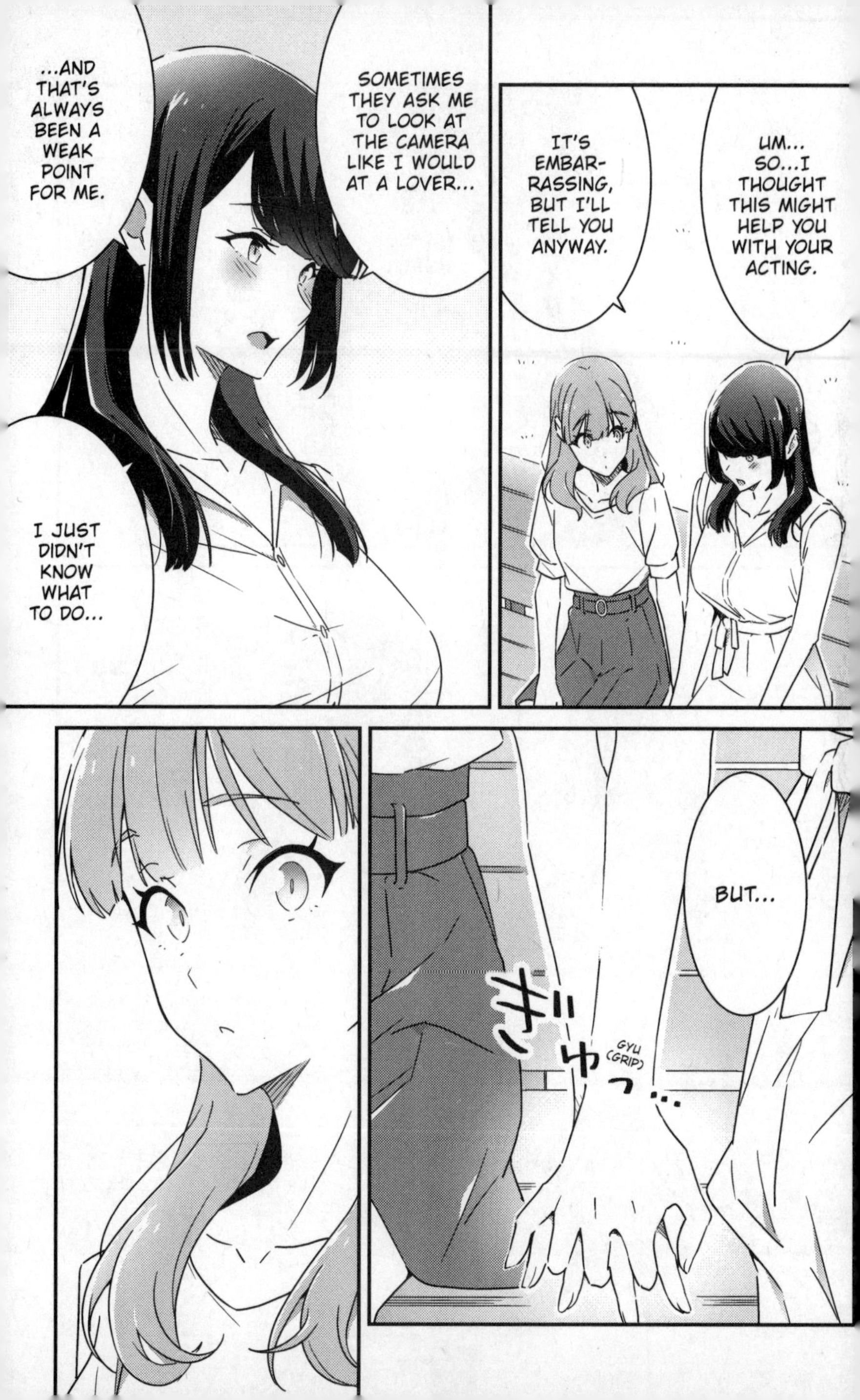
UM... SO...I THOUGHT THIS MIGHT HELP YOU WITH YOUR ACTING.
IT'S EMBAR-RASSING, BUT I'LL TELL YOU ANYWAY.
SOMETIMES THEY ASK ME TO LOOK AT THE CAMERA LIKE I WOULD AT A LOVER...
...AND THAT'S ALWAYS BEEN A WEAK POINT FOR ME.
I JUST DIDN'T KNOW WHAT TO DO...
BUT...
ぎゅっ...
GYU (GRIP)

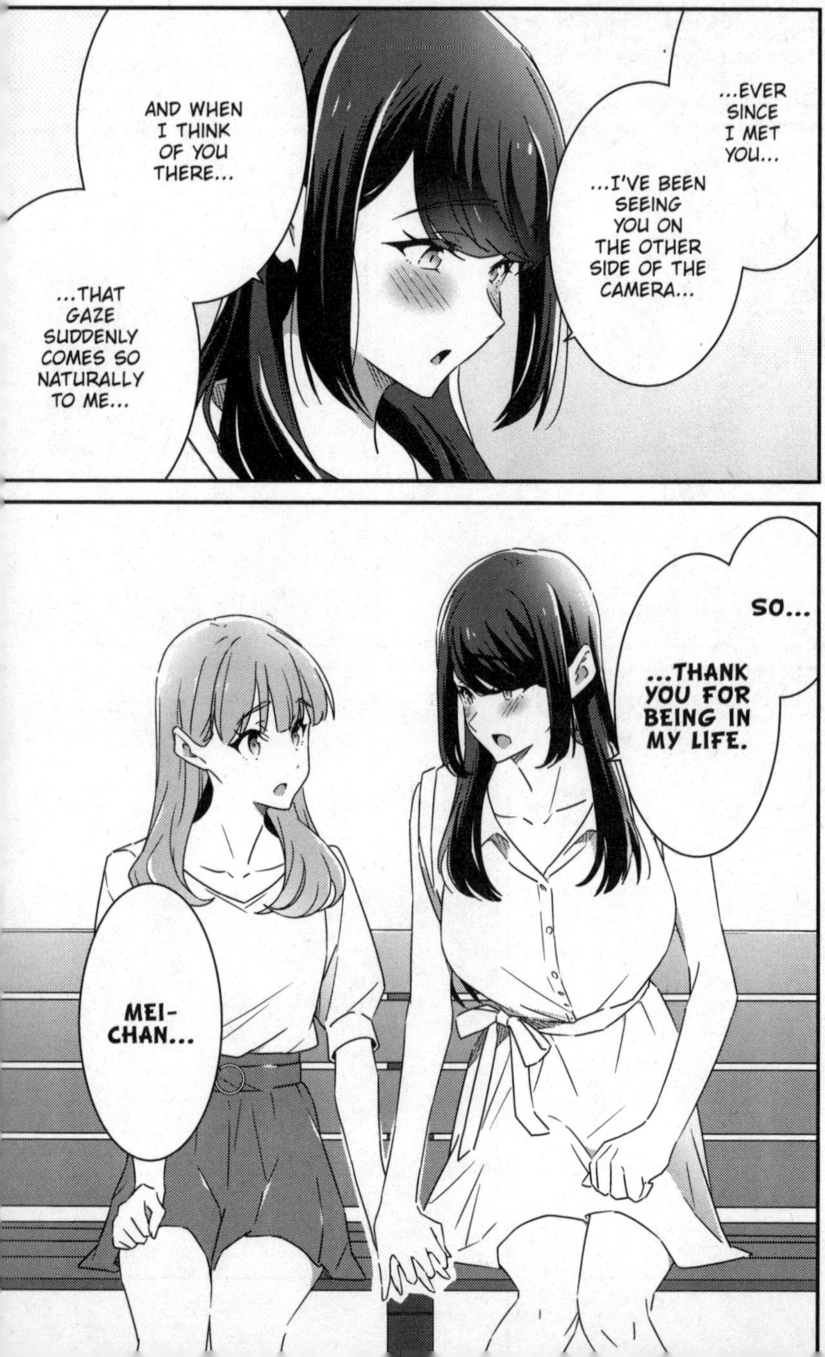
...EVER SINCE I MET YOU...
...I'VE BEEN SEEING YOU ON THE OTHER SIDE OF THE CAMERA...
AND WHEN I THINK OF YOU THERE...
...THAT GAZE SUDDENLY COMES SO NATURALLY TO ME...
SO...
...THANK YOU FOR BEING IN MY LIFE.
MEI-CHAN...

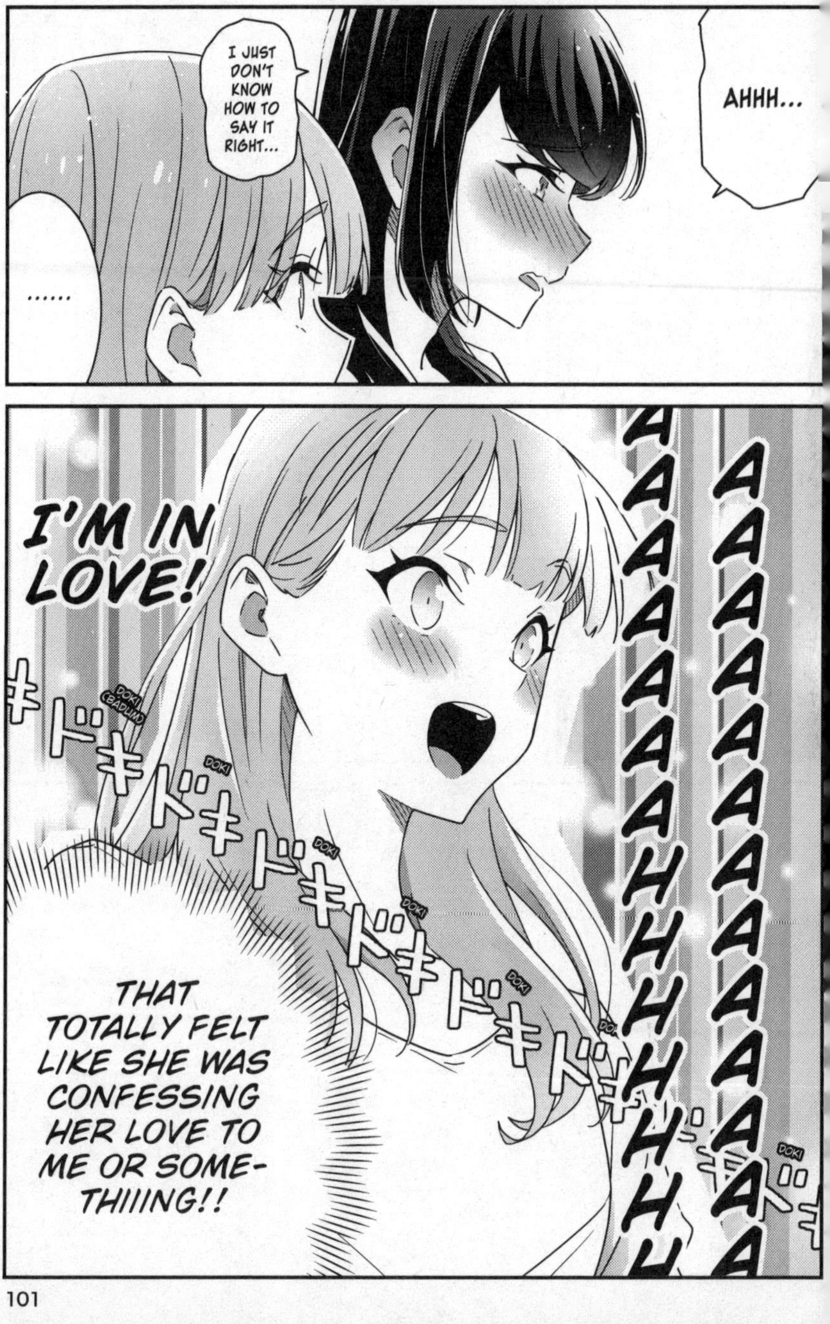
AHHH...
I JUST DON'T KNOW HOW TO SAY IT RIGHT...
......
AAAAAAAAAAAAAAAAAA
AAAAAAAAAAHHHHHHHHH
I'M IN LOVE!
ドキドキドキドキドキドキ
DOKI (BADUMP)
DOKI
DOKI
DOKI
DOKI
DOKI
THAT TOTALLY FELT LIKE SHE WAS CONFESSING HER LOVE TO ME OR SOME-THIIING!!

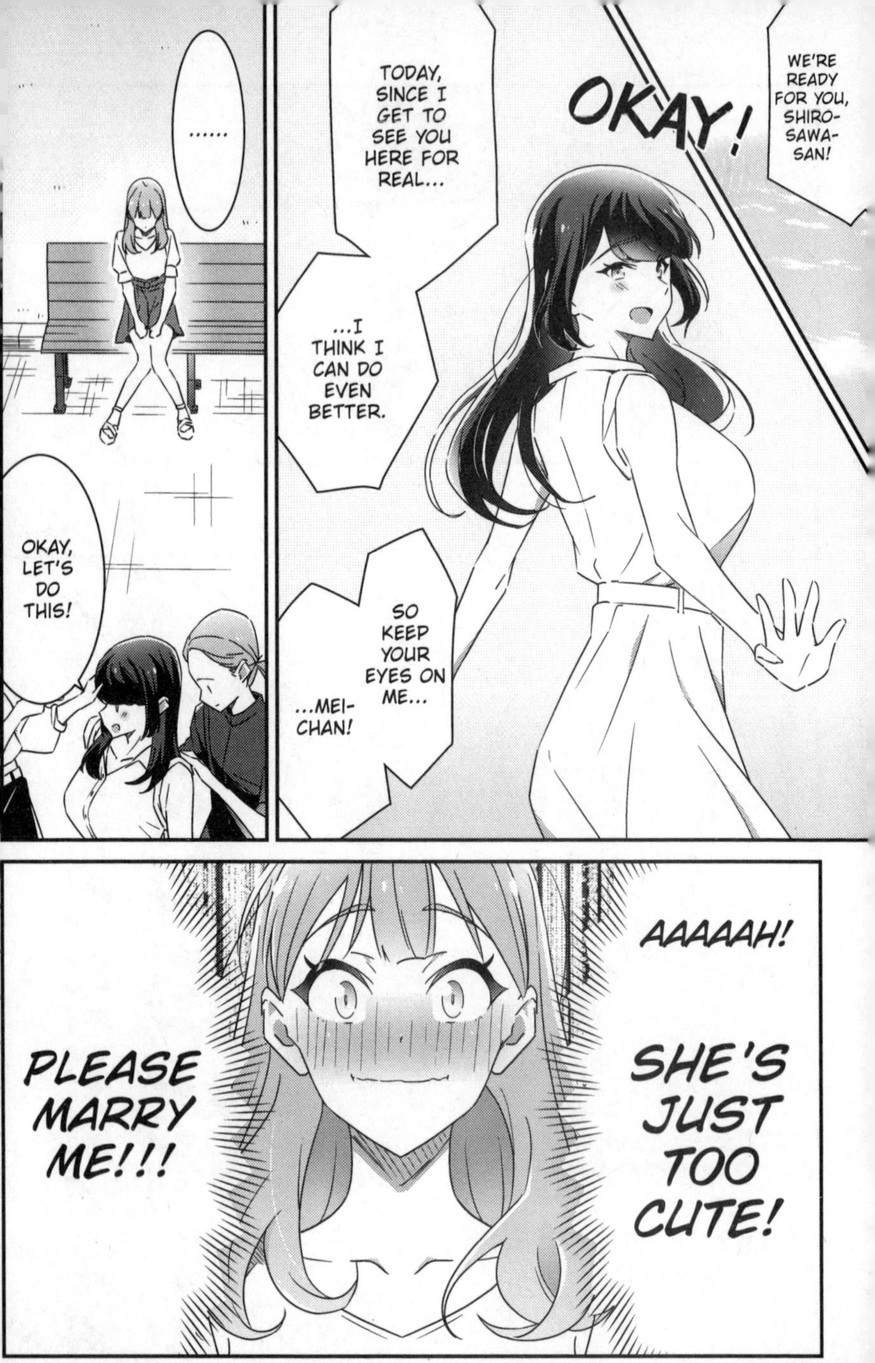
WE'RE READY FOR YOU, SHIRO-SAWA-SAN!
OKAY!
TODAY, SINCE I GET TO SEE YOU HERE FOR REAL...
...I THINK I CAN DO EVEN BETTER.
SO KEEP YOUR EYES ON ME...
...MEI-CHAN!
......
OKAY, LET'S DO THIS!
AAAAAH!
SHE'S JUST TOO CUTE!
PLEASE MARRY ME!!!

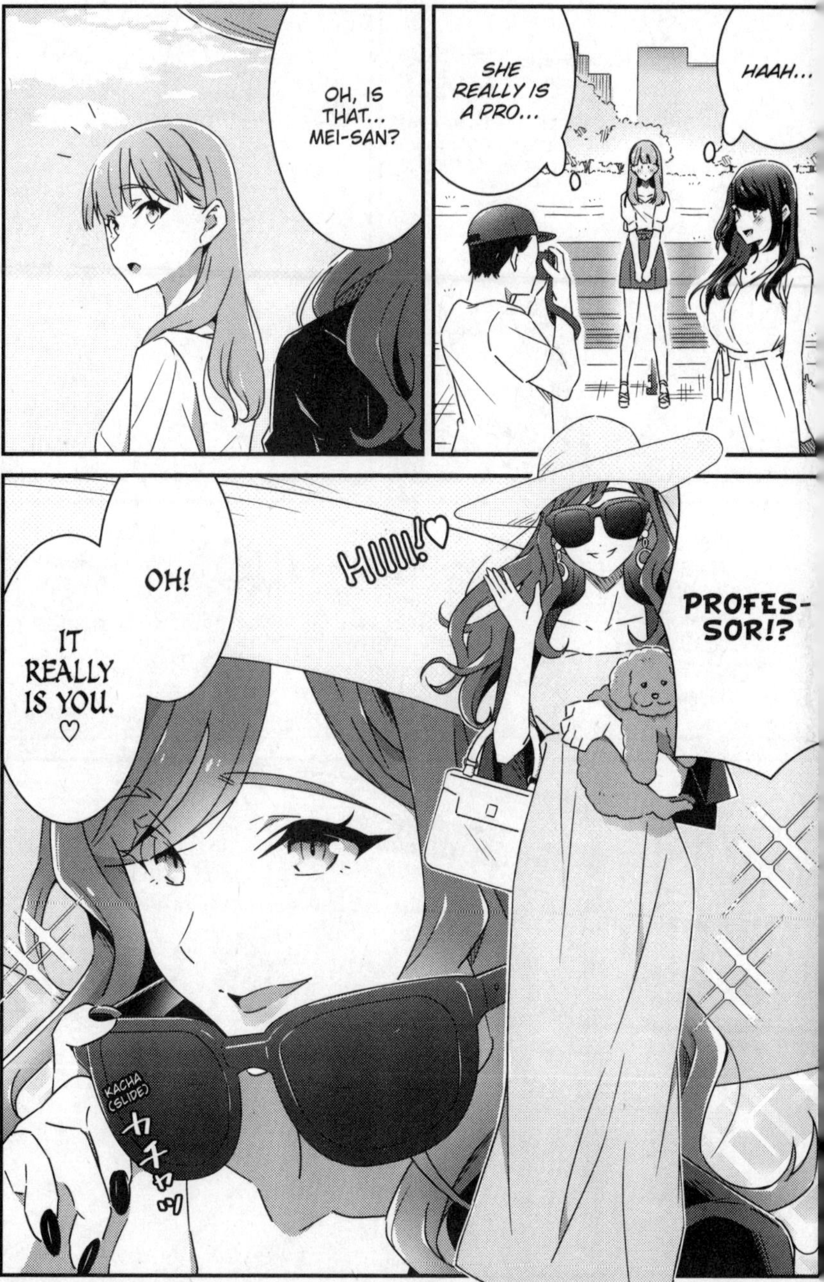
HAAH...
SHE REALLY IS A PRO...
OH, IS THAT... MEI-SAN?
PROFES-SOR!?
HIIII!♡
OH! IT REALLY IS YOU. ♡
KACHA (SLIDE)
カチャッ

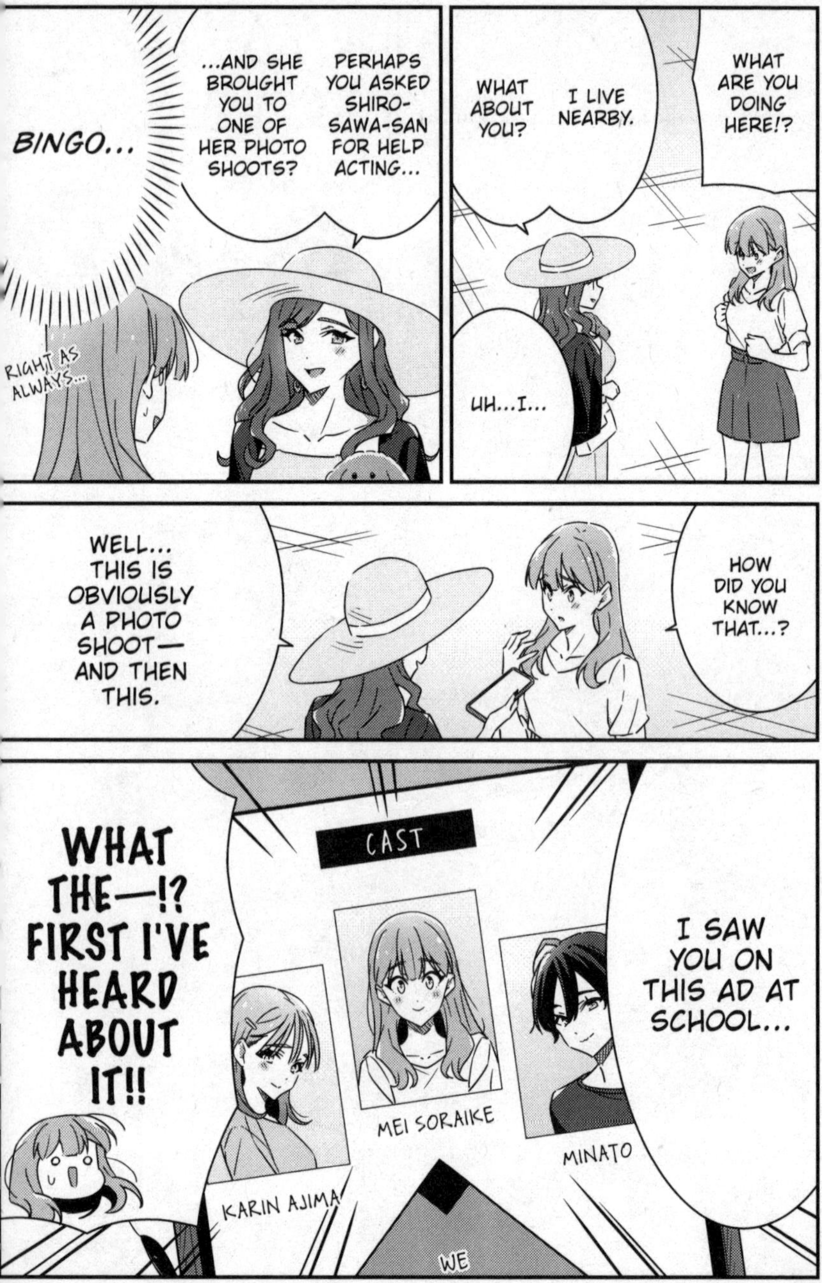
WHAT ARE YOU DOING HERE!?
I LIVE NEARBY.
WHAT ABOUT YOU?
UH...I...
PERHAPS YOU ASKED SHIRO-SAWA-SAN FOR HELP ACTING...
...AND SHE BROUGHT YOU TO ONE OF HER PHOTO SHOOTS?
BINGO...
RIGHT AS ALWAYS...
HOW DID YOU KNOW THAT...?
WELL... THIS IS OBVIOUSLY A PHOTO SHOOT—AND THEN THIS.
I SAW YOU ON THIS AD AT SCHOOL...
CAST
MINATO
MEI SORAIKE
KARIN AJIMA
WE
WHAT THE—!? FIRST I'VE HEARD ABOUT IT!!

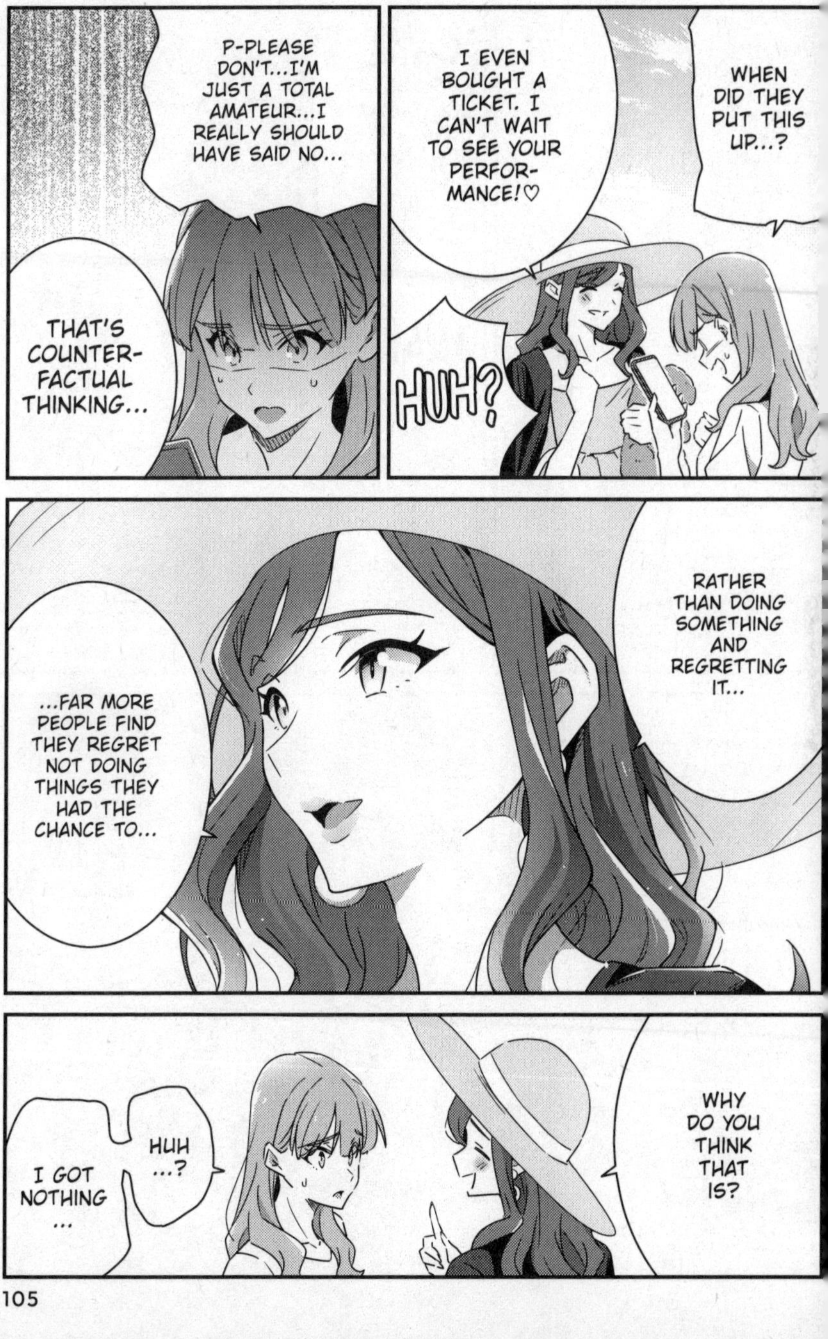
WHEN DID THEY PUT THIS UP...?
I EVEN BOUGHT A TICKET. I CAN'T WAIT TO SEE YOUR PERFOR-MANCE!♡
HUH?
P-PLEASE DON'T...I'M JUST A TOTAL AMATEUR...I REALLY SHOULD HAVE SAID NO...
THAT'S COUNTER-FACTUAL THINKING...
RATHER THAN DOING SOMETHING AND REGRETTING IT...
...FAR MORE PEOPLE FIND THEY REGRET NOT DOING THINGS THEY HAD THE CHANCE TO...
WHY DO YOU THINK THAT IS?
HUH ...?
I GOT NOTHING ...

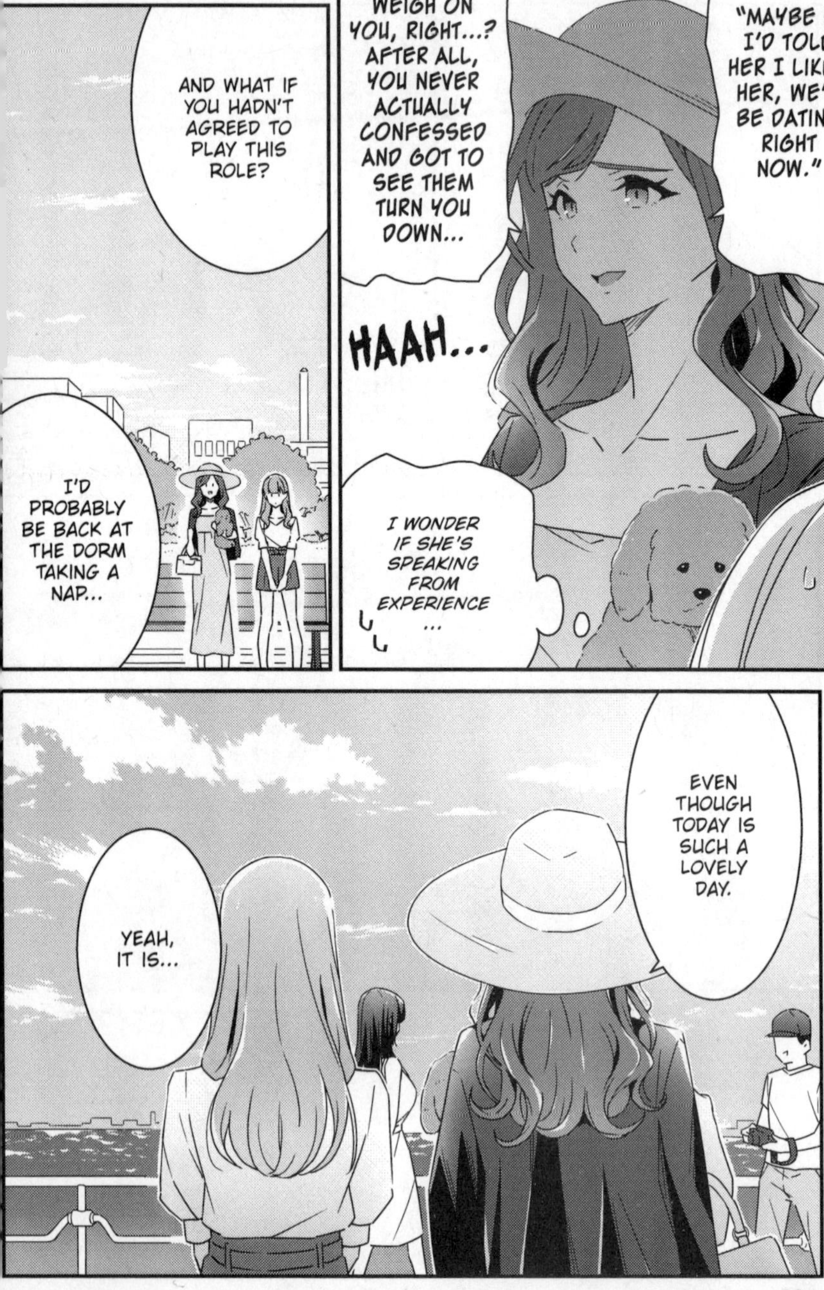
"MAYBE IF I'D TOLD HER I LIKED HER, WE'D BE DATING RIGHT NOW."
THAT WOULD WEIGH ON YOU, RIGHT...? AFTER ALL, YOU NEVER ACTUALLY CONFESSED AND GOT TO SEE THEM TURN YOU DOWN...
HAAH...
I WONDER IF SHE'S SPEAKING FROM EXPERIENCE...
AND WHAT IF YOU HADN'T AGREED TO PLAY THIS ROLE?
I'D PROBABLY BE BACK AT THE DORM TAKING A NAP...
EVEN THOUGH TODAY IS SUCH A LOVELY DAY.
YEAH, IT IS...

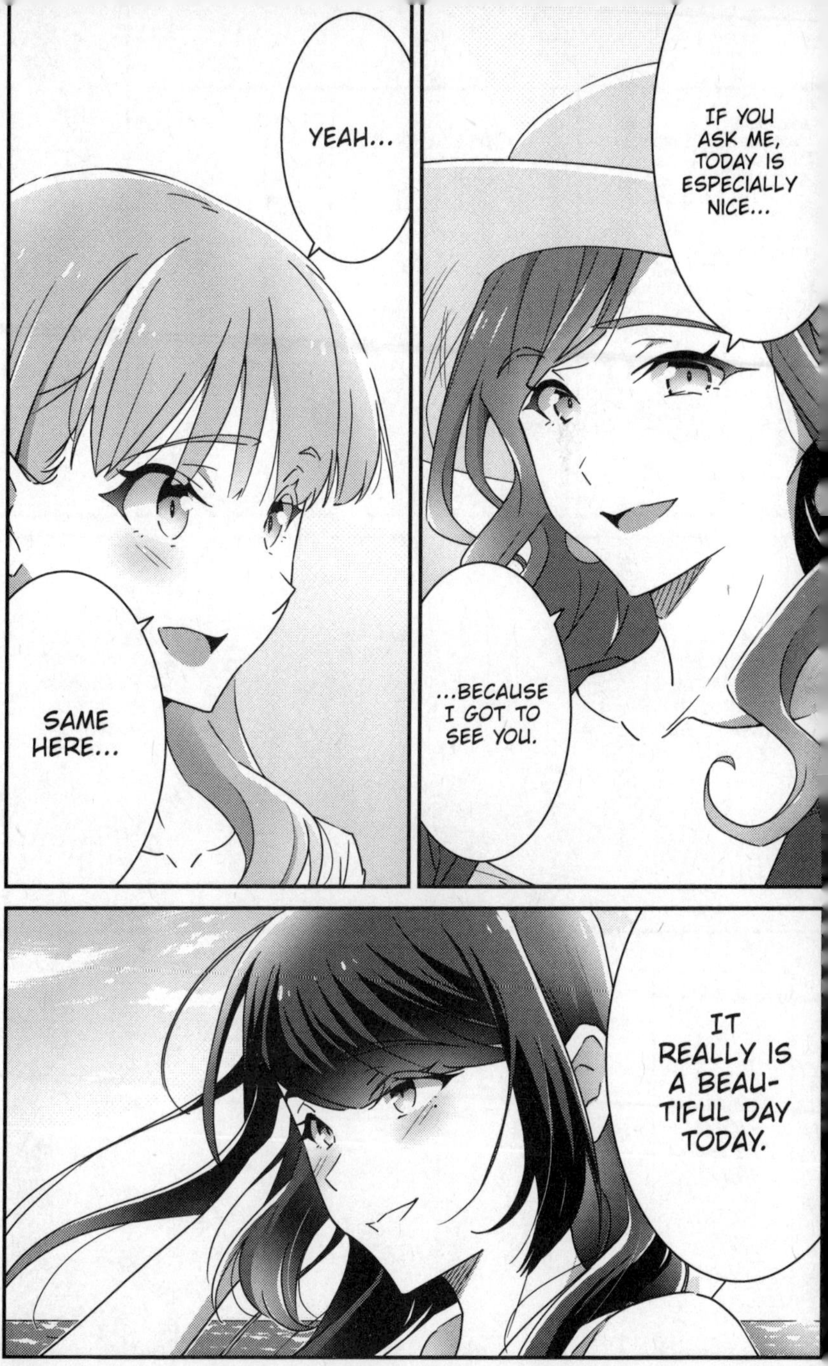
IF YOU ASK ME, TODAY IS ESPECIALLY NICE...
...BECAUSE I GOT TO SEE YOU.
YEAH...
SAME HERE...
IT REALLY IS A BEAU-TIFUL DAY TODAY.

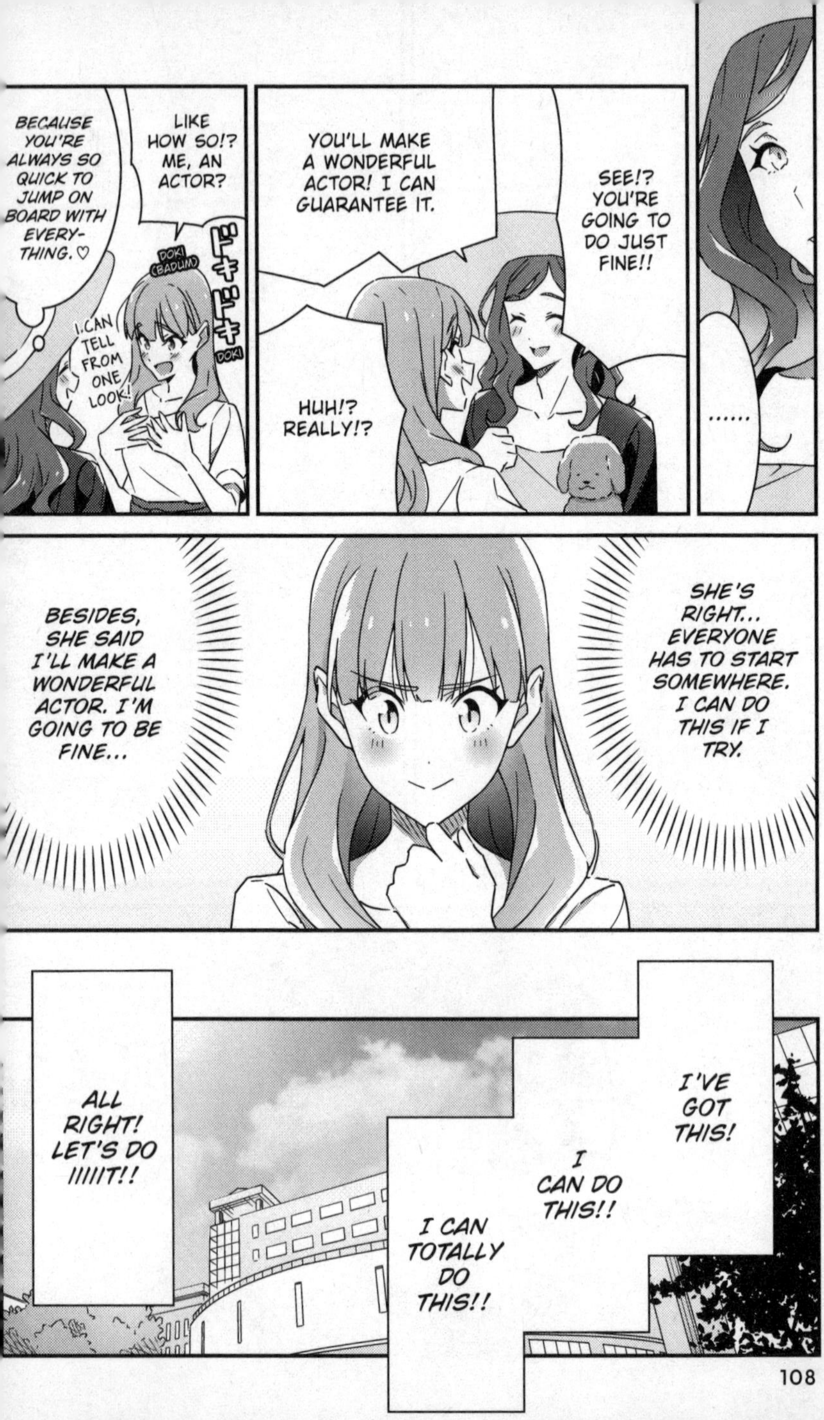
......
SEE!? YOU'RE GOING TO DO JUST FINE!!
YOU'LL MAKE A WONDERFUL ACTOR! I CAN GUARANTEE IT.
HUH!? REALLY!?
LIKE HOW SO!? ME, AN ACTOR?
DOKI (BADUM) DOKI
I CAN TELL FROM ONE LOOK!
BECAUSE YOU'RE ALWAYS SO QUICK TO JUMP ON BOARD WITH EVERY-THING.♡
SHE'S RIGHT... EVERYONE HAS TO START SOMEWHERE. I CAN DO THIS IF I TRY.
BESIDES, SHE SAID I'LL MAKE A WONDERFUL ACTOR. I'M GOING TO BE FINE...
I'VE GOT THIS!
I CAN DO THIS!!
I CAN TOTALLY DO THIS!!
ALL RIGHT! LET'S DO IIIIIT!!

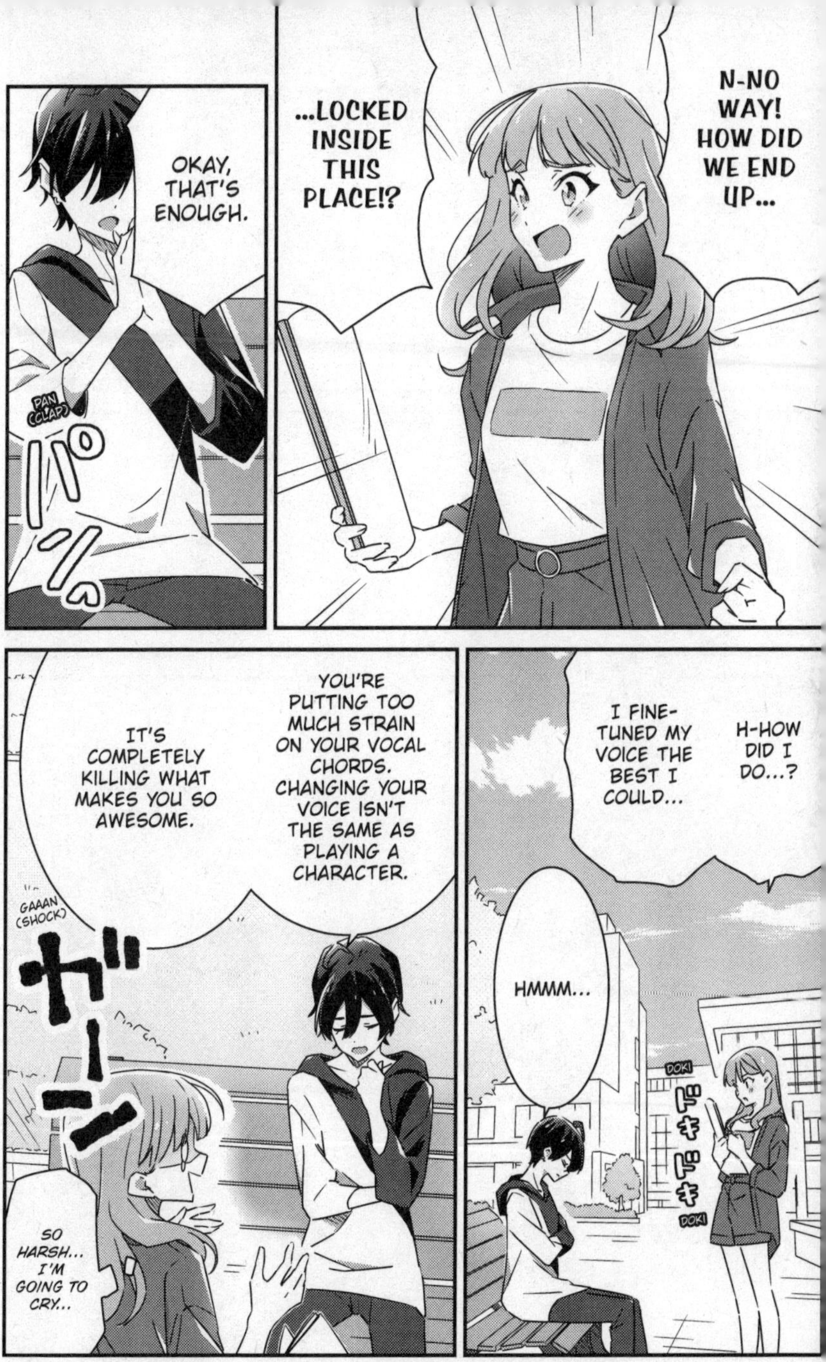
N-NO WAY! HOW DID WE END UP...
...LOCKED INSIDE THIS PLACE!?
OKAY, THAT'S ENOUGH.
PAN (CLAP)
H-HOW DID I DO...?
I FINE-TUNED MY VOICE THE BEST I COULD...
HMMM...
DOKI
DOKI
YOU'RE PUTTING TOO MUCH STRAIN ON YOUR VOCAL CHORDS. CHANGING YOUR VOICE ISN'T THE SAME AS PLAYING A CHARACTER.
IT'S COMPLETELY KILLING WHAT MAKES YOU SO AWESOME.
GAAAN (SHOCK)
SO HARSH... I'M GOING TO CRY...

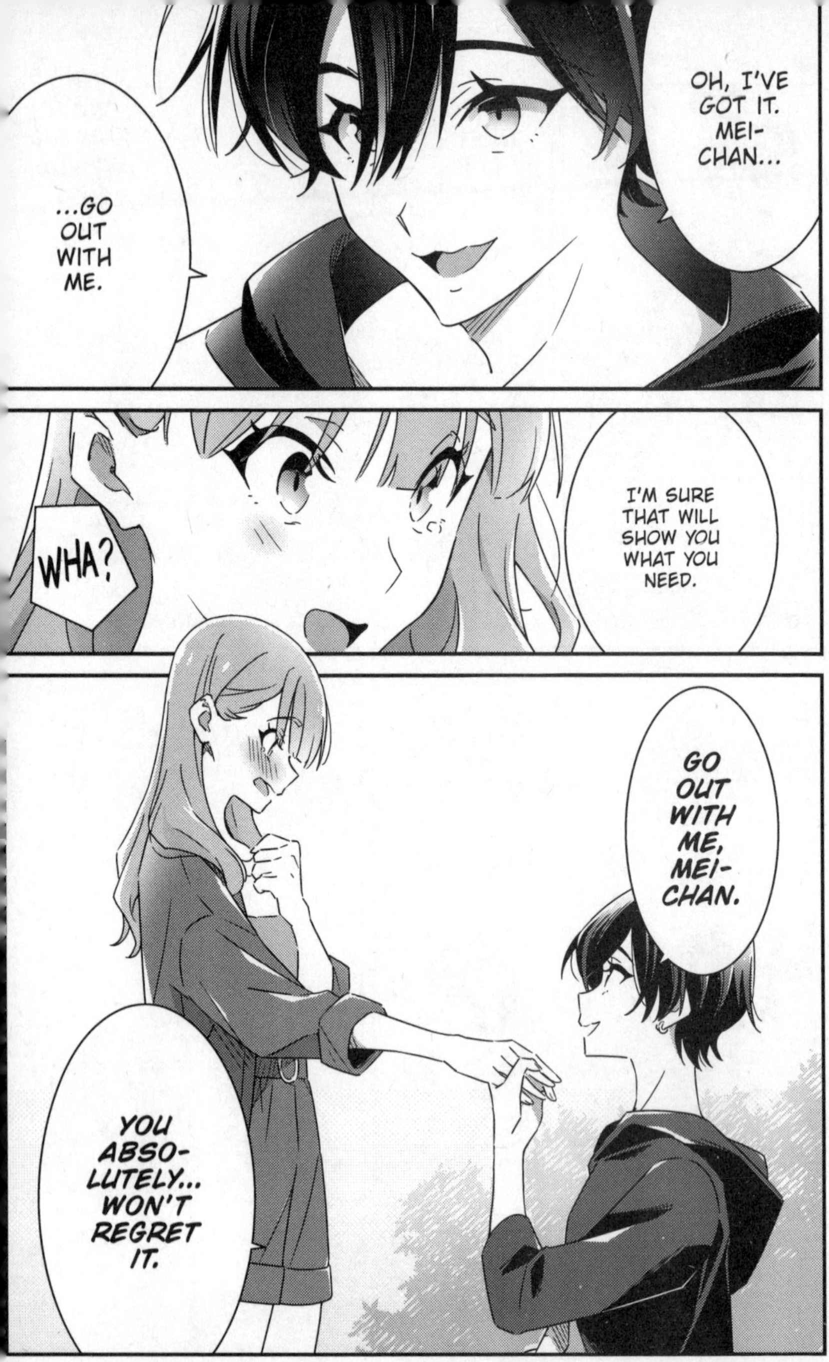
OH, I'VE GOT IT. MEI-CHAN...
...GO OUT WITH ME.
I'M SURE THAT WILL SHOW YOU WHAT YOU NEED.
WHA?
GO OUT WITH ME, MEI-CHAN.
YOU ABSOLUTELY... WON'T REGRET IT.

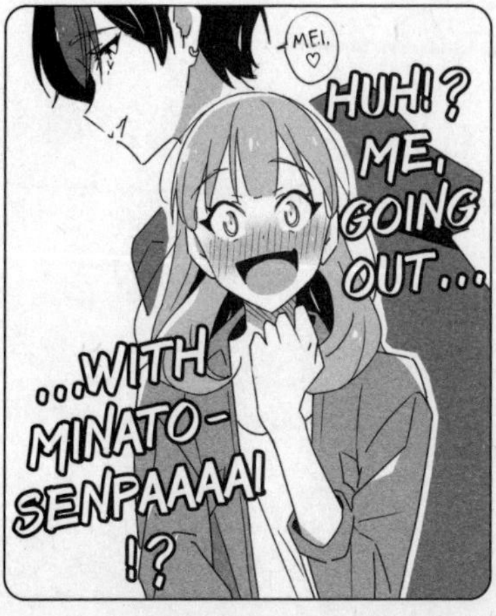
MEI. ♡
HUH!? ME, GOING OUT...
...WITH MINATO-SENPAAAAI!?

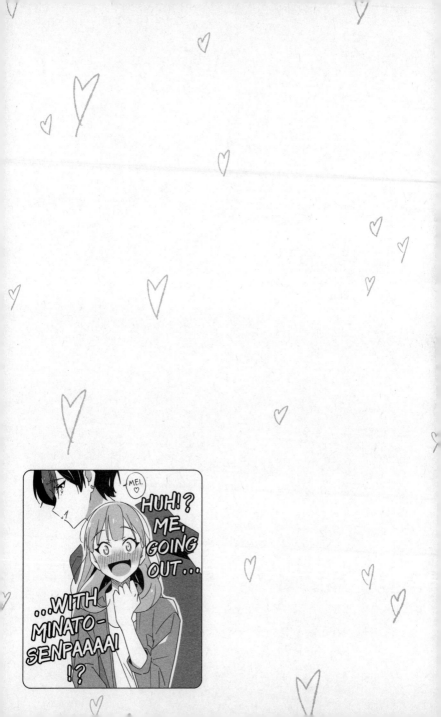

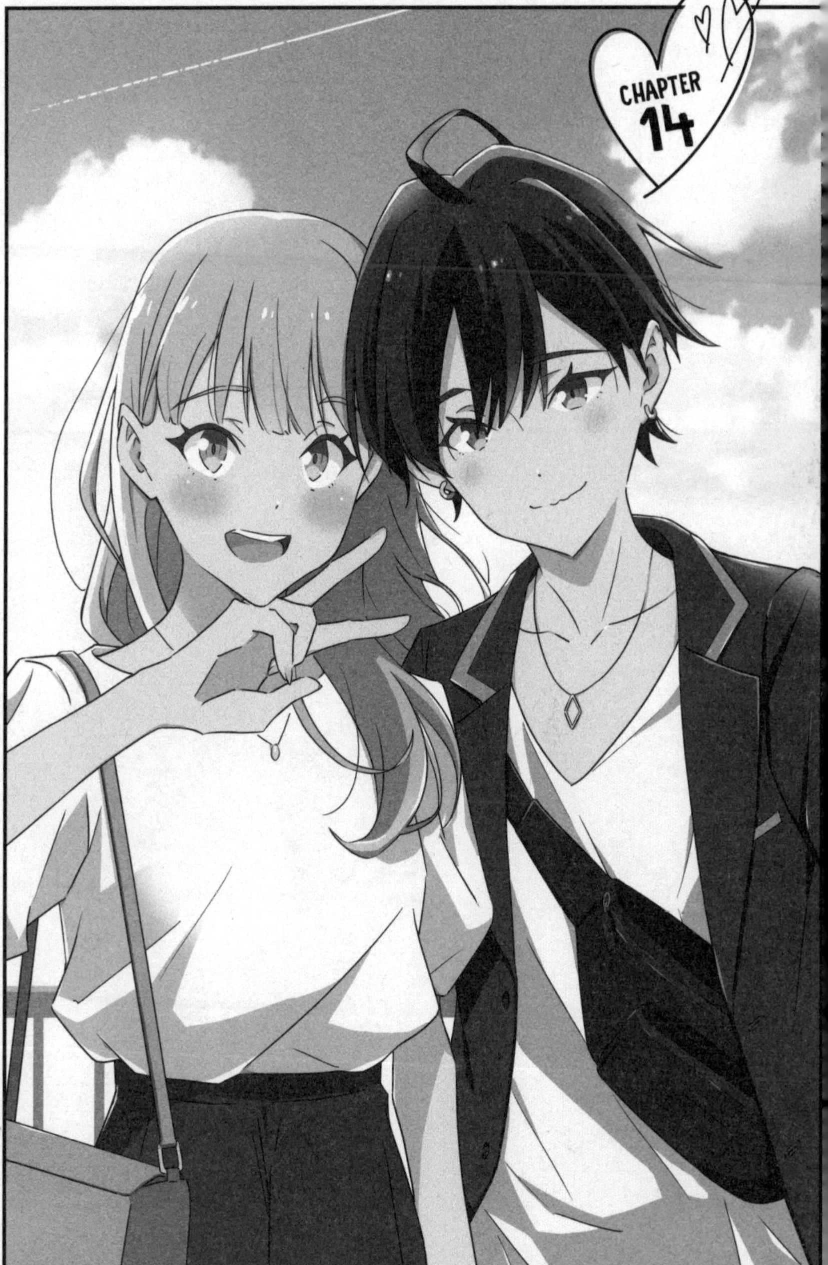
CHAPTER
14

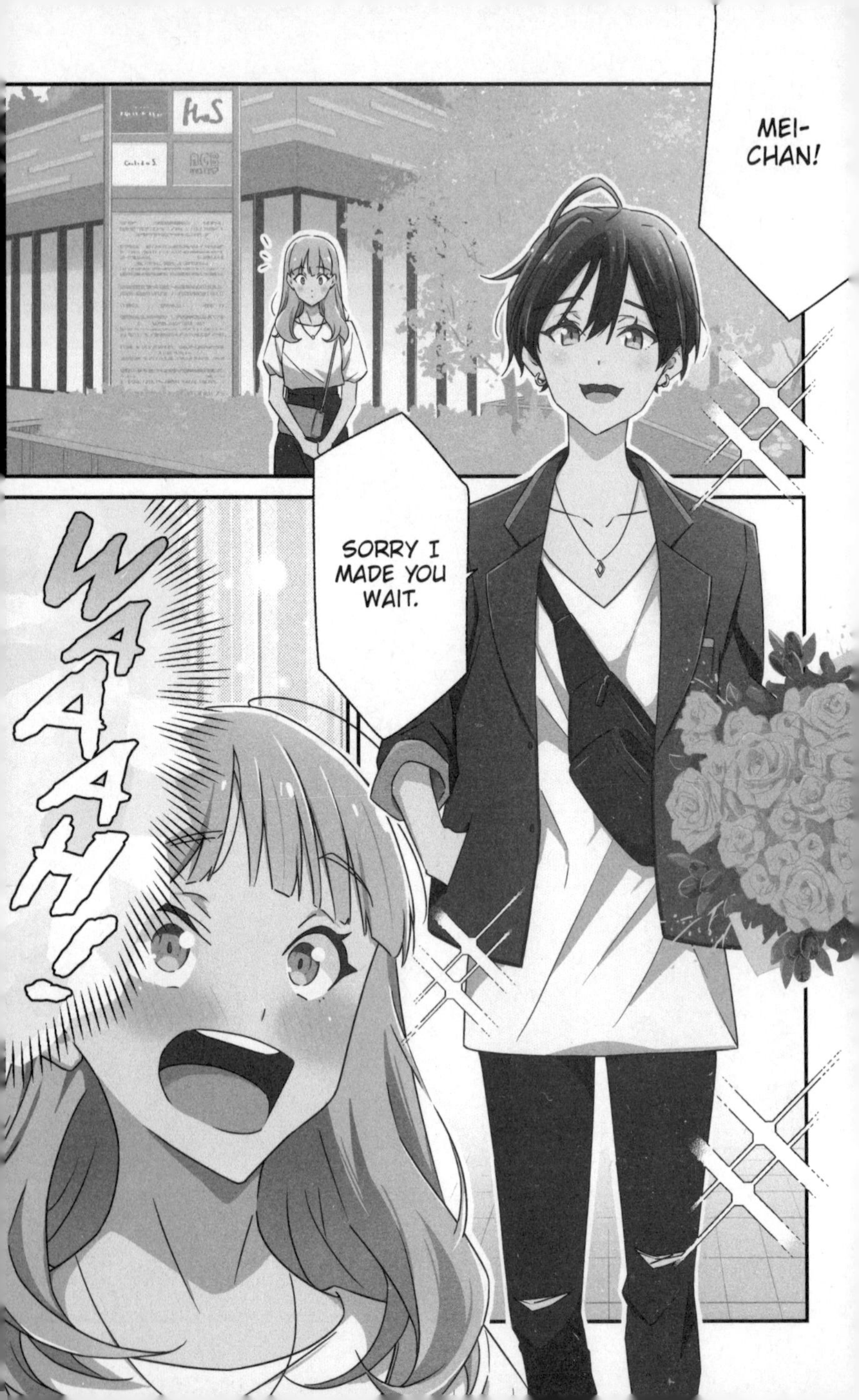
MEI-CHAN!
SORRY I MADE YOU WAIT.
WAAAH!!

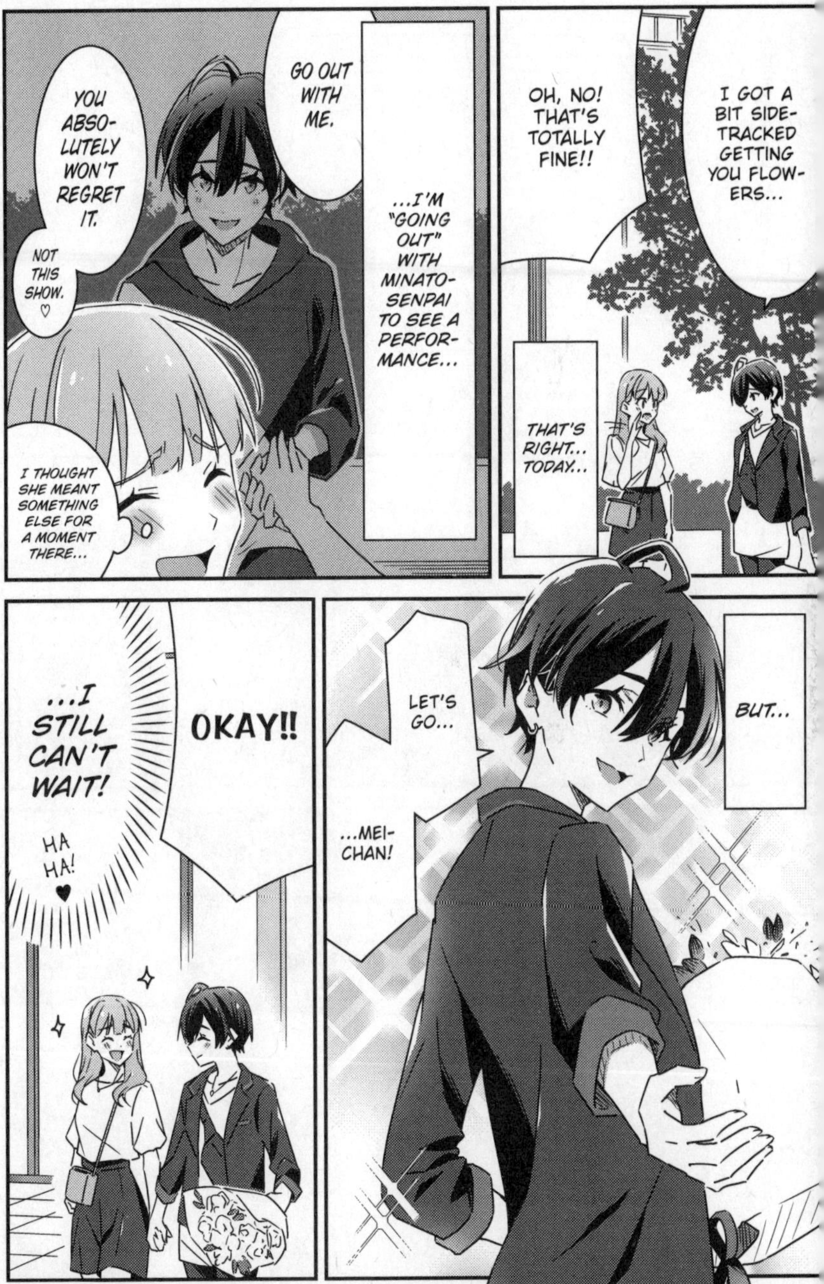
I GOT A BIT SIDE-TRACKED GETTING YOU FLOWERS...
OH, NO! THAT'S TOTALLY FINE!!
THAT'S RIGHT... TODAY...
GO OUT WITH ME.
YOU ABSO-LUTELY WON'T REGRET IT.
NOT THIS SHOW. ♡
...I'M "GOING OUT" WITH MINATO-SENPAI TO SEE A PERFOR-MANCE...
I THOUGHT SHE MEANT SOMETHING ELSE FOR A MOMENT THERE...
BUT...
LET'S GO...
...MEI-CHAN!
OKAY!!
...I STILL CAN'T WAIT!
HA HA! ♥

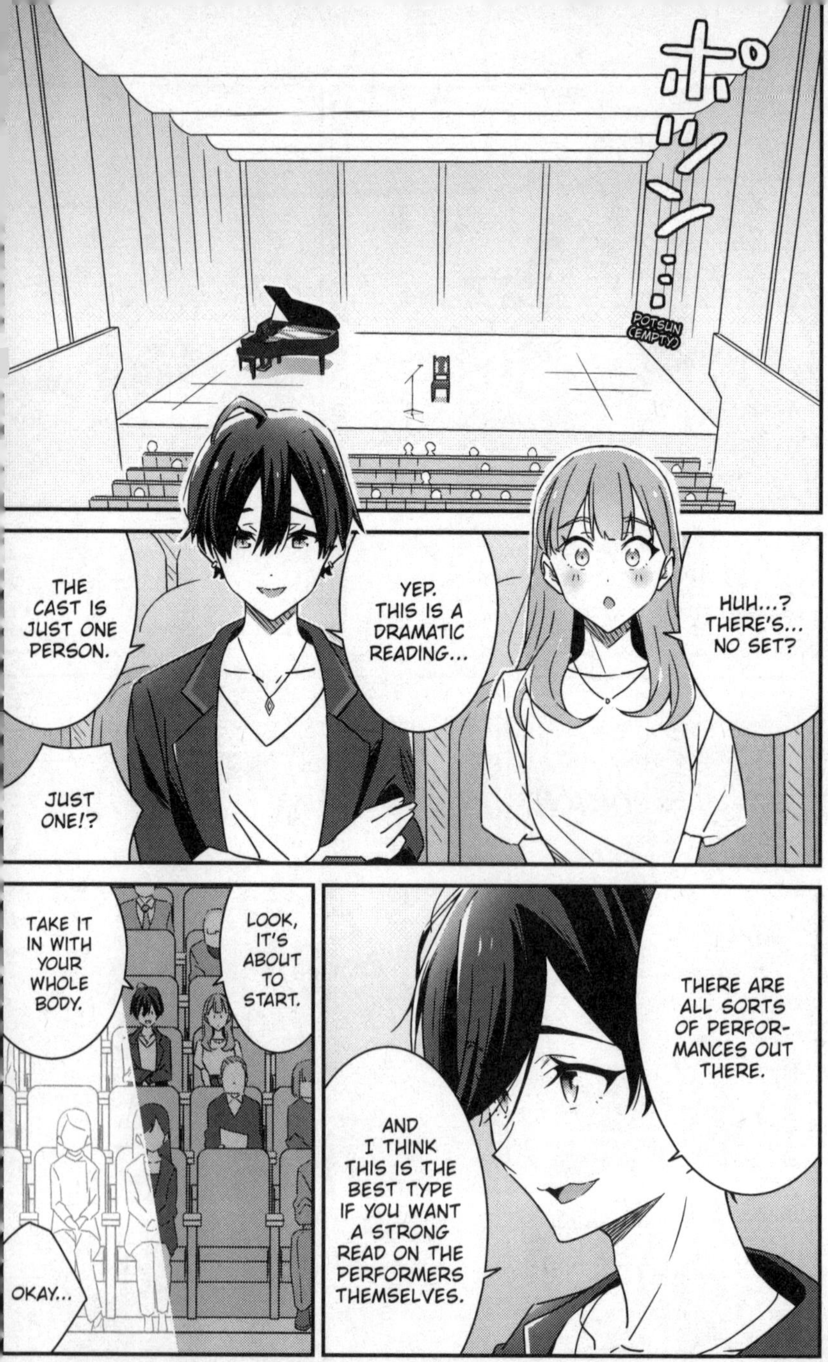
POTSUN (EMPTY)
HUH...? THERE'S... NO SET?
YEP. THIS IS A DRAMATIC READING...
THE CAST IS JUST ONE PERSON.
JUST ONE!?
THERE ARE ALL SORTS OF PERFOR-MANCES OUT THERE.
AND I THINK THIS IS THE BEST TYPE IF YOU WANT A STRONG READ ON THE PERFORMERS THEMSELVES.
LOOK, IT'S ABOUT TO START.
TAKE IT IN WITH YOUR WHOLE BODY.
OKAY...

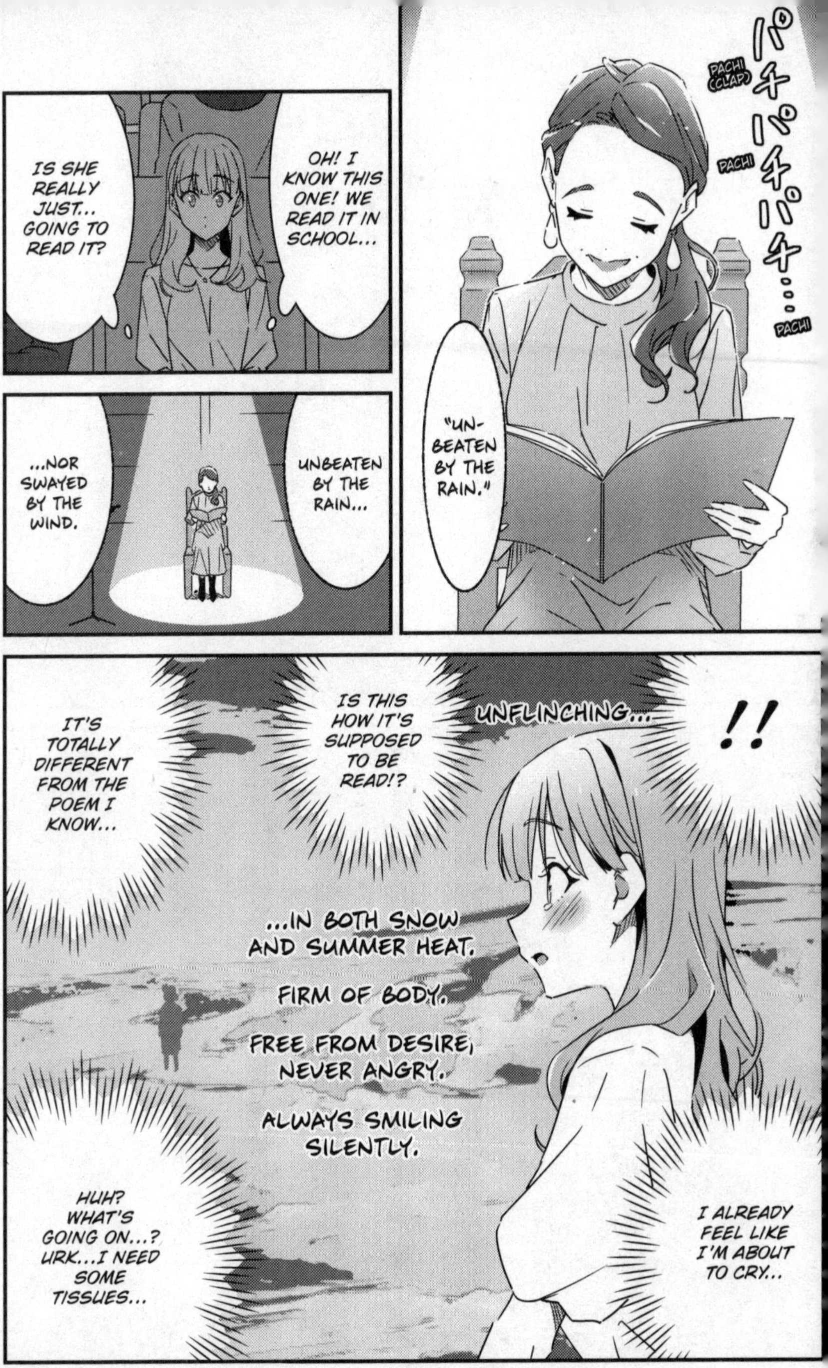

パチパチパチ…
PACHI (CLAP)
PACHI
PACHI
"UN-BEATEN BY THE RAIN."
OH! I KNOW THIS ONE! WE READ IT IN SCHOOL...
IS SHE REALLY JUST... GOING TO READ IT?
UNBEATEN BY THE RAIN...
...NOR SWAYED BY THE WIND.
!!
UNFLINCHING...
IS THIS HOW IT'S SUPPOSED TO BE READ!?
IT'S TOTALLY DIFFERENT FROM THE POEM I KNOW...
...IN BOTH SNOW AND SUMMER HEAT.
FIRM OF BODY.
FREE FROM DESIRE, NEVER ANGRY.
ALWAYS SMILING SILENTLY.
I ALREADY FEEL LIKE I'M ABOUT TO CRY...
HUH? WHAT'S GOING ON...? URK...I NEED SOME TISSUES...

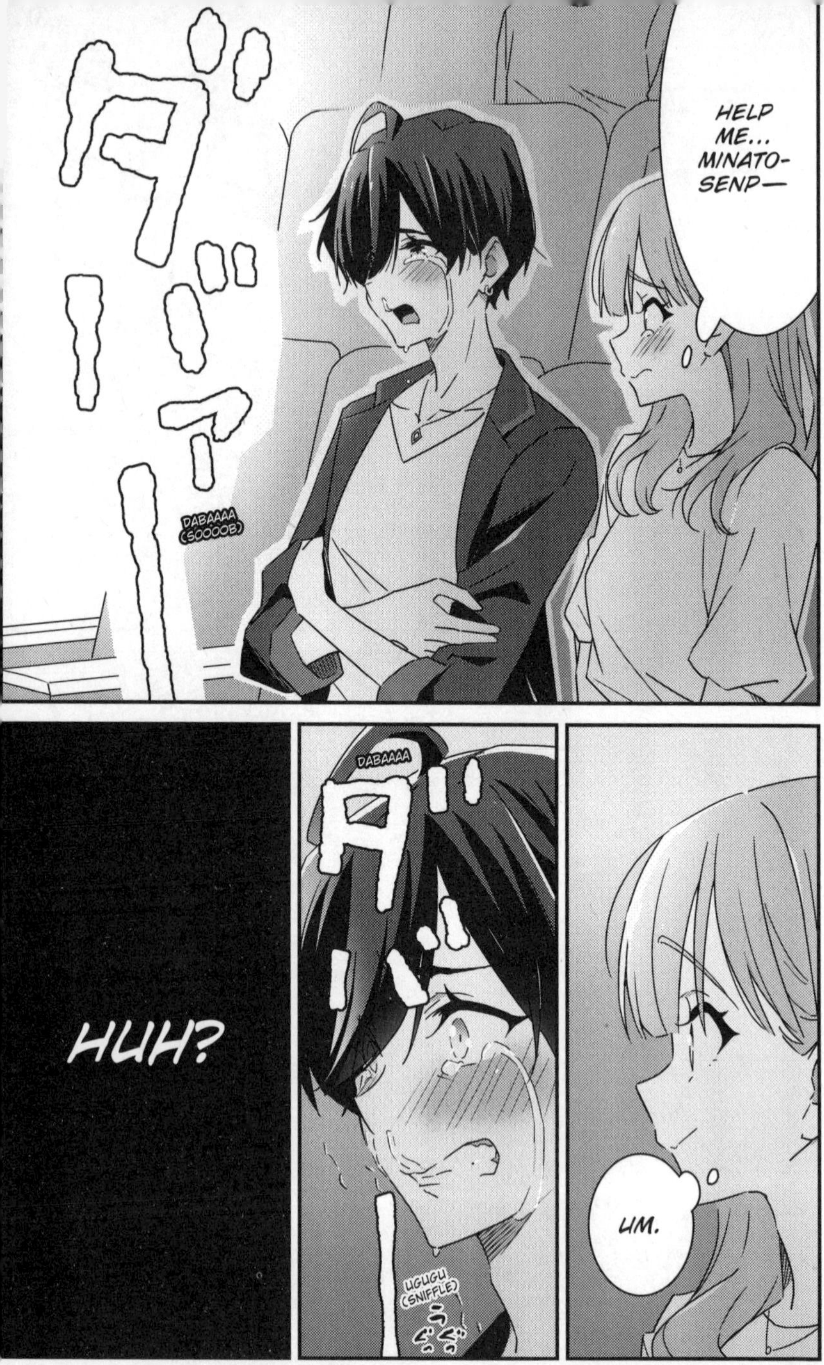
HELP ME... MINATO-SENP—
ダバァー
DABAAAA (SOOOOB)
UM.
DABAAAA
ダバ
UGUGU (SNIFFLE)
うぐぐ
HUH?

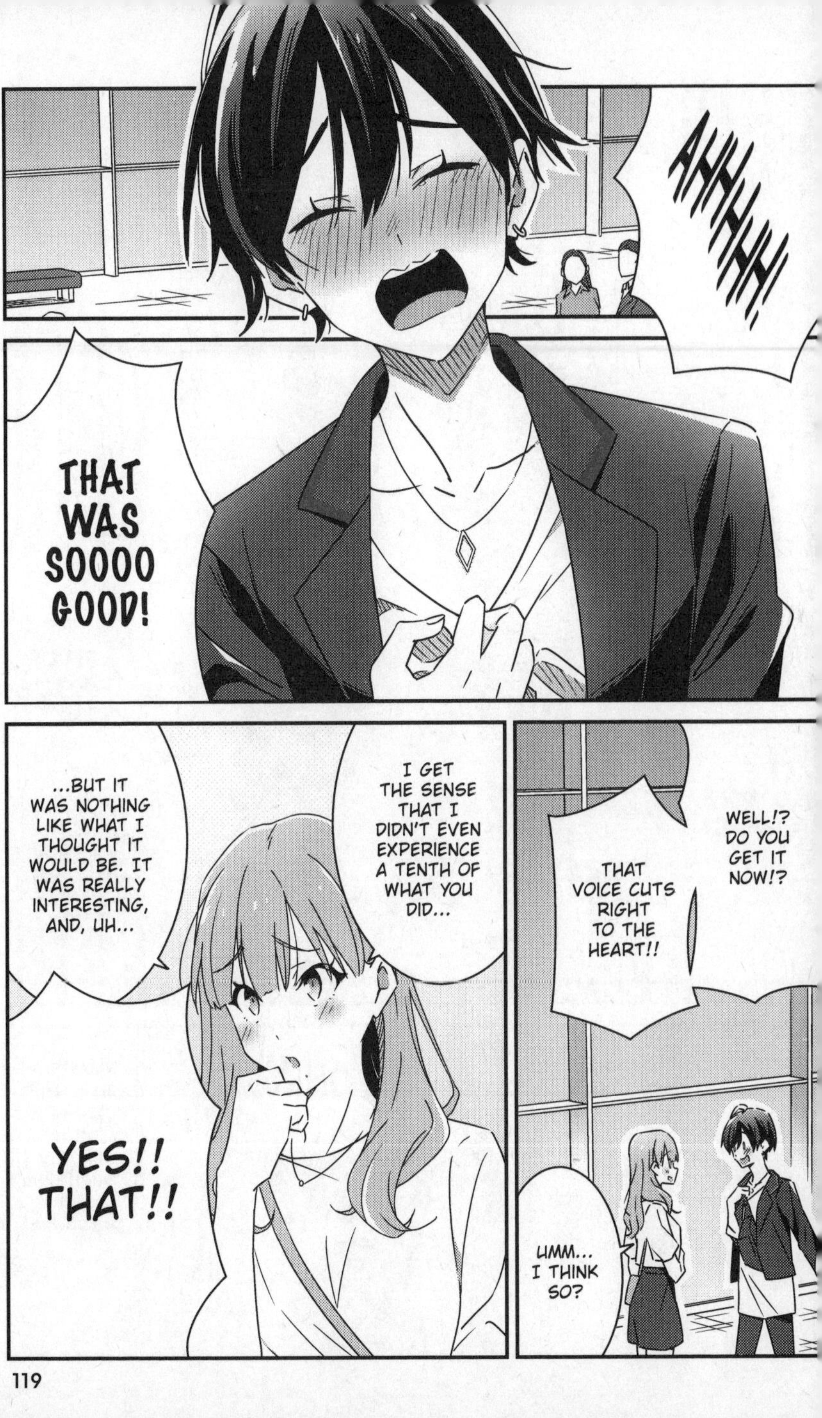
AHHHH!
THAT WAS SOOOO GOOD!
WELL!? DO YOU GET IT NOW!?
THAT VOICE CUTS RIGHT TO THE HEART!!
UMM... I THINK SO?
I GET THE SENSE THAT I DIDN'T EVEN EXPERIENCE A TENTH OF WHAT YOU DID...
...BUT IT WAS NOTHING LIKE WHAT I THOUGHT IT WOULD BE. IT WAS REALLY INTERESTING, AND, UH...
YES!! THAT!!

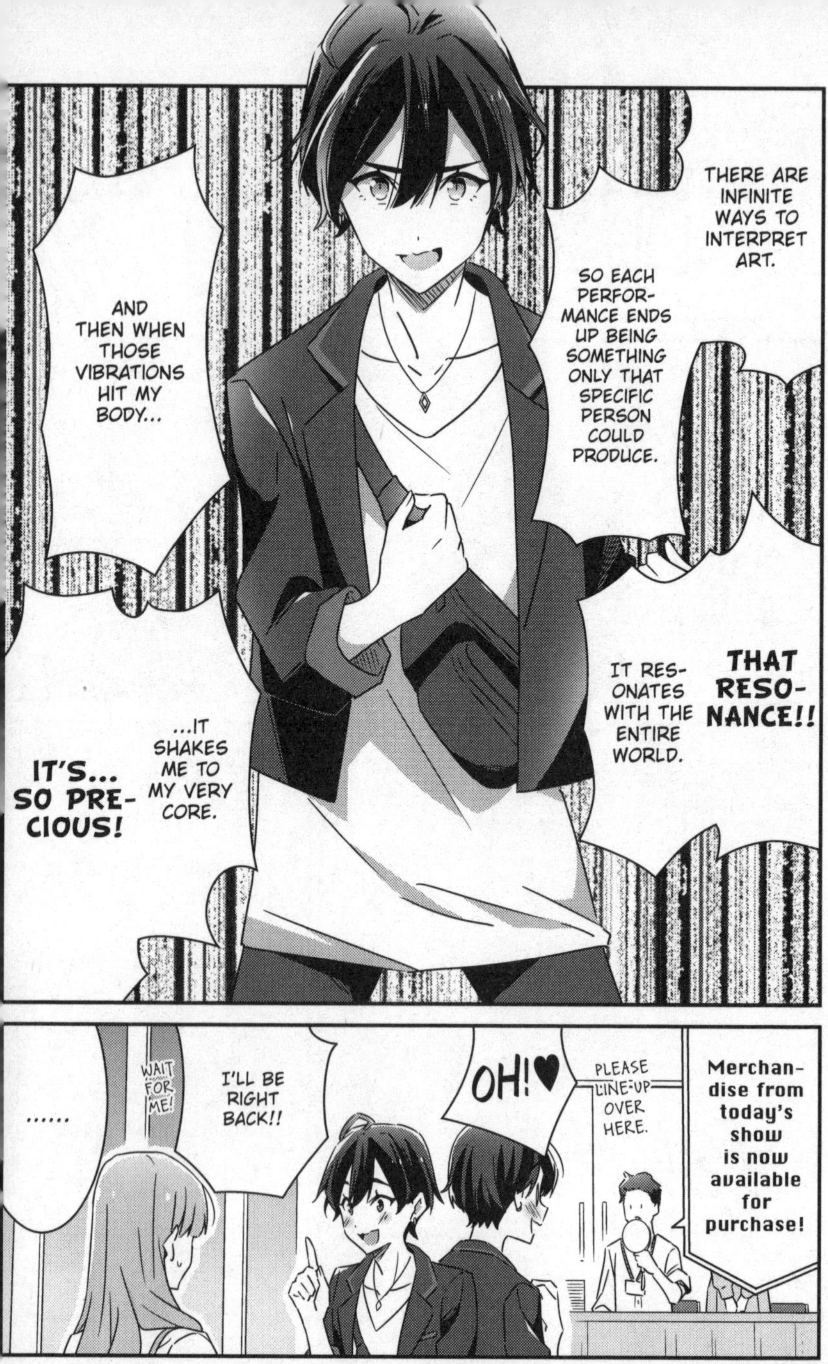
THERE ARE INFINITE WAYS TO INTERPRET ART.
SO EACH PERFORMANCE ENDS UP BEING SOMETHING ONLY THAT SPECIFIC PERSON COULD PRODUCE.
AND THEN WHEN THOSE VIBRATIONS HIT MY BODY...
THAT RESONANCE!!
IT RESONATES WITH THE ENTIRE WORLD.
...IT SHAKES ME TO MY VERY CORE.
IT'S... SO PRECIOUS!
Merchandise from today's show is now available for purchase!
PLEASE LINE-UP OVER HERE.
OH!♥
I'LL BE RIGHT BACK!!
WAIT FOR ME!
......

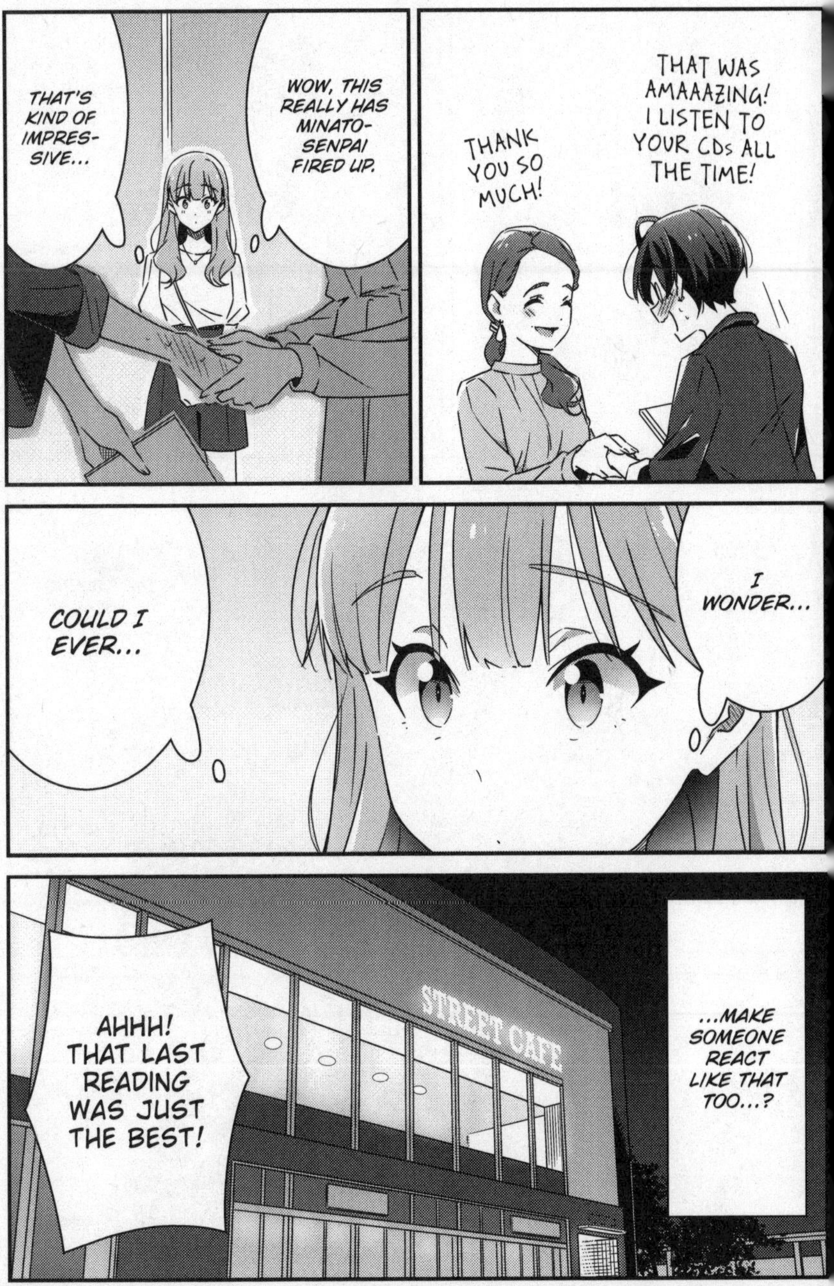
THAT WAS AMAAAZING! I LISTEN TO YOUR CDs ALL THE TIME!
THANK YOU SO MUCH!
WOW, THIS REALLY HAS MINATO-SENPAI FIRED UP.
THAT'S KIND OF IMPRES-SIVE...
I WONDER...
COULD I EVER...
...MAKE SOMEONE REACT LIKE THAT TOO...?
STREET CAFE
AHHH! THAT LAST READING WAS JUST THE BEST!

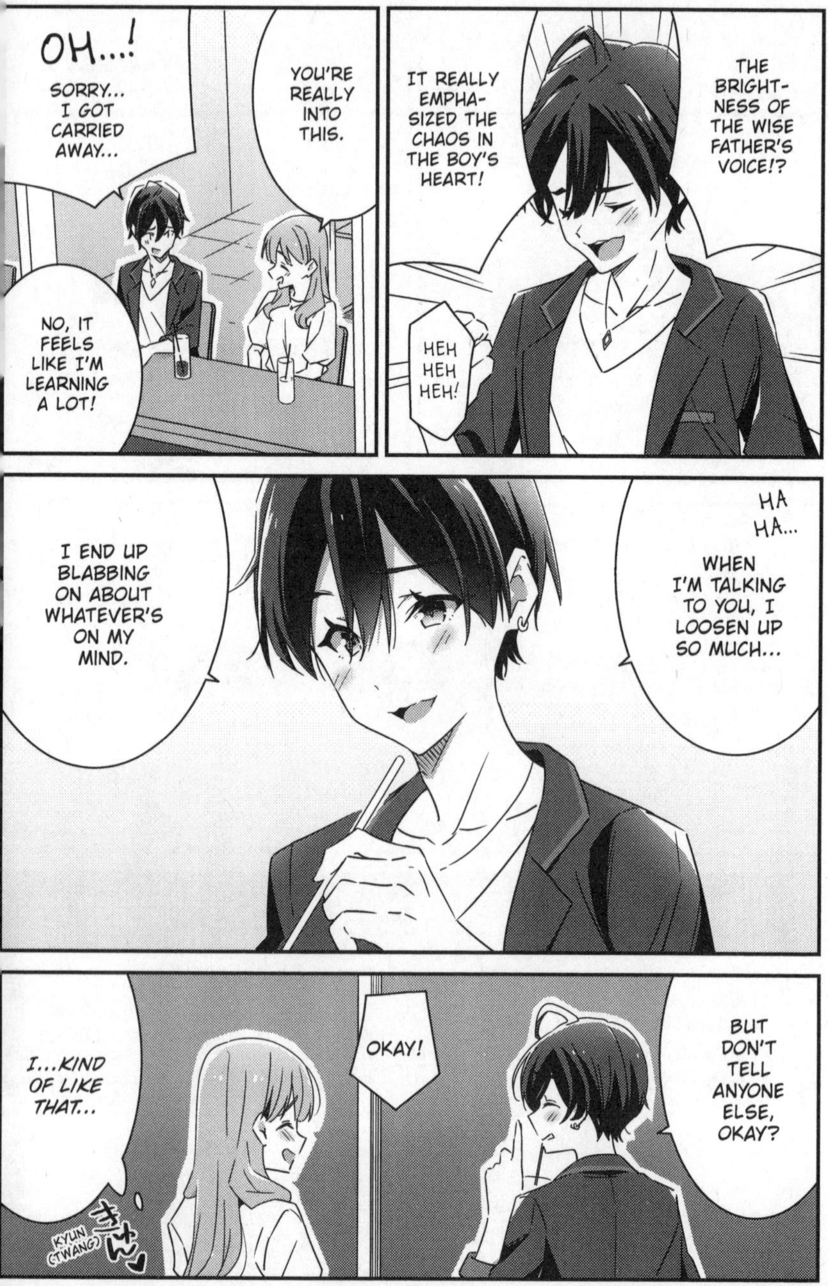
THE BRIGHT-NESS OF THE WISE FATHER'S VOICE!?
IT REALLY EMPHA-SIZED THE CHAOS IN THE BOY'S HEART!
HEH HEH HEH!
YOU'RE REALLY INTO THIS.
OH...!
SORRY... I GOT CARRIED AWAY...
NO, IT FEELS LIKE I'M LEARNING A LOT!
HA HA...
WHEN I'M TALKING TO YOU, I LOOSEN UP SO MUCH...
I END UP BLABBING ON ABOUT WHATEVER'S ON MY MIND.
BUT DON'T TELL ANYONE ELSE, OKAY?
OKAY!
I...KIND OF LIKE THAT...
きゅん
KYUN (TWANG)

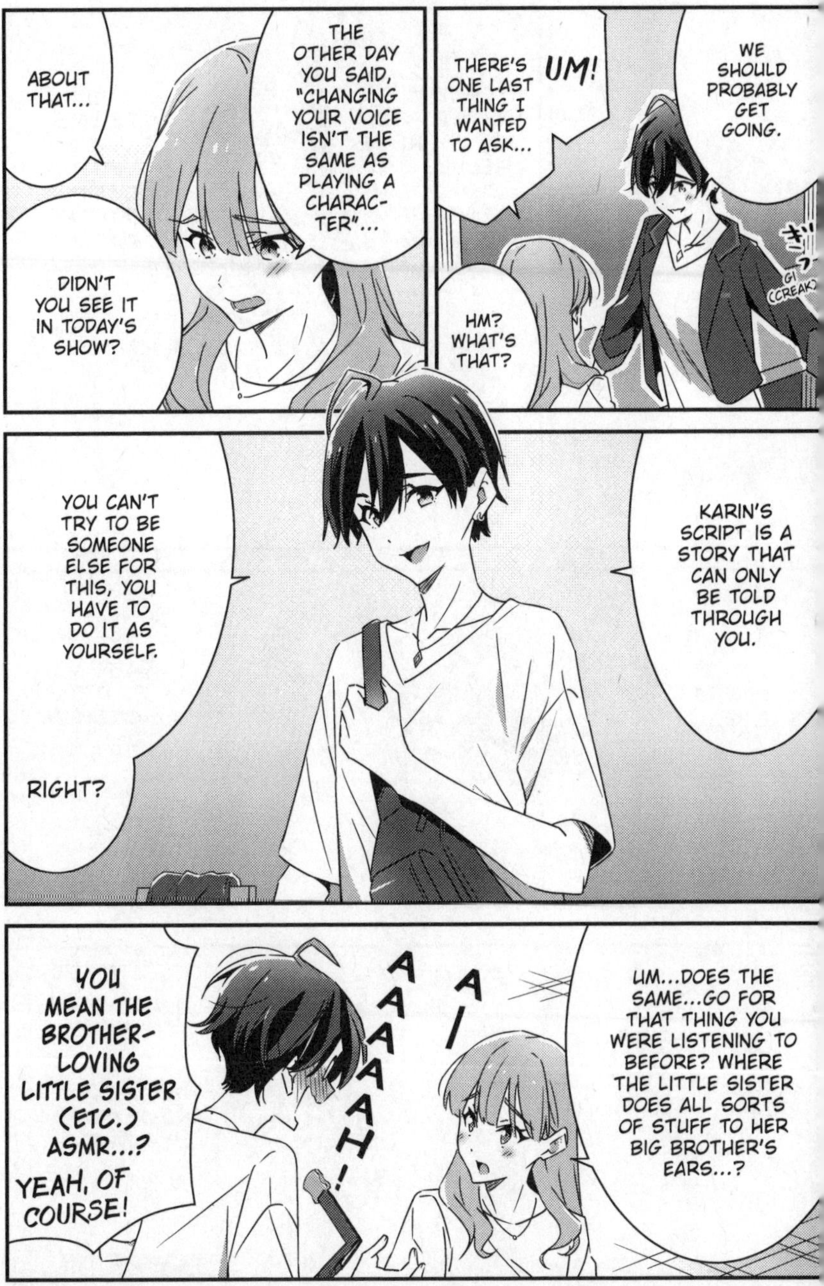
WE SHOULD PROBABLY GET GOING.
GI (CREAK)
UM!
THERE'S ONE LAST THING I WANTED TO ASK...
HM? WHAT'S THAT?
THE OTHER DAY YOU SAID, "CHANGING YOUR VOICE ISN'T THE SAME AS PLAYING A CHARAC-TER"...
ABOUT THAT...
DIDN'T YOU SEE IT IN TODAY'S SHOW?
KARIN'S SCRIPT IS A STORY THAT CAN ONLY BE TOLD THROUGH YOU.
YOU CAN'T TRY TO BE SOMEONE ELSE FOR THIS, YOU HAVE TO DO IT AS YOURSELF.
RIGHT?
UM...DOES THE SAME...GO FOR THAT THING YOU WERE LISTENING TO BEFORE? WHERE THE LITTLE SISTER DOES ALL SORTS OF STUFF TO HER BIG BROTHER'S EARS...?
A/
AAAAAAH!
YOU MEAN THE BROTHER-LOVING LITTLE SISTER (ETC.) ASMR...?
YEAH, OF COURSE!

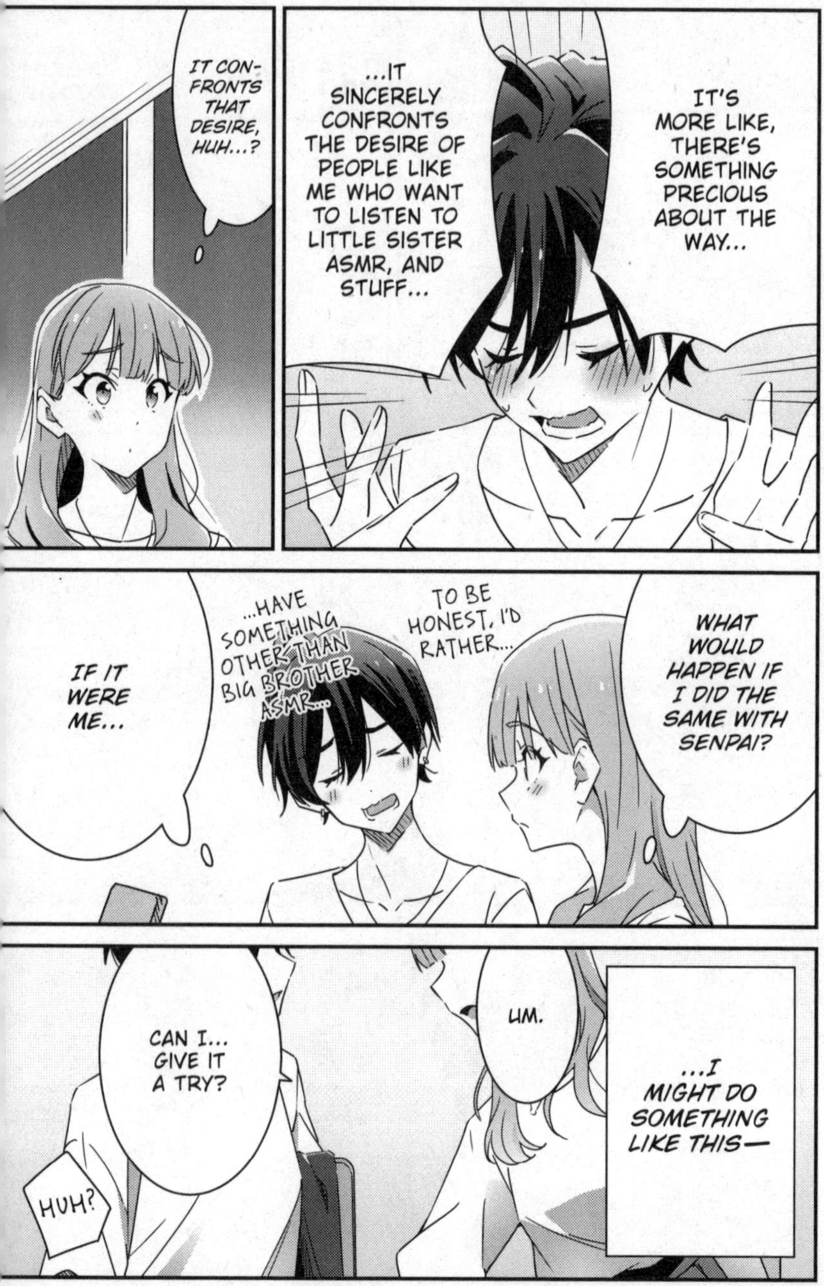
IT'S MORE LIKE, THERE'S SOMETHING PRECIOUS ABOUT THE WAY...
...IT SINCERELY CONFRONTS THE DESIRE OF PEOPLE LIKE ME WHO WANT TO LISTEN TO LITTLE SISTER ASMR, AND STUFF...
IT CON-FRONTS THAT DESIRE, HUH...?
WHAT WOULD HAPPEN IF I DID THE SAME WITH SENPAI?
TO BE HONEST, I'D RATHER...
...HAVE SOMETHING OTHER THAN BIG BROTHER ASMR...
IF IT WERE ME...
...I MIGHT DO SOMETHING LIKE THIS—
UM.
CAN I... GIVE IT A TRY?
HUH?

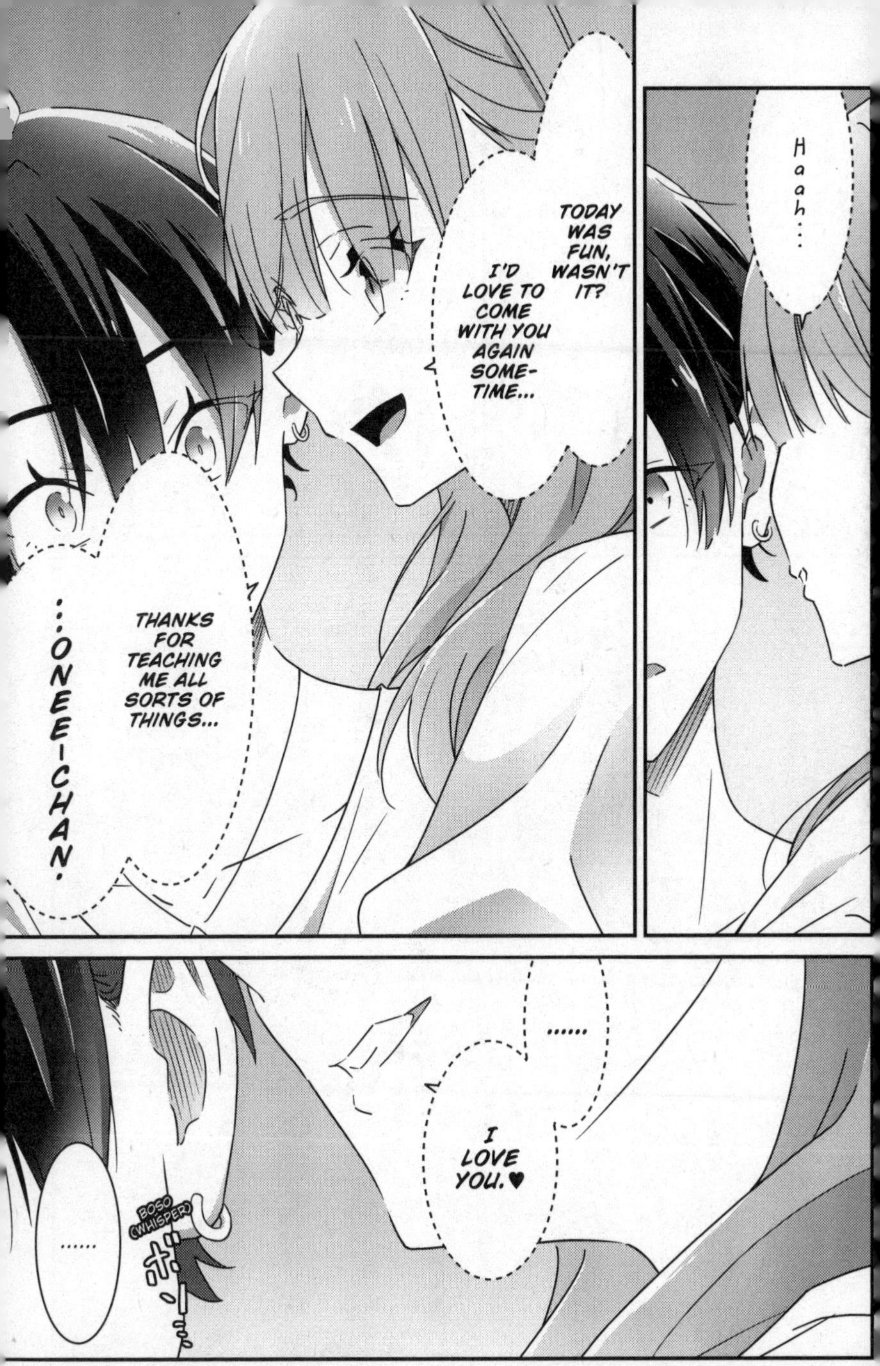
Haaah...
TODAY WAS FUN, WASN'T IT?
I'D LOVE TO COME WITH YOU AGAIN SOMETIME...
THANKS FOR TEACHING ME ALL SORTS OF THINGS...
...ONEE-CHAN.
......
I LOVE YOU.♥
BOSO (WHISPER)
......

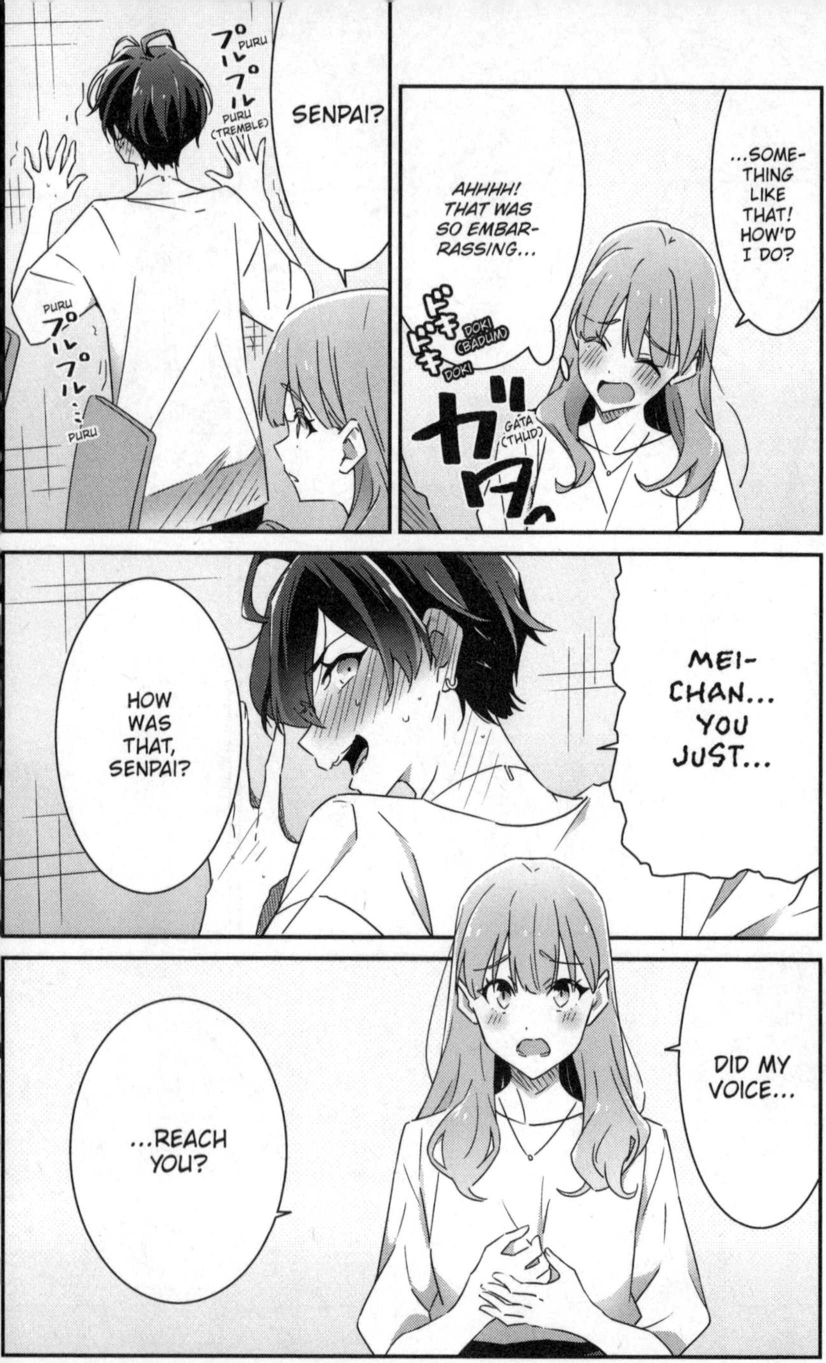
...SOME-THING LIKE THAT! HOW'D I DO?
AHHHH! THAT WAS SO EMBAR-RASSING...
ドキドキ DOKI (BADUM) DOKI
ガタ GATA (THUD)
SENPAI?
プルプル PURU PURU (TREMBLE)
プルプル PURU PURU
MEI-CHAN... YOU JUST...
HOW WAS THAT, SENPAI?
DID MY VOICE...
...REACH YOU?

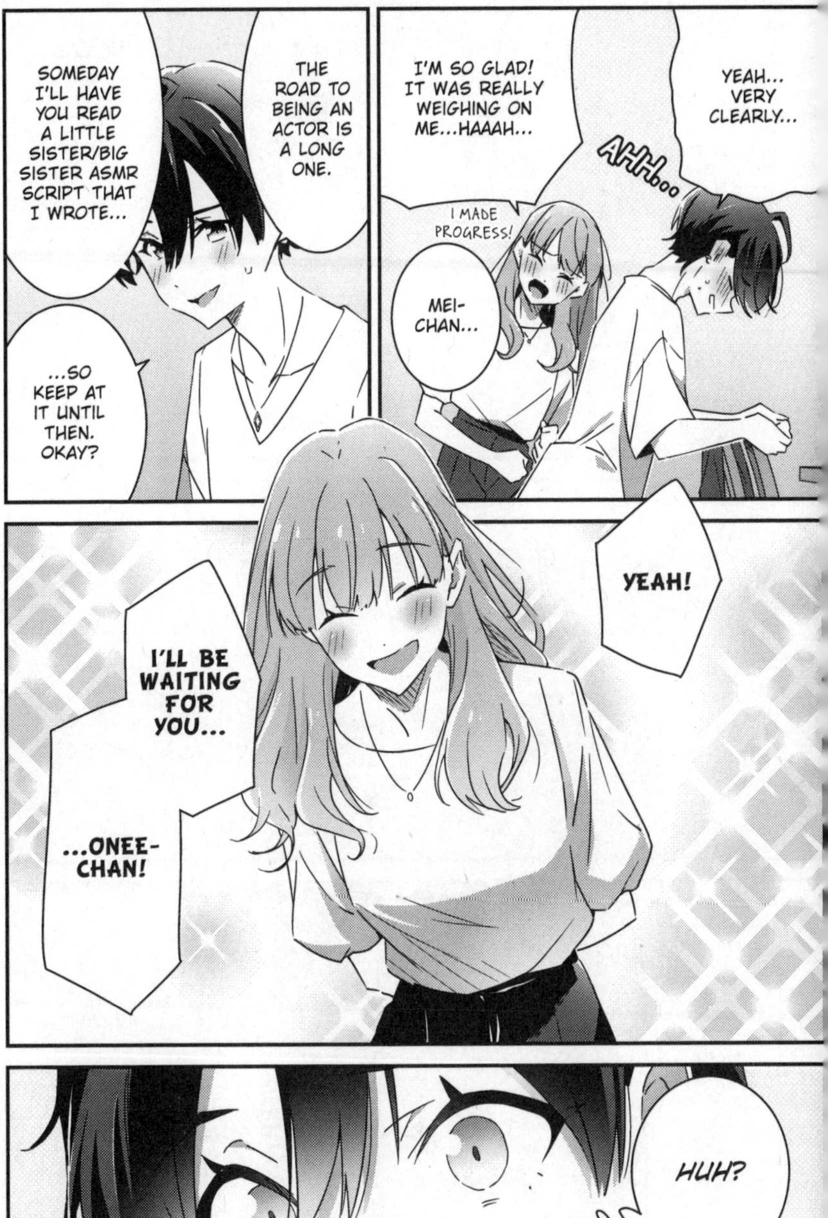
YEAH... VERY CLEARLY...
AHH...
I'M SO GLAD! IT WAS REALLY WEIGHING ON ME...HAAAH...
I MADE PROGRESS!
MEI-CHAN...
THE ROAD TO BEING AN ACTOR IS A LONG ONE.
SOMEDAY I'LL HAVE YOU READ A LITTLE SISTER/BIG SISTER ASMR SCRIPT THAT I WROTE...
...SO KEEP AT IT UNTIL THEN. OKAY?
YEAH!
I'LL BE WAITING FOR YOU...
...ONEE-CHAN!
HUH?

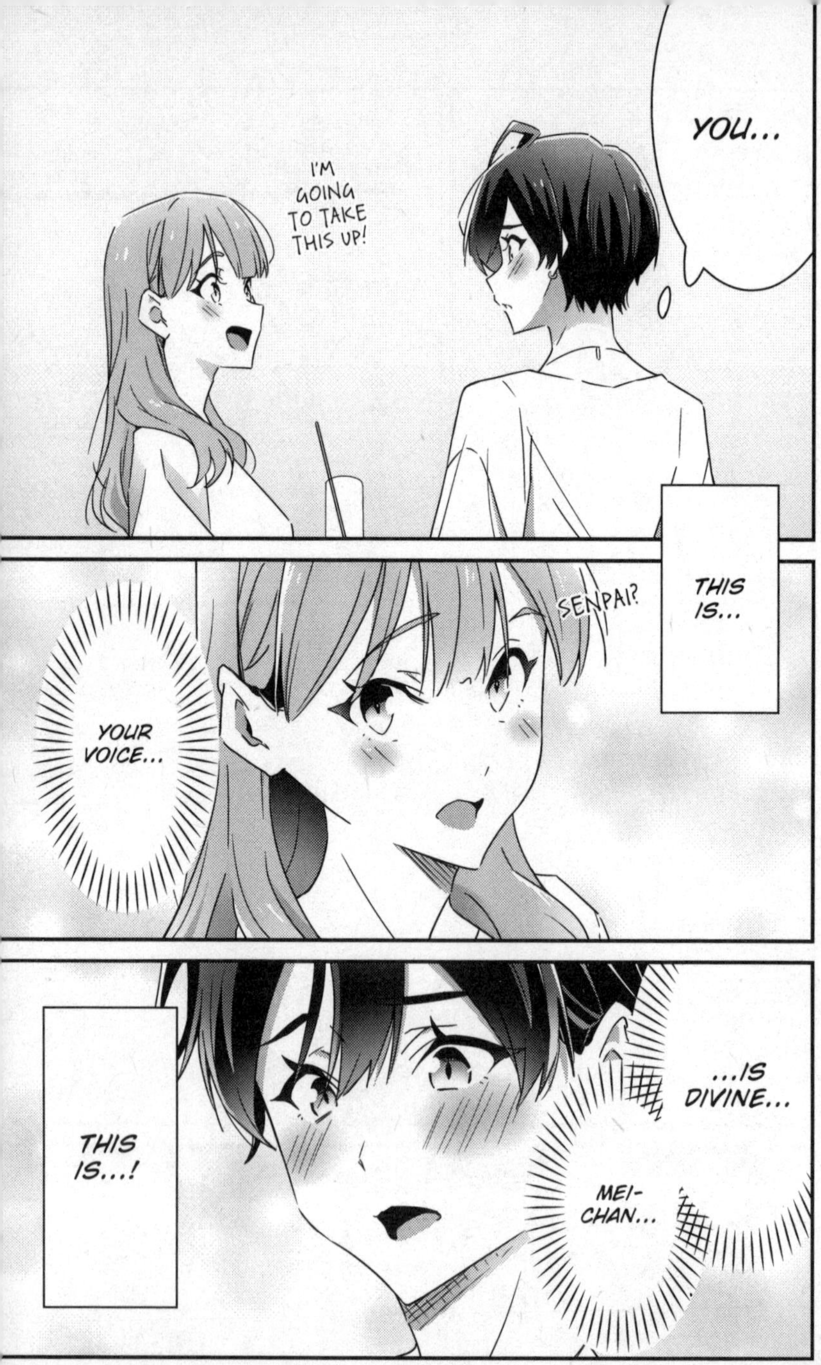
YOU...
I'M GOING TO TAKE THIS UP!
THIS IS...
SENPAI?
YOUR VOICE...
...IS DIVINE...
MEI-CHAN...
THIS IS...!

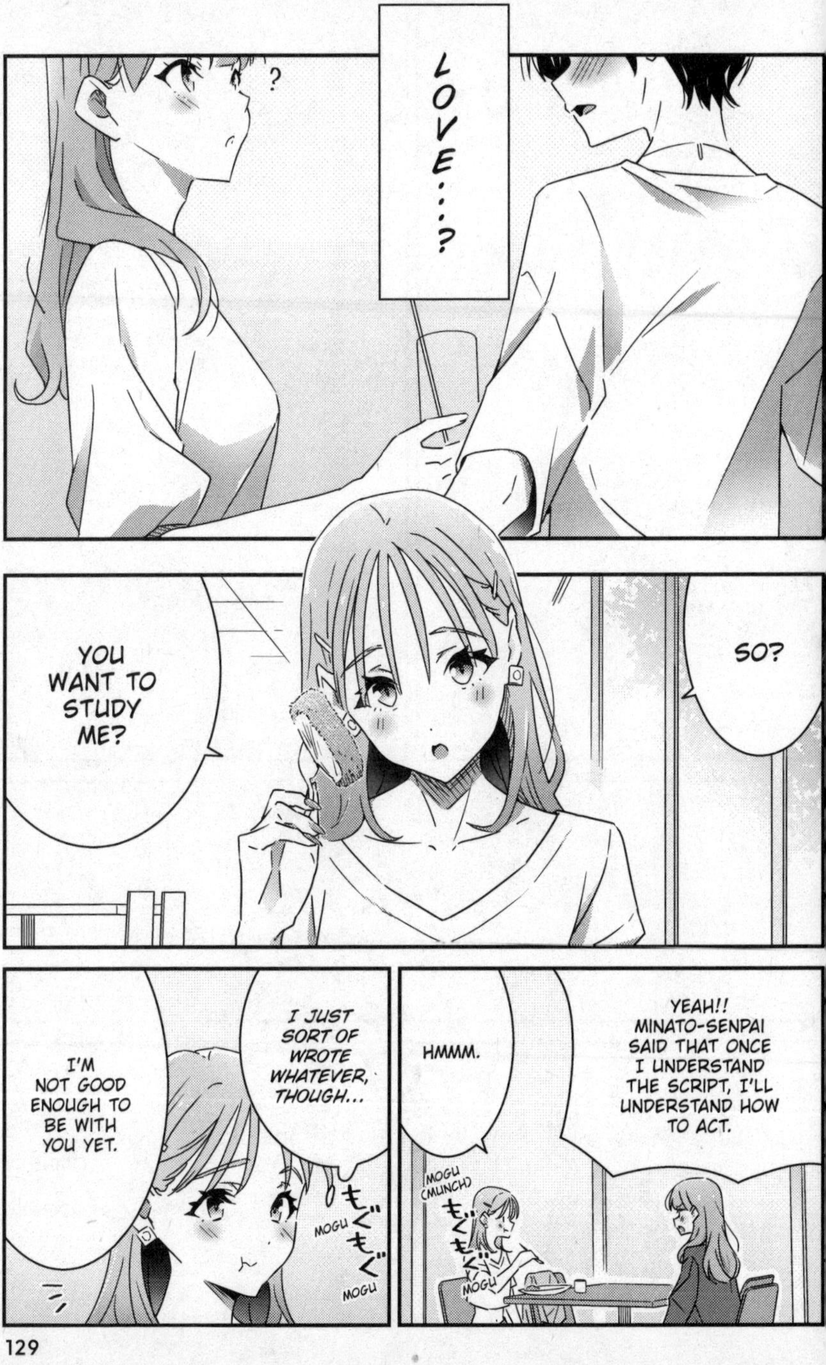
LOVE...?
?
SO?
YOU WANT TO STUDY ME?
YEAH!! MINATO-SENPAI SAID THAT ONCE I UNDERSTAND THE SCRIPT, I'LL UNDERSTAND HOW TO ACT.
HMMM.
MOGU (MUNCH)
もぐもぐ
MOGU
I JUST SORT OF WROTE WHATEVER, THOUGH...
I'M NOT GOOD ENOUGH TO BE WITH YOU YET.
もぐもぐ
MOGU
MOGU

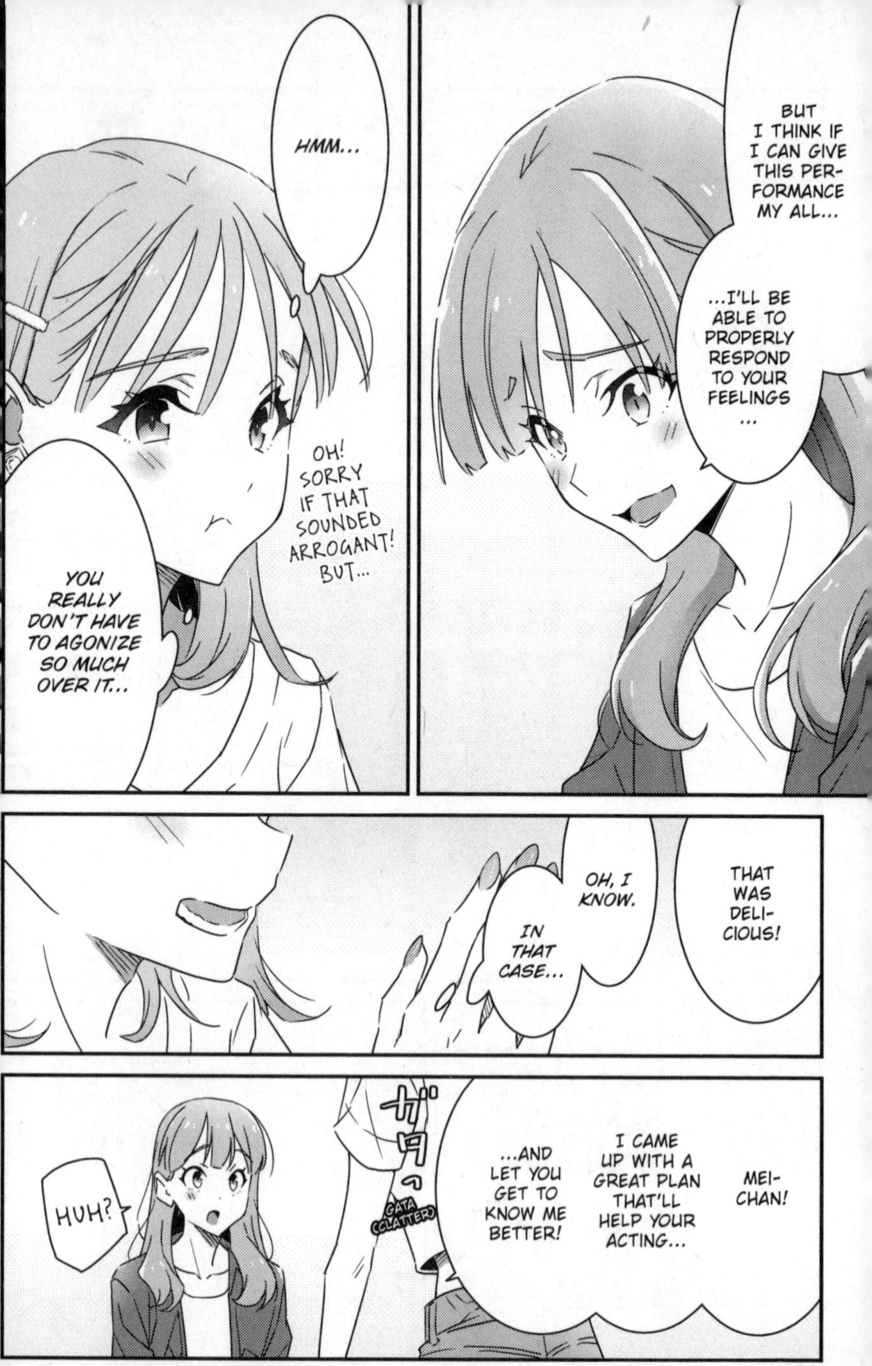
BUT I THINK IF I CAN GIVE THIS PERFORMANCE MY ALL...
...I'LL BE ABLE TO PROPERLY RESPOND TO YOUR FEELINGS...
HMM...
OH! SORRY IF THAT SOUNDED ARROGANT! BUT...
YOU REALLY DON'T HAVE TO AGONIZE SO MUCH OVER IT...
THAT WAS DELICIOUS!
OH, I KNOW.
IN THAT CASE...
MEI-CHAN!
I CAME UP WITH A GREAT PLAN THAT'LL HELP YOUR ACTING...
...AND LET YOU GET TO KNOW ME BETTER!
GATA (CLATTER)
HUH?

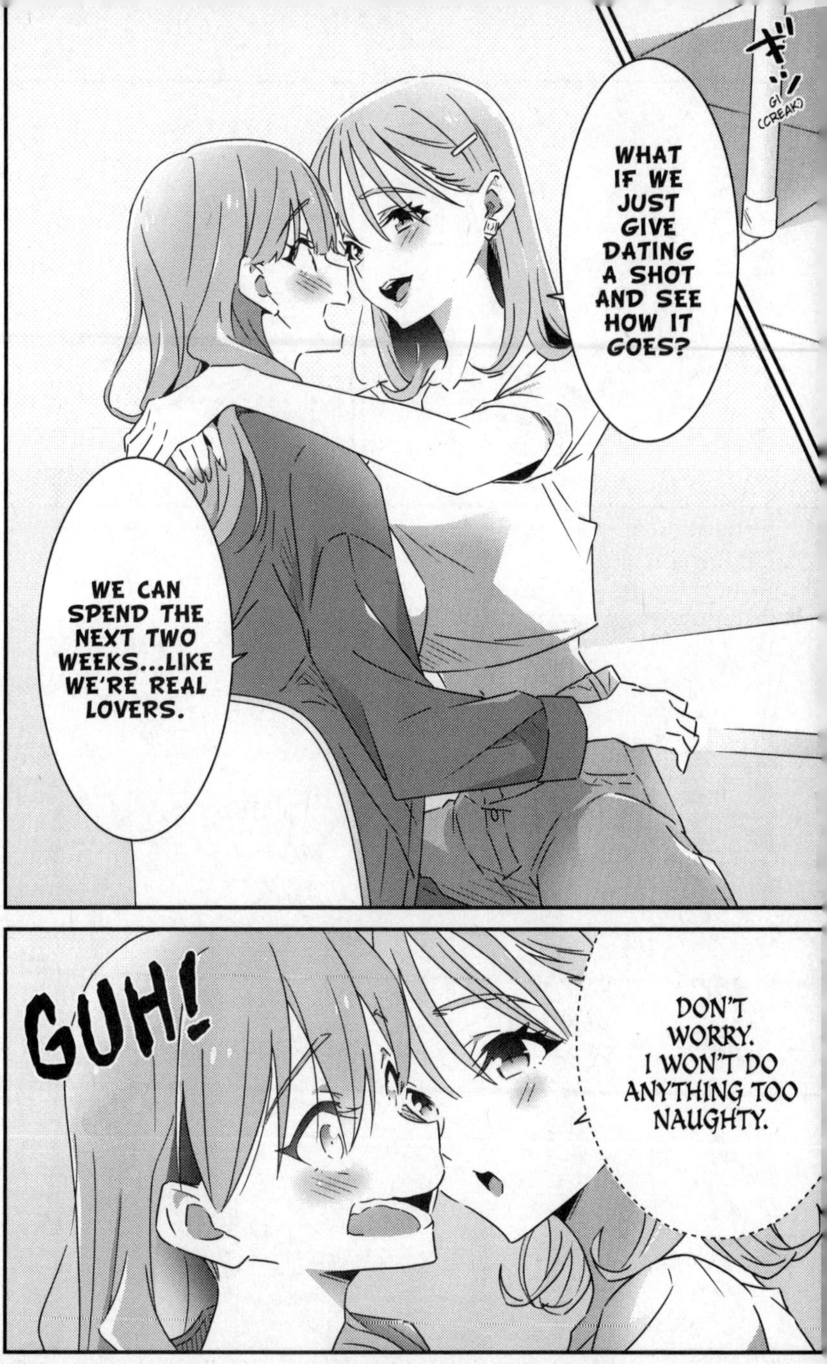
ギッ
GI (CREAK)
WHAT IF WE JUST GIVE DATING A SHOT AND SEE HOW IT GOES?
WE CAN SPEND THE NEXT TWO WEEKS...LIKE WE'RE REAL LOVERS.
DON'T WORRY. I WON'T DO ANYTHING TOO NAUGHTY.
GUH!

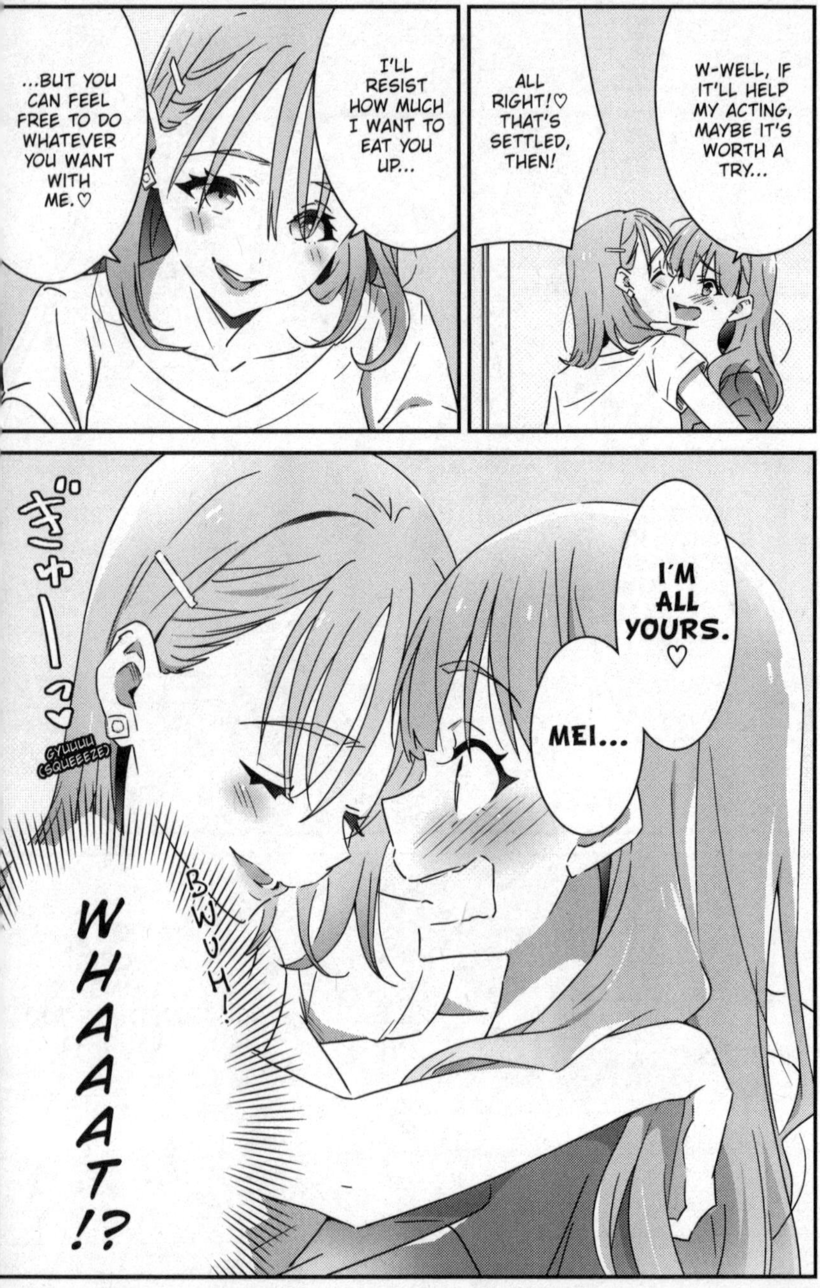
W-WELL, IF IT'LL HELP MY ACTING, MAYBE IT'S WORTH A TRY...
ALL RIGHT!♡ THAT'S SETTLED, THEN!
I'LL RESIST HOW MUCH I WANT TO EAT YOU UP...
...BUT YOU CAN FEEL FREE TO DO WHATEVER YOU WANT WITH ME.♡
I'M ALL YOURS.♡
MEI...
ぎゅーっ♡
GYUUUU (SQUEEEZE)
BWUH!
WHAAAAT!?

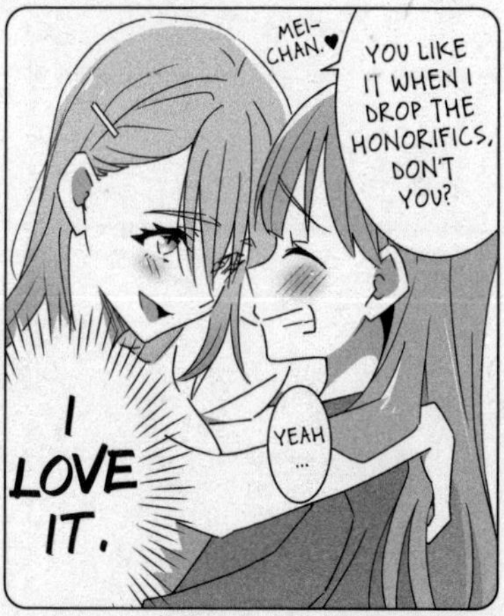
YOU LIKE IT WHEN I DROP THE HONORIFICS, DON'T YOU?
MEI-CHAN.♥
YEAH...
I LOVE IT.

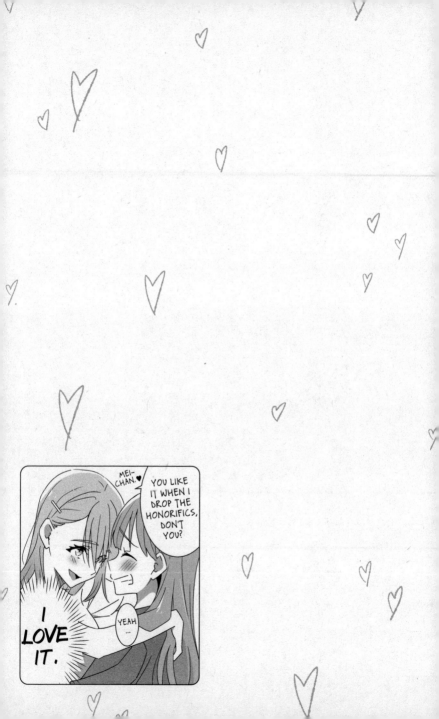

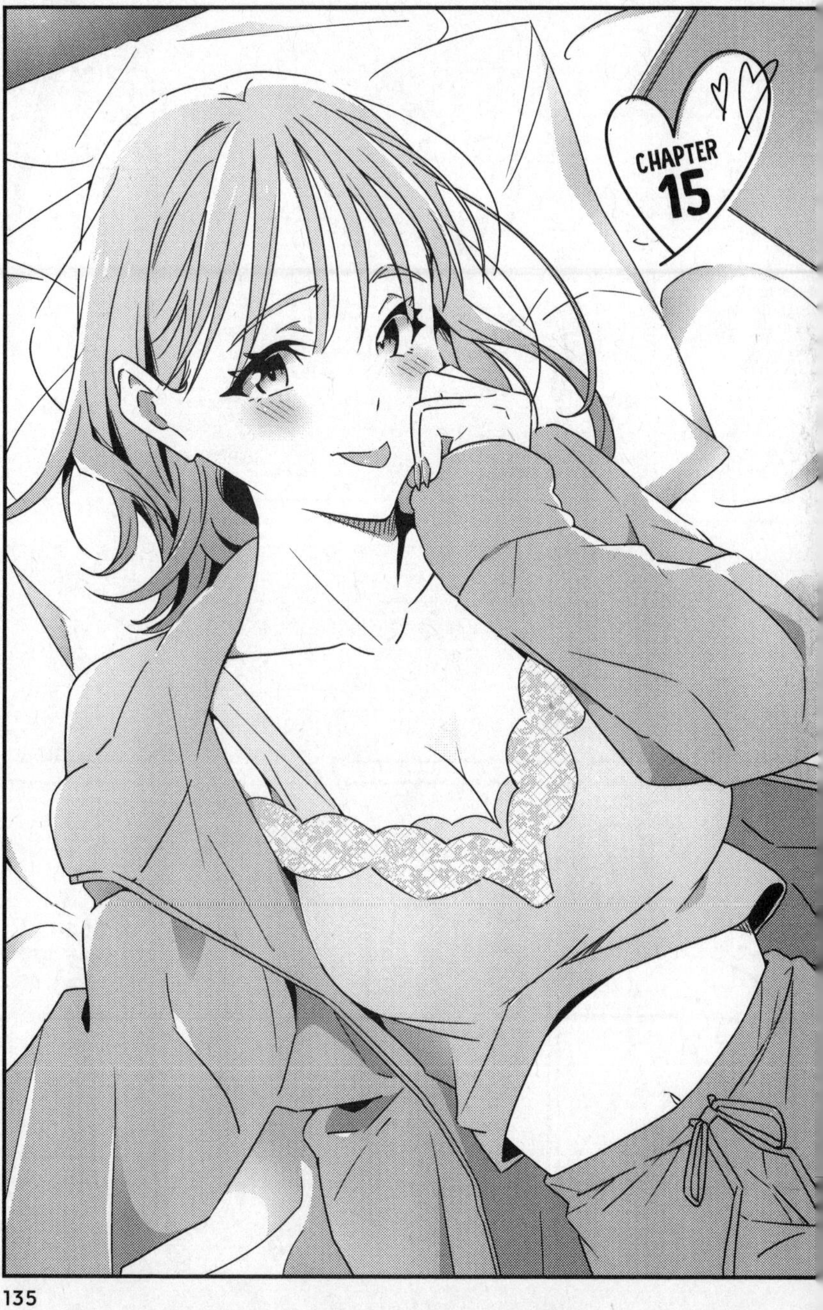
CHAPTER
15

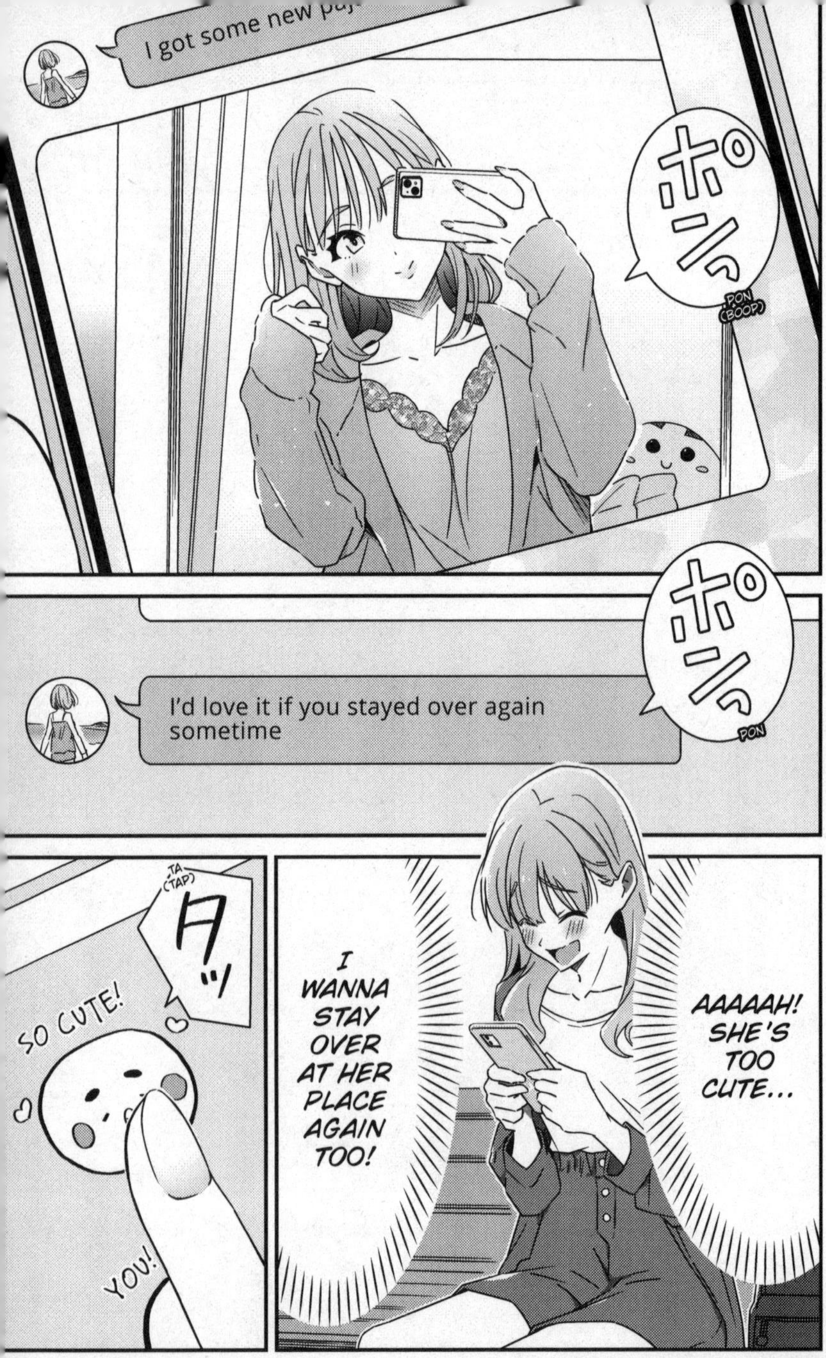

I got some new pa
ポンッ
PON (BOOP)
ポンッ
PON
I'd love it if you stayed over again sometime
AAAAAH! SHE'S TOO CUTE...
I WANNA STAY OVER AT HER PLACE AGAIN TOO!
タッ
TA (TAP)
SO CUTE!
YOU!

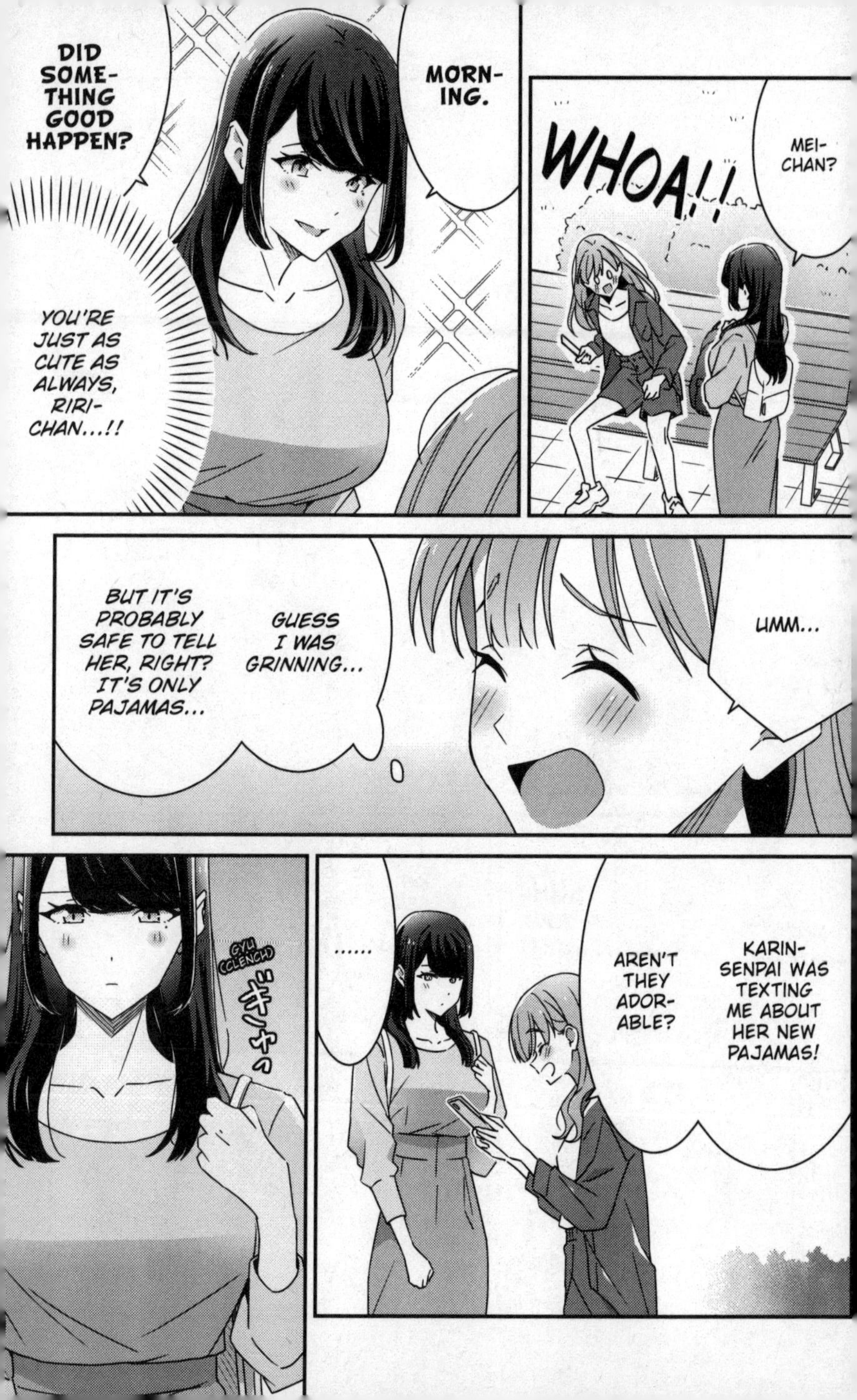
MEI-CHAN?
WHOA!!
MORNING.
DID SOMETHING GOOD HAPPEN?
YOU'RE JUST AS CUTE AS ALWAYS, RIRI-CHAN...!!
UMM...
GUESS I WAS GRINNING...
BUT IT'S PROBABLY SAFE TO TELL HER, RIGHT? IT'S ONLY PAJAMAS...
KARIN-SENPAI WAS TEXTING ME ABOUT HER NEW PAJAMAS!
AREN'T THEY ADORABLE?
......
GYU (CLENCH)

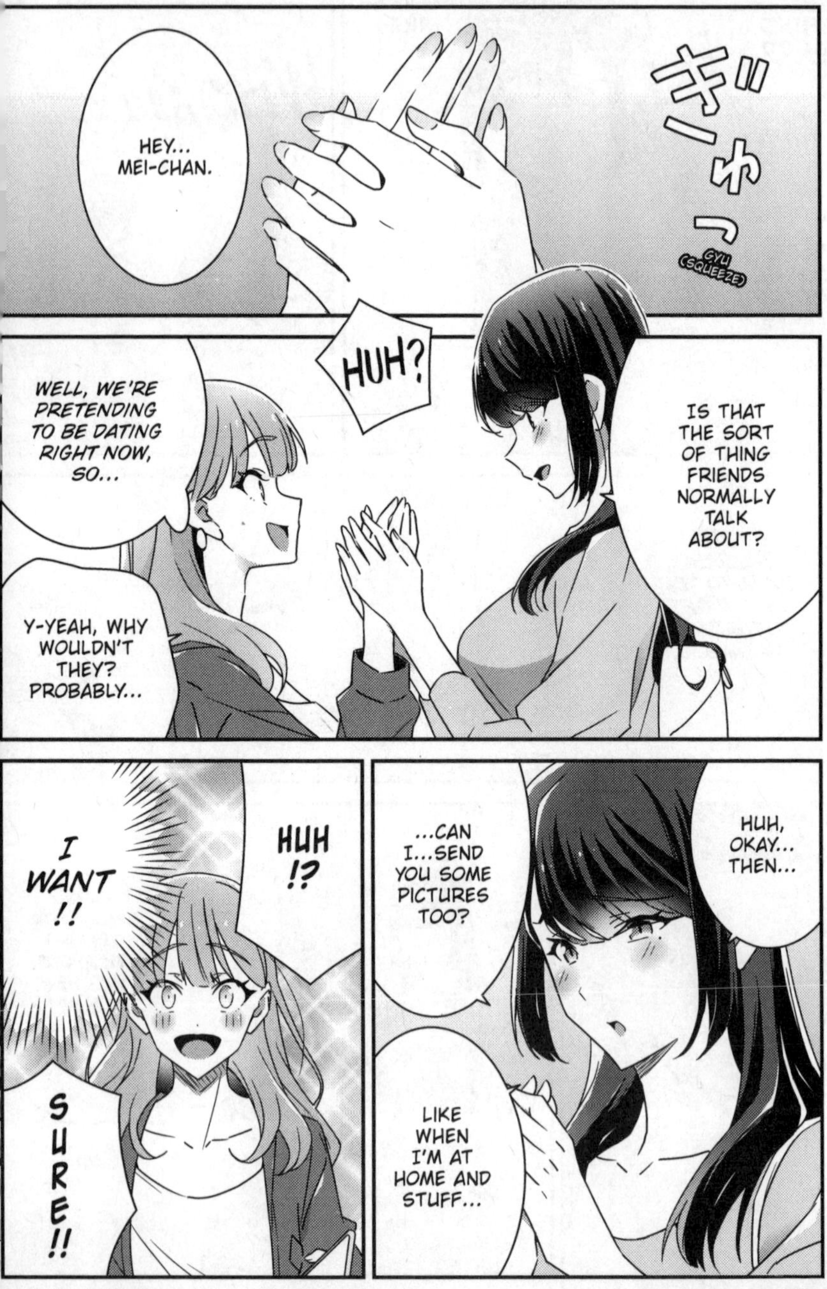
ぎゅーっ
GYU (SQUEEZE)
HEY... MEI-CHAN.
HUH?
IS THAT THE SORT OF THING FRIENDS NORMALLY TALK ABOUT?
WELL, WE'RE PRETENDING TO BE DATING RIGHT NOW, SO...
Y-YEAH, WHY WOULDN'T THEY? PROBABLY...
HUH, OKAY... THEN...
...CAN I...SEND YOU SOME PICTURES TOO?
LIKE WHEN I'M AT HOME AND STUFF...
HUH!?
I WANT!!
SURE!!

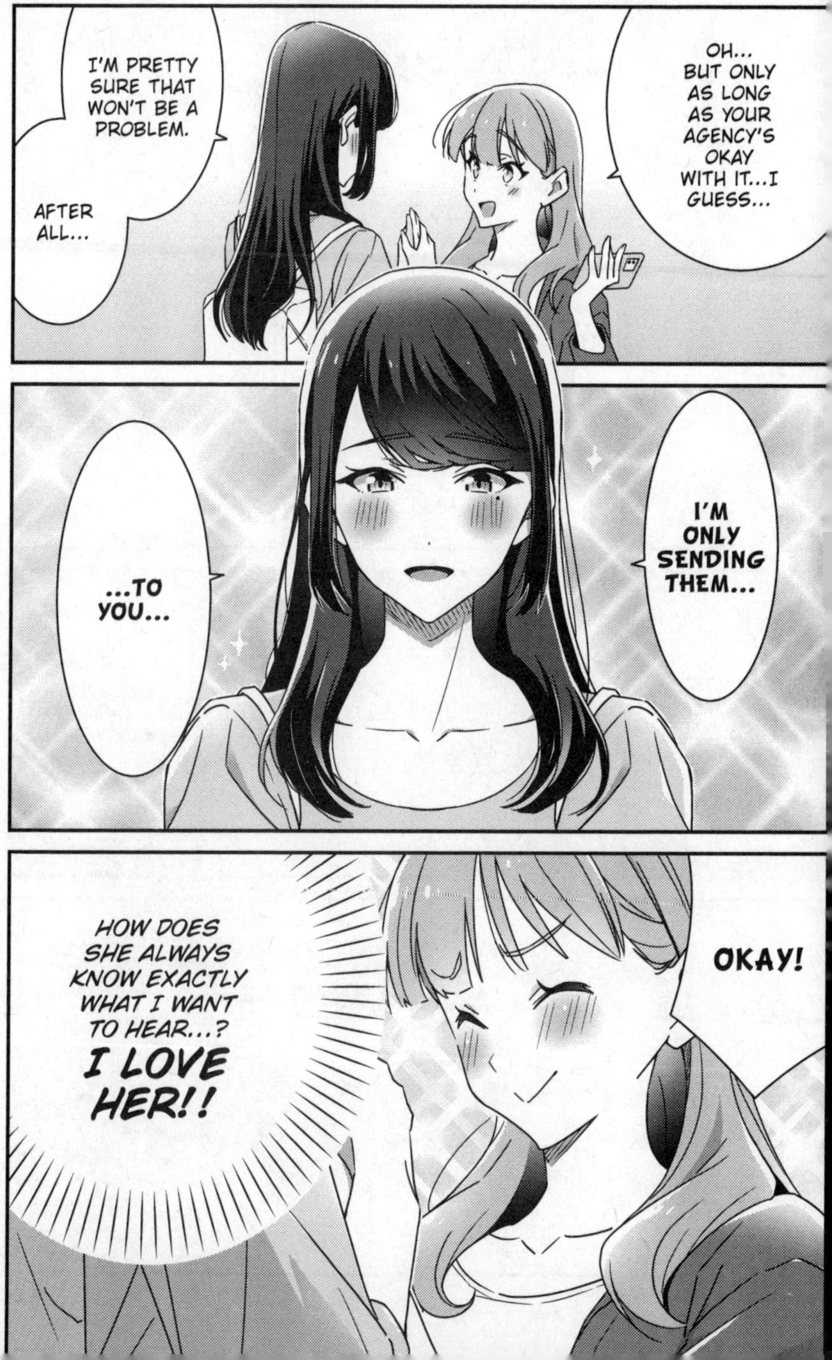
OH... BUT ONLY AS LONG AS YOUR AGENCY'S OKAY WITH IT...I GUESS...
I'M PRETTY SURE THAT WON'T BE A PROBLEM.
AFTER ALL...
I'M ONLY SENDING THEM...
...TO YOU...
OKAY!
HOW DOES SHE ALWAYS KNOW EXACTLY WHAT I WANT TO HEAR...? I LOVE HER!!

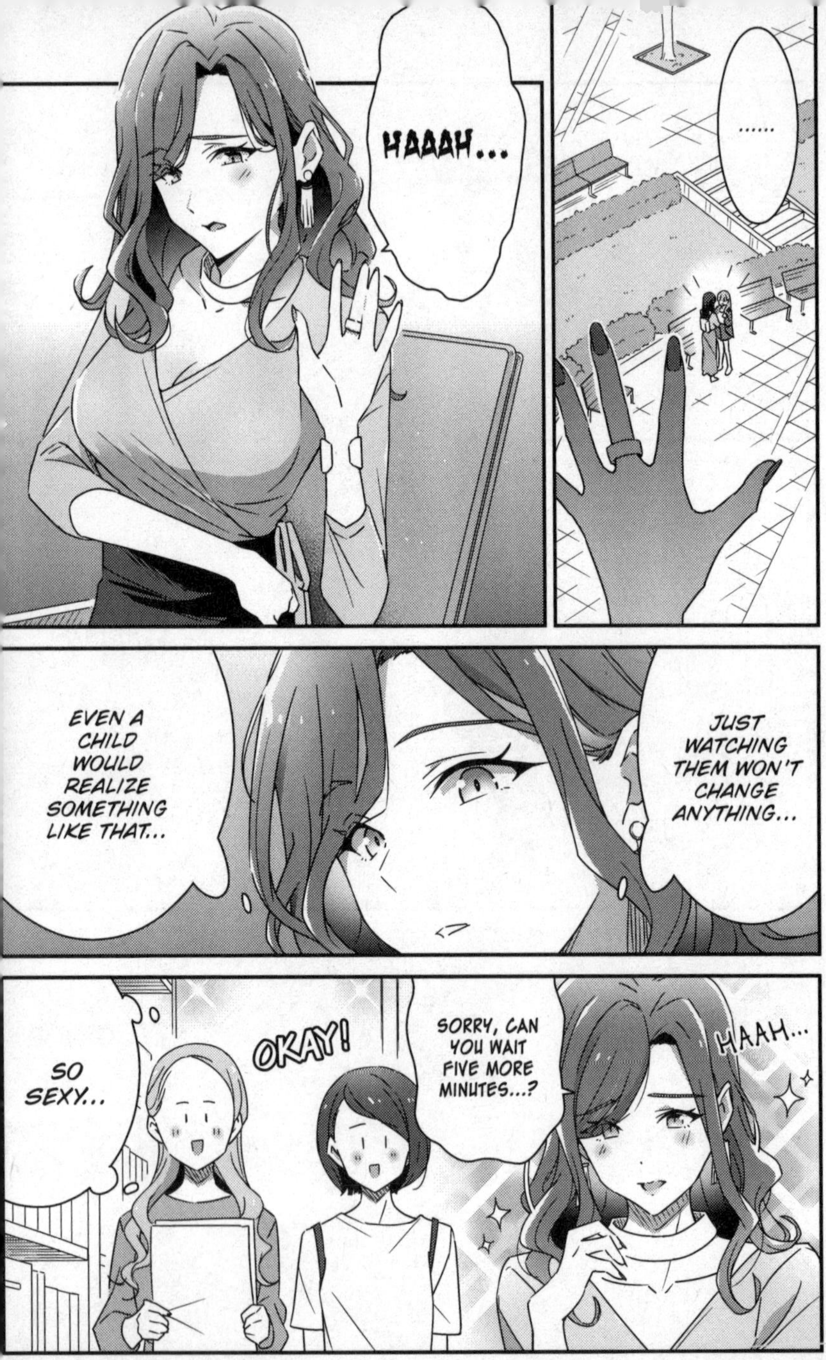
......
HAAAH...
JUST WATCHING THEM WON'T CHANGE ANYTHING...
EVEN A CHILD WOULD REALIZE SOMETHING LIKE THAT...
HAAH...
SORRY, CAN YOU WAIT FIVE MORE MINUTES...?
OKAY!
SO SEXY...

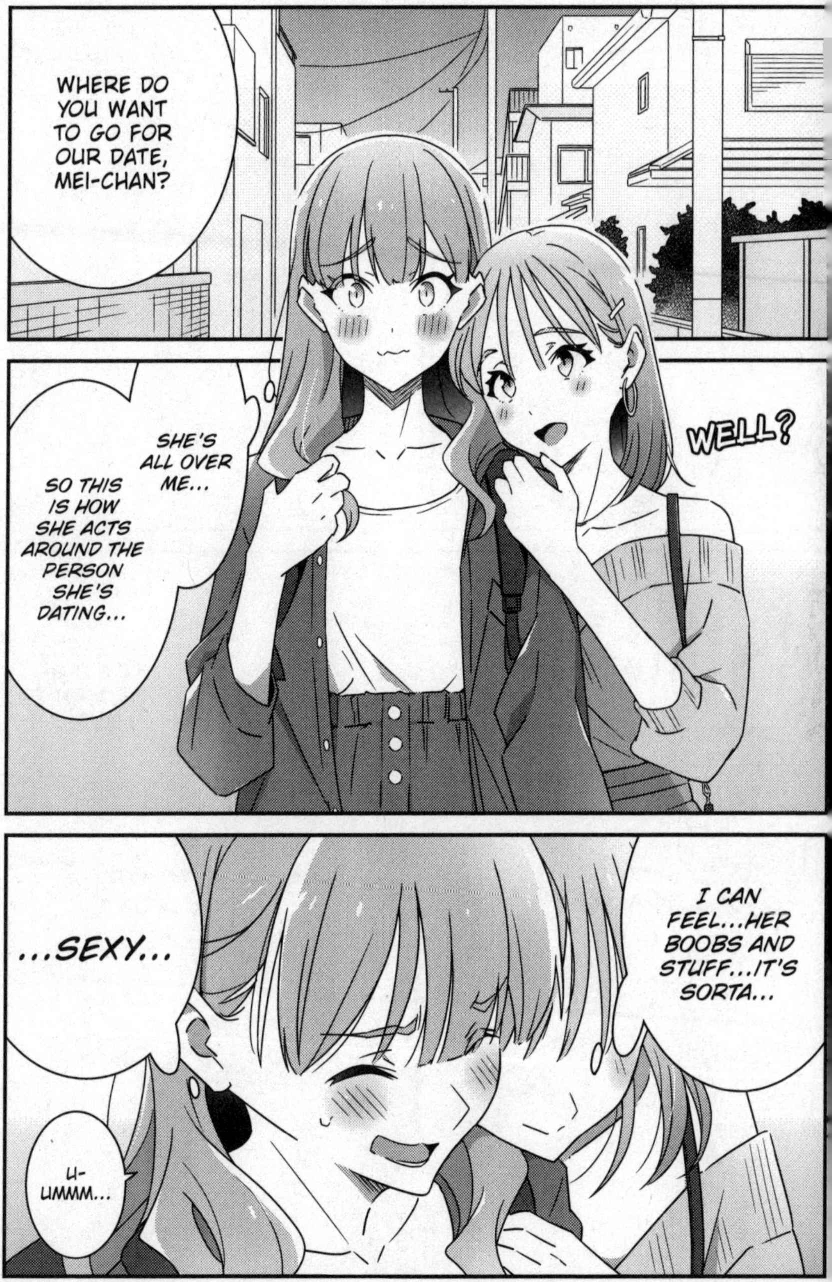
WHERE DO YOU WANT TO GO FOR OUR DATE, MEI-CHAN?
WELL?
SHE'S ALL OVER ME...
SO THIS IS HOW SHE ACTS AROUND THE PERSON SHE'S DATING...
I CAN FEEL...HER BOOBS AND STUFF...IT'S SORTA...
...SEXY...
U-UMMM...

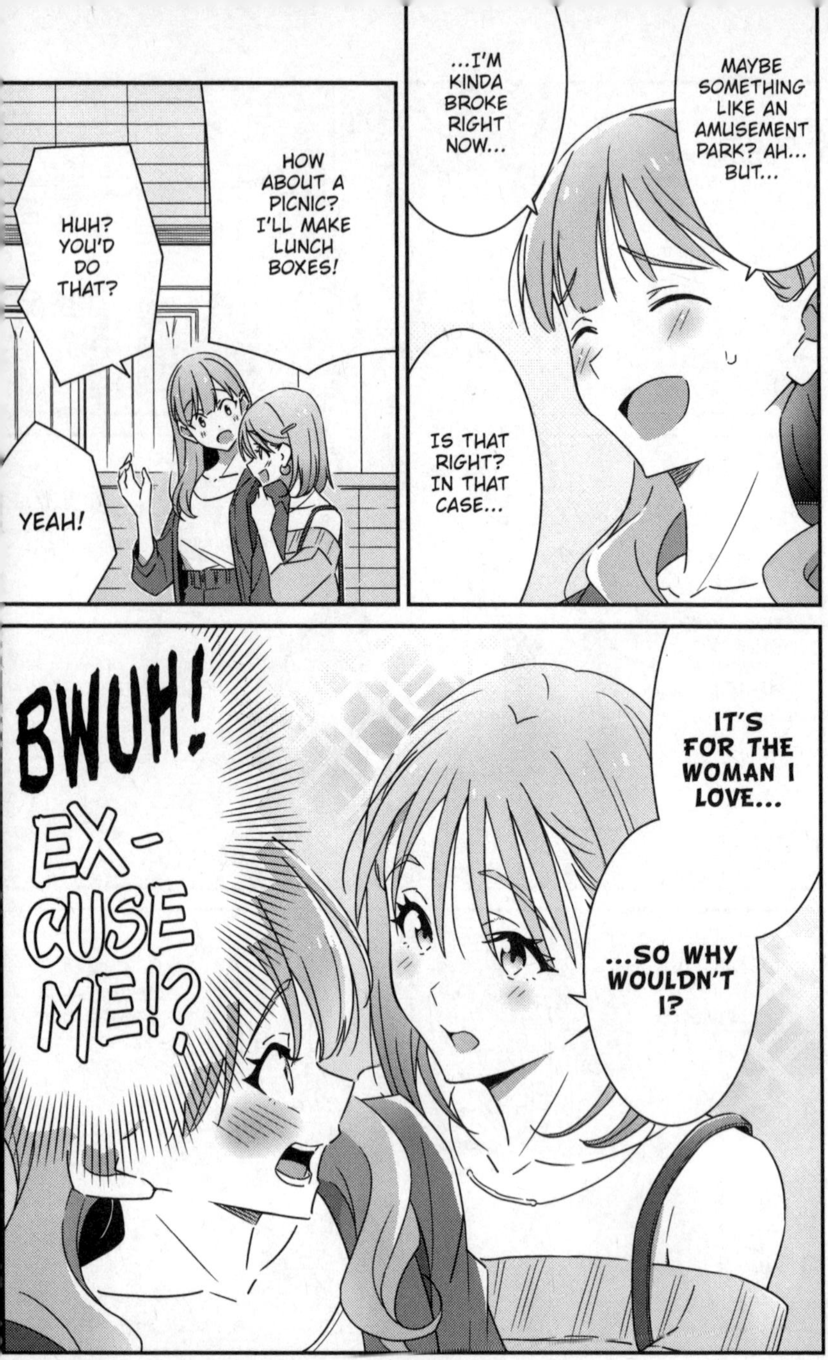
MAYBE SOMETHING LIKE AN AMUSEMENT PARK? AH... BUT...
...I'M KINDA BROKE RIGHT NOW...
IS THAT RIGHT? IN THAT CASE...
HOW ABOUT A PICNIC? I'LL MAKE LUNCH BOXES!
HUH? YOU'D DO THAT?
YEAH!
IT'S FOR THE WOMAN I LOVE...
...SO WHY WOULDN'T I?
BWUH!
EX-CUSE ME!?

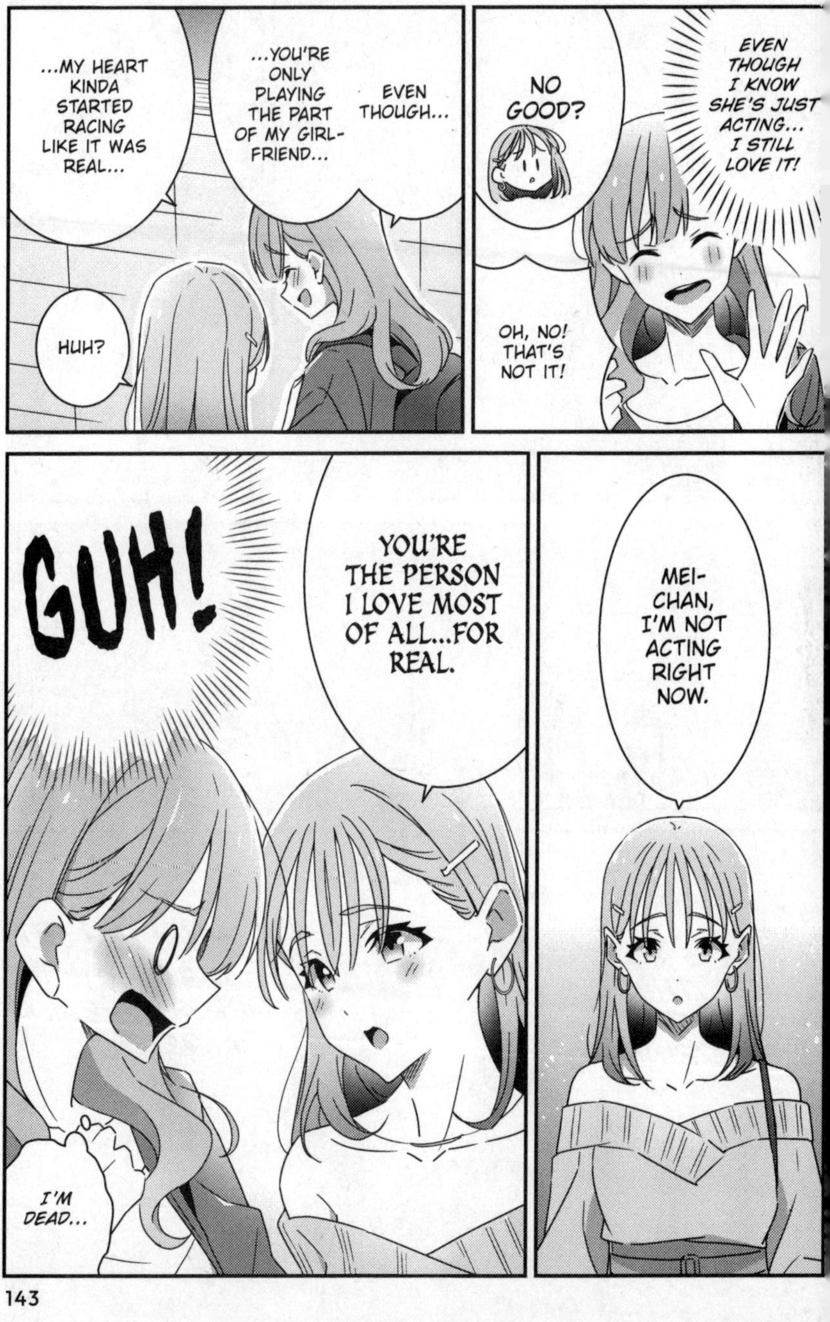
EVEN THOUGH I KNOW SHE'S JUST ACTING... I STILL LOVE IT!
NO GOOD?
OH, NO! THAT'S NOT IT!
EVEN THOUGH...
...YOU'RE ONLY PLAYING THE PART OF MY GIRL-FRIEND...
...MY HEART KINDA STARTED RACING LIKE IT WAS REAL...
HUH?
MEI-CHAN, I'M NOT ACTING RIGHT NOW.
YOU'RE THE PERSON I LOVE MOST OF ALL...FOR REAL.
GUH!
I'M DEAD...

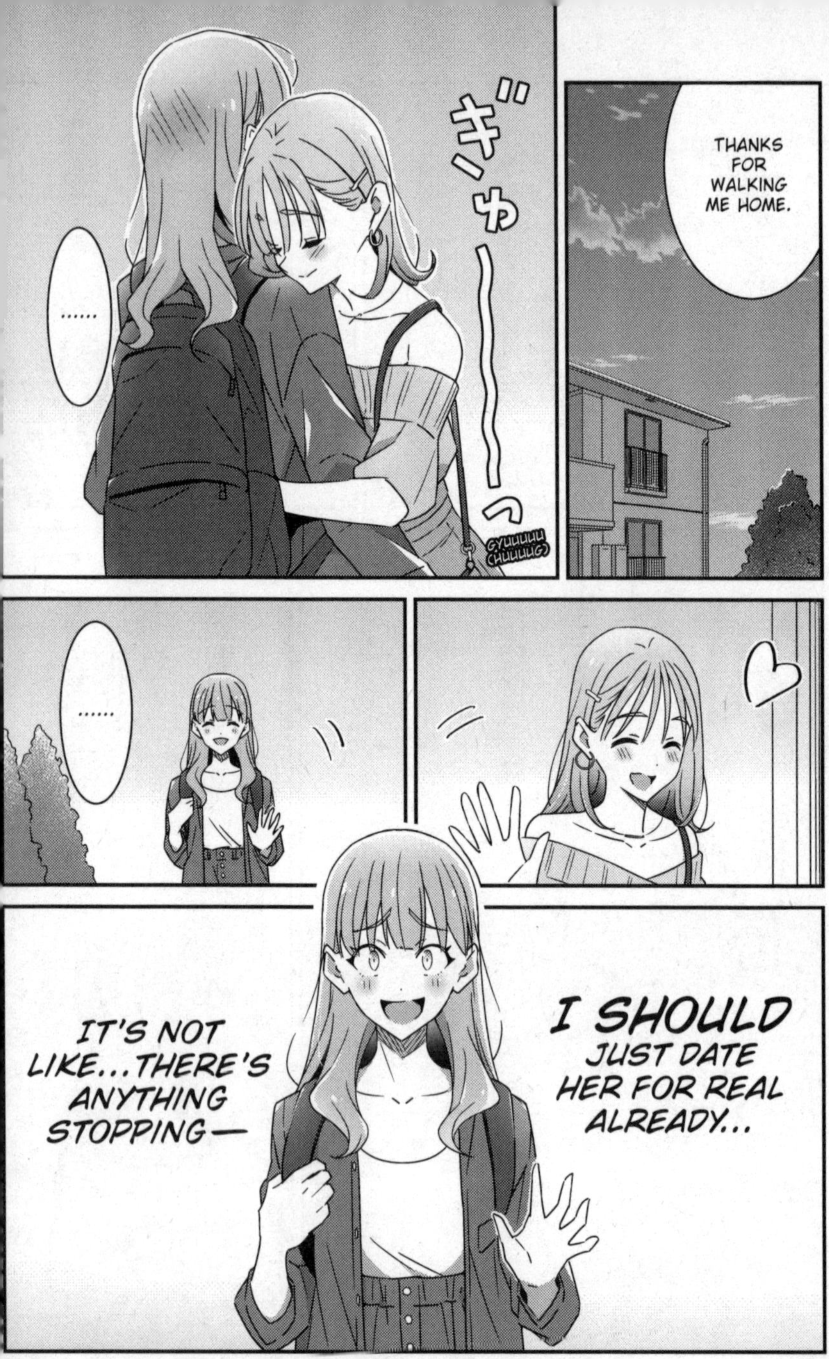
THANKS FOR WALKING ME HOME.
ぎゅーっ
GYUUUUU (HUUUUUG)
......
......
I SHOULD JUST DATE HER FOR REAL ALREADY...
IT'S NOT LIKE...THERE'S ANYTHING STOPPING—

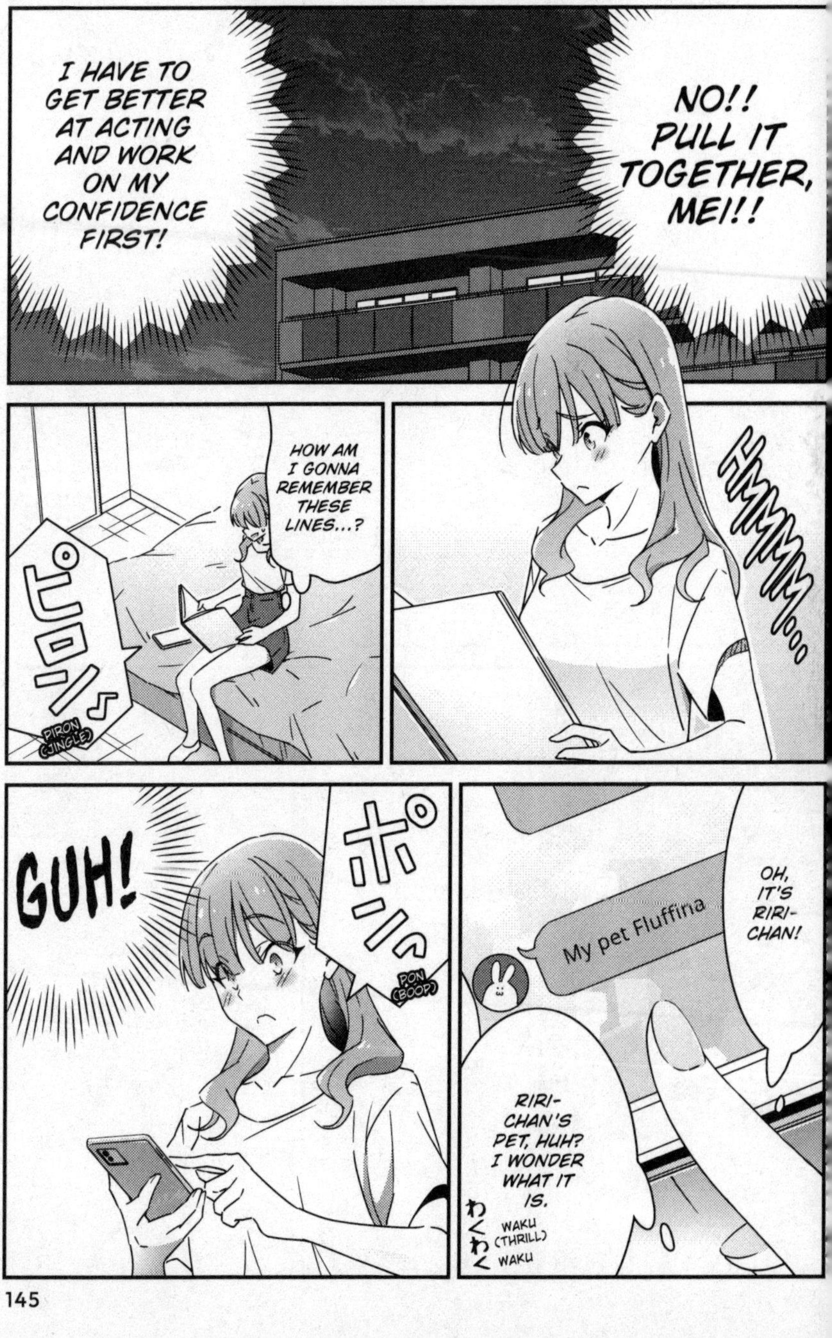
NO!! PULL IT TOGETHER, MEI!!
I HAVE TO GET BETTER AT ACTING AND WORK ON MY CONFIDENCE FIRST!
HMMMMM...
HOW AM I GONNA REMEMBER THESE LINES...?
ピロン♪
PIRON (JINGLE)
OH, IT'S RIRI-CHAN!
My pet Fluffina
RIRI-CHAN'S PET, HUH? I WONDER WHAT IT IS.
わくわく
WAKU (THRILL) WAKU
ポン♪
PON (BOOP)
GUH!

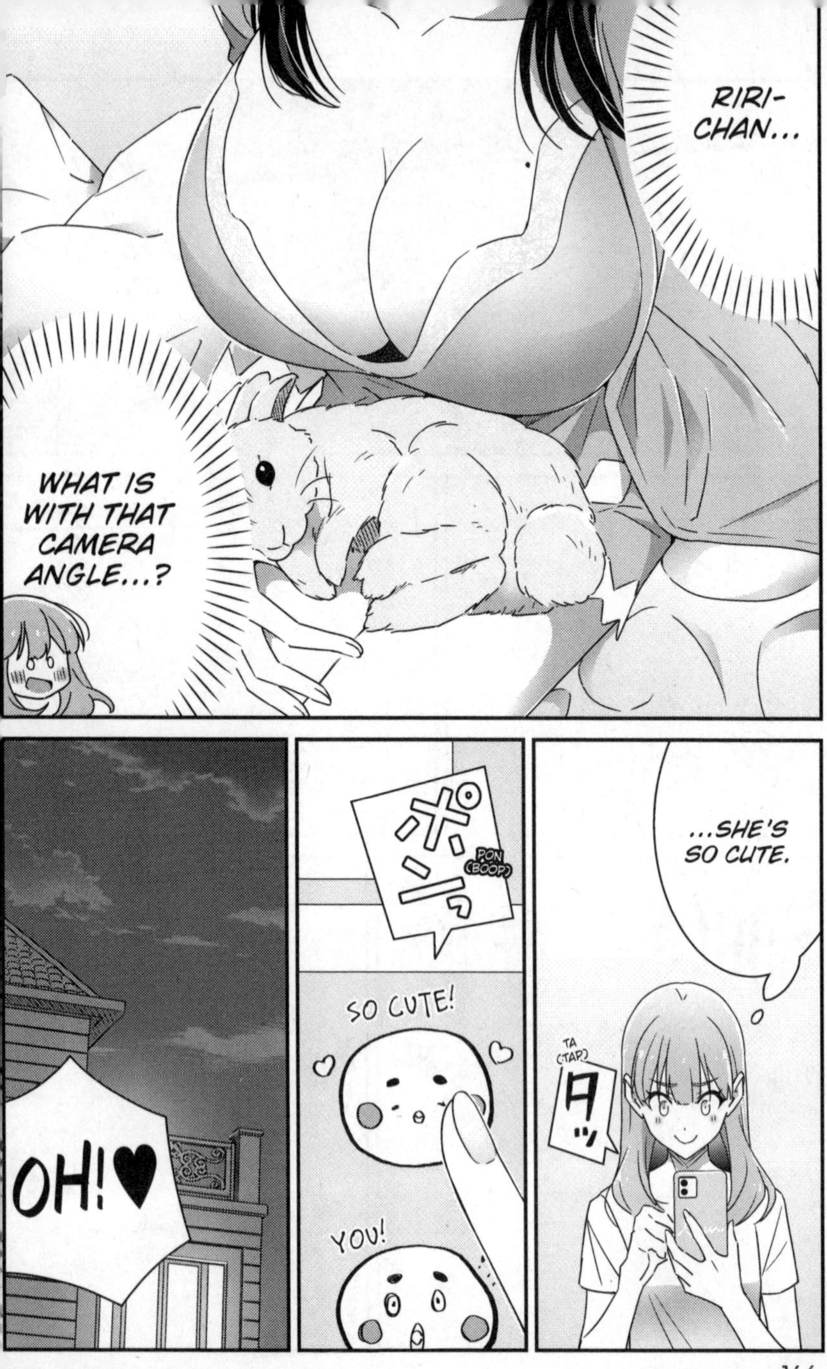
RIRI-CHAN...
WHAT IS WITH THAT CAMERA ANGLE...?
...SHE'S SO CUTE.
タッ
TA (TAP)
ポンッ
PON (BOOP)
SO CUTE!
YOU!
OH!♥

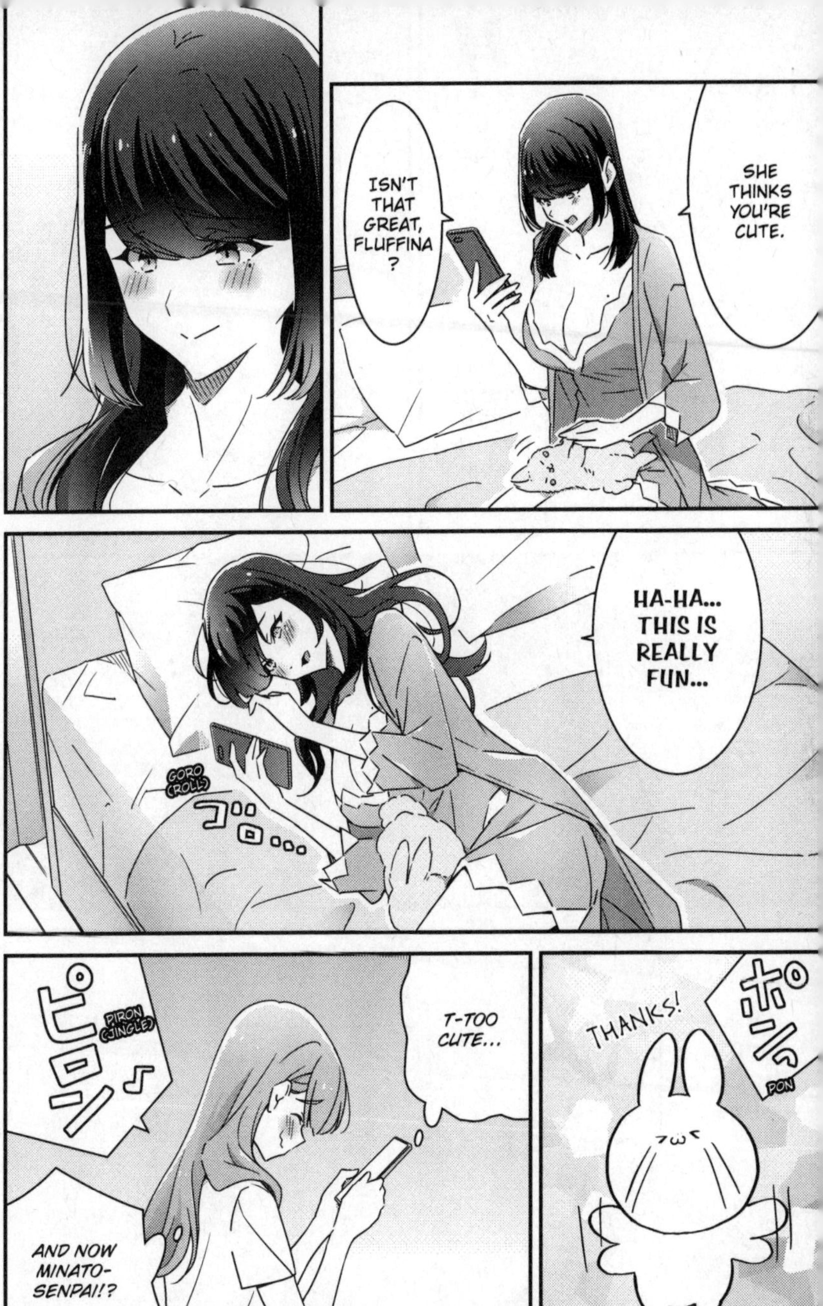
SHE THINKS YOU'RE CUTE.
ISN'T THAT GREAT, FLUFFINA?
HA-HA... THIS IS REALLY FUN...
GORO (ROLL)
ゴロ…
ポンッ
PON
THANKS!
ピロン♪
PIRON (JINGLE)
T-TOO CUTE...
AND NOW MINATO-SENPAI!?

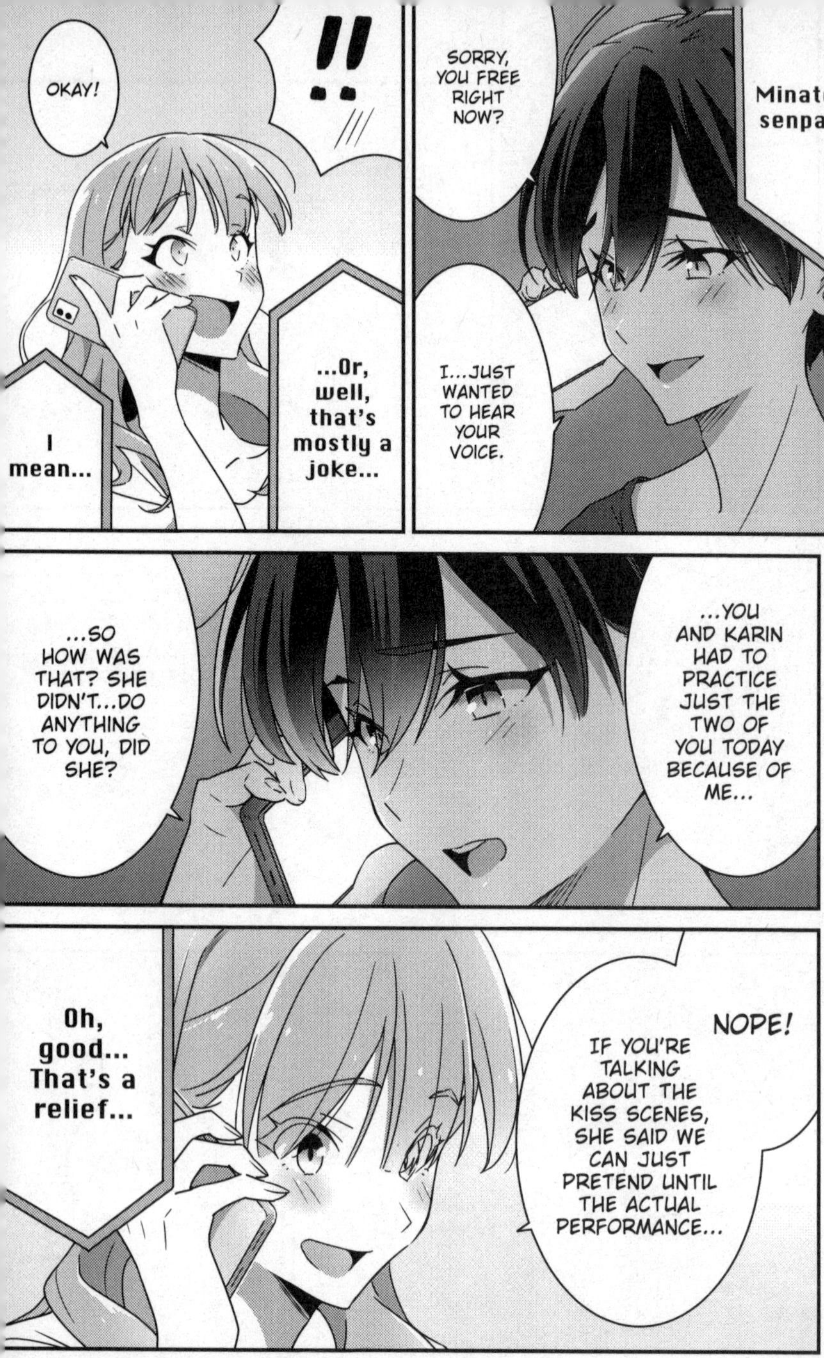
Minato-senpai!
SORRY, YOU FREE RIGHT NOW?
I...JUST WANTED TO HEAR YOUR VOICE.
!!
OKAY!
...Or, well, that's mostly a joke...
I mean...
...YOU AND KARIN HAD TO PRACTICE JUST THE TWO OF YOU TODAY BECAUSE OF ME...
...SO HOW WAS THAT? SHE DIDN'T...DO ANYTHING TO YOU, DID SHE?
NOPE!
IF YOU'RE TALKING ABOUT THE KISS SCENES, SHE SAID WE CAN JUST PRETEND UNTIL THE ACTUAL PERFORMANCE...
Oh, good... That's a relief...

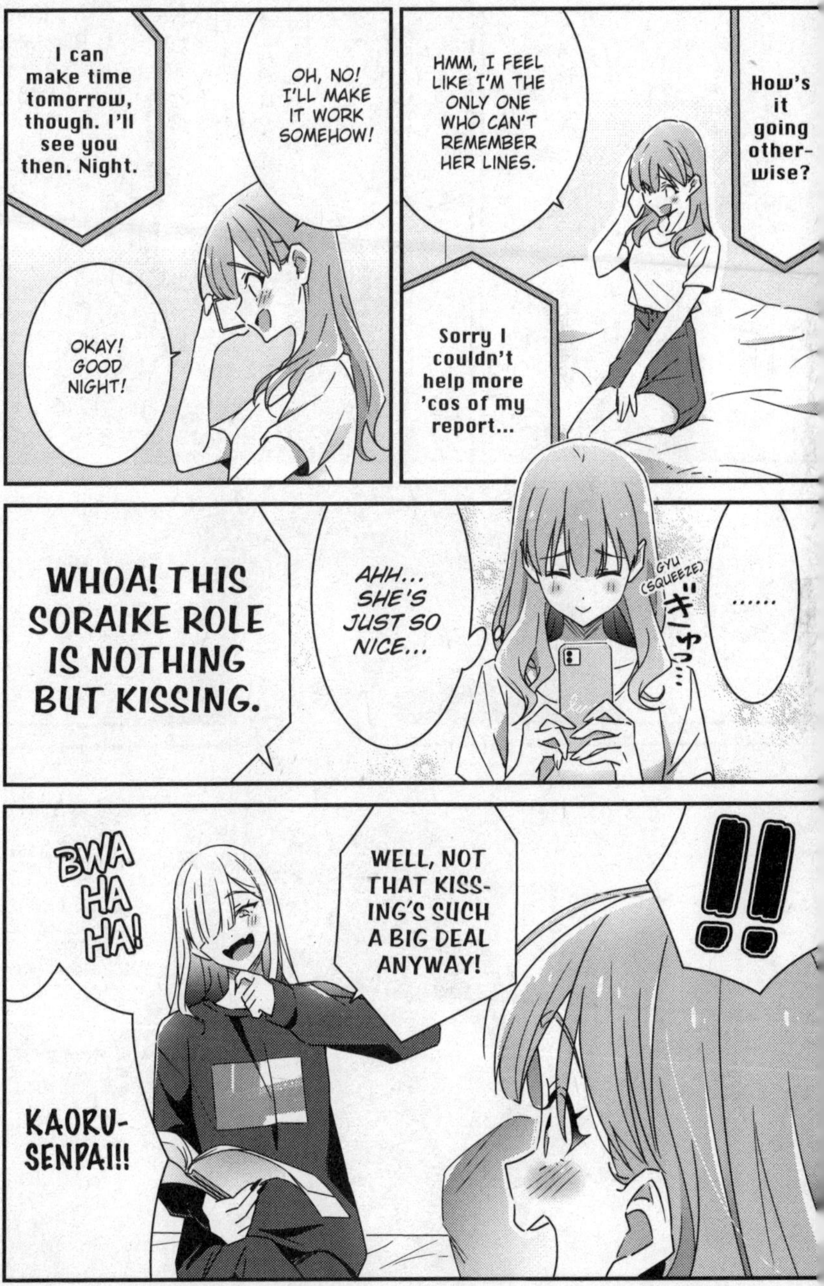
How's it going otherwise?
HMM, I FEEL LIKE I'M THE ONLY ONE WHO CAN'T REMEMBER HER LINES.
Sorry I couldn't help more 'cos of my report...
OH, NO! I'LL MAKE IT WORK SOMEHOW!
I can make time tomorrow, though. I'll see you then. Night.
OKAY! GOOD NIGHT!
......
GYU (SQUEEZE)
ギュッ…
AHH... SHE'S JUST SO NICE...
WHOA! THIS SORAIKE ROLE IS NOTHING BUT KISSING.
!!
WELL, NOT THAT KISSING'S SUCH A BIG DEAL ANYWAY!
BWA HA HA!
KAORU-SENPAI!!

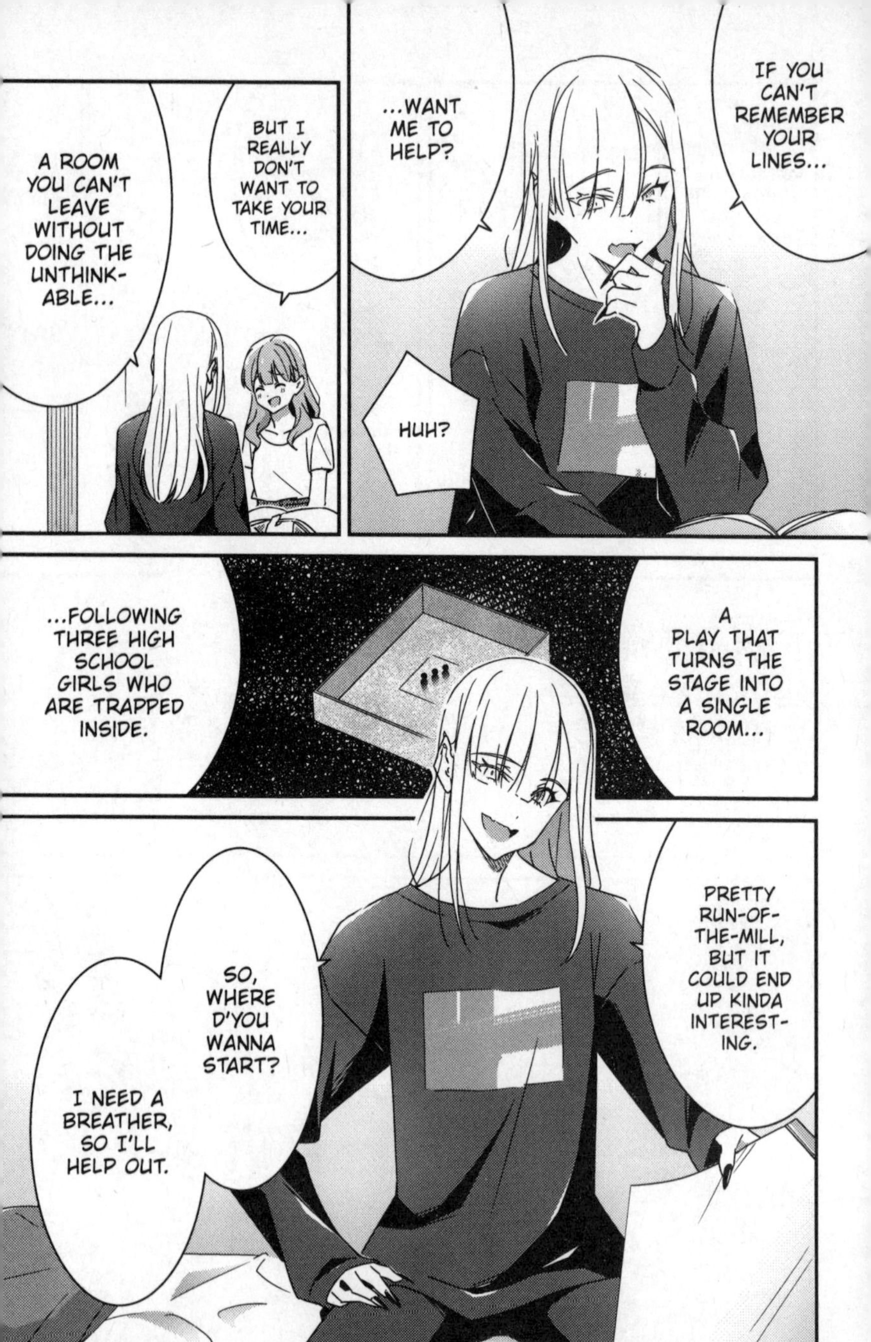
IF YOU CAN'T REMEMBER YOUR LINES...
...WANT ME TO HELP?
HUH?
BUT I REALLY DON'T WANT TO TAKE YOUR TIME...
A ROOM YOU CAN'T LEAVE WITHOUT DOING THE UNTHINK-ABLE...
A PLAY THAT TURNS THE STAGE INTO A SINGLE ROOM...
...FOLLOWING THREE HIGH SCHOOL GIRLS WHO ARE TRAPPED INSIDE.
PRETTY RUN-OF-THE-MILL, BUT IT COULD END UP KINDA INTEREST-ING.
SO, WHERE D'YOU WANNA START?
I NEED A BREATHER, SO I'LL HELP OUT.

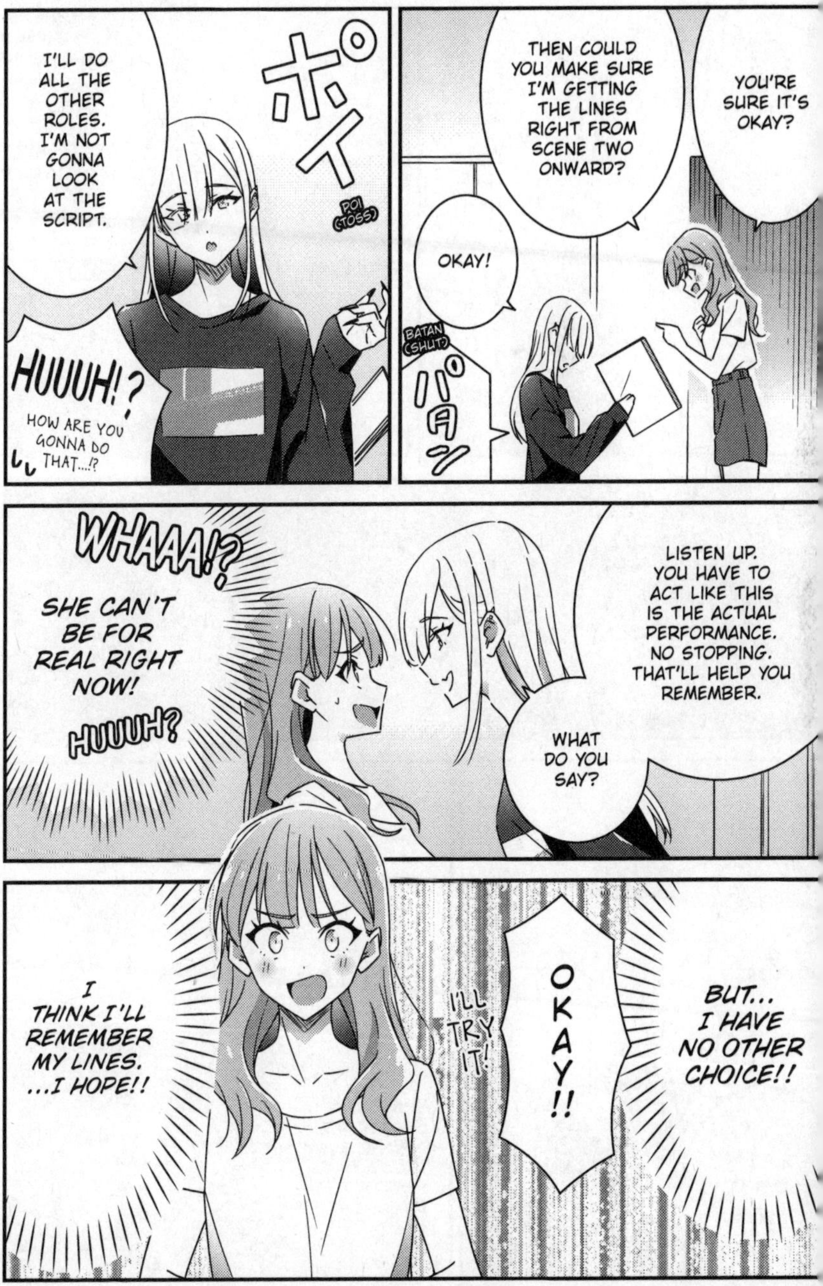
YOU'RE SURE IT'S OKAY?
THEN COULD YOU MAKE SURE I'M GETTING THE LINES RIGHT FROM SCENE TWO ONWARD?
OKAY!
BATAN (SHUT)
I'LL DO ALL THE OTHER ROLES. I'M NOT GONNA LOOK AT THE SCRIPT.
POI (TOSS)
HUUUH!?
HOW ARE YOU GONNA DO THAT...!?
LISTEN UP. YOU HAVE TO ACT LIKE THIS IS THE ACTUAL PERFORMANCE. NO STOPPING. THAT'LL HELP YOU REMEMBER.
WHAT DO YOU SAY?
WHAAA!?
SHE CAN'T BE FOR REAL RIGHT NOW!
HUUUH?
BUT... I HAVE NO OTHER CHOICE!!
OKAY!!
I'LL TRY IT!
I THINK I'LL REMEMBER MY LINES. ...I HOPE!!

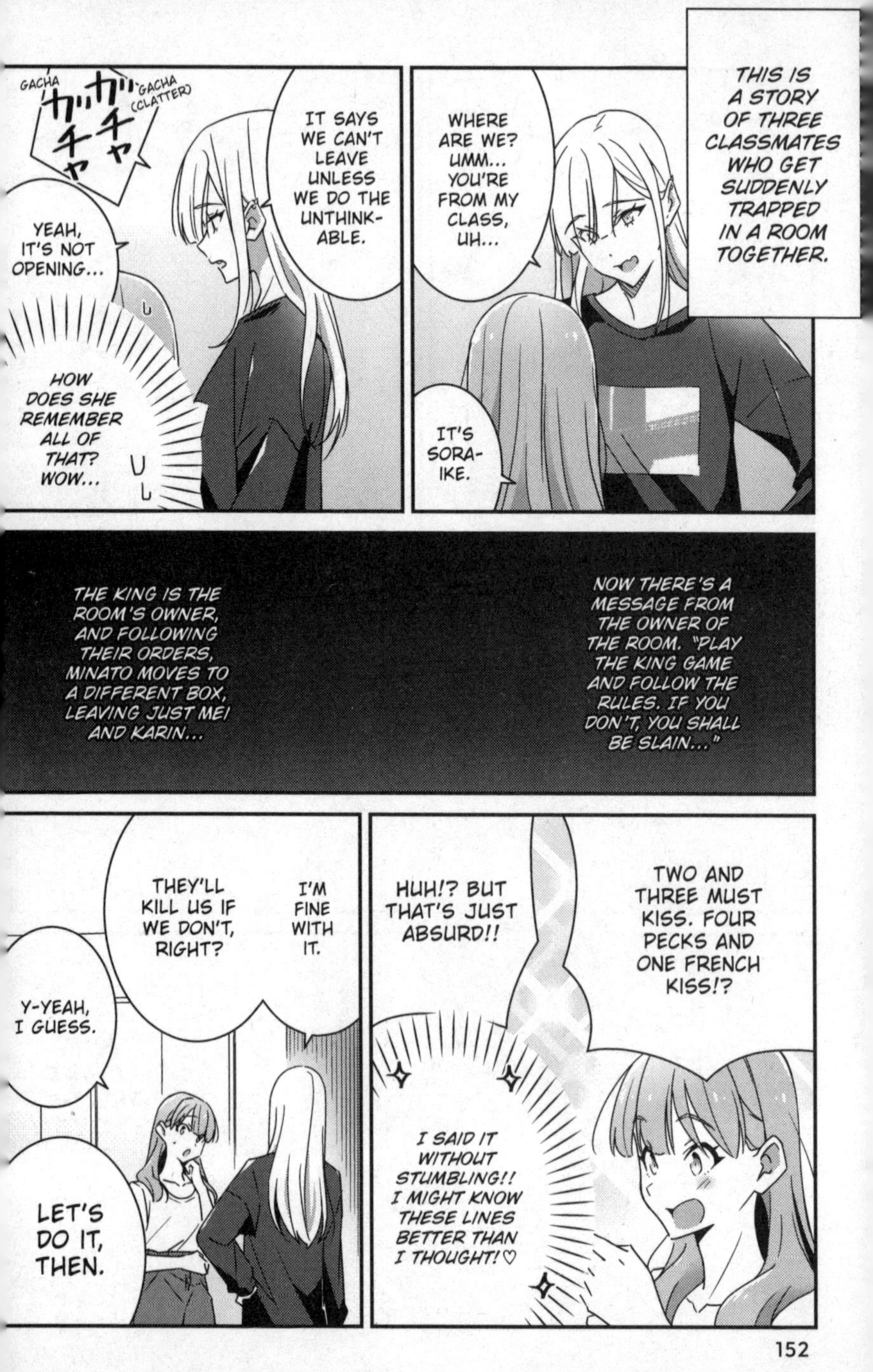
THIS IS A STORY OF THREE CLASSMATES WHO GET SUDDENLY TRAPPED IN A ROOM TOGETHER.
WHERE ARE WE? UMM... YOU'RE FROM MY CLASS, UH...
IT'S SORA-IKE.
IT SAYS WE CAN'T LEAVE UNLESS WE DO THE UNTHINK-ABLE.
GACHA ガッガチャチャ GACHA (CLATTER)
YEAH, IT'S NOT OPENING...
HOW DOES SHE REMEMBER ALL OF THAT? WOW...
NOW THERE'S A MESSAGE FROM THE OWNER OF THE ROOM. "PLAY THE KING GAME AND FOLLOW THE RULES. IF YOU DON'T, YOU SHALL BE SLAIN..."
THE KING IS THE ROOM'S OWNER, AND FOLLOWING THEIR ORDERS, MINATO MOVES TO A DIFFERENT BOX, LEAVING JUST MEI AND KARIN...
TWO AND THREE MUST KISS. FOUR PECKS AND ONE FRENCH KISS!?
HUH!? BUT THAT'S JUST ABSURD!!
I SAID IT WITHOUT STUMBLING!! I MIGHT KNOW THESE LINES BETTER THAN I THOUGHT!♡
I'M FINE WITH IT.
THEY'LL KILL US IF WE DON'T, RIGHT?
Y-YEAH, I GUESS.
LET'S DO IT, THEN.

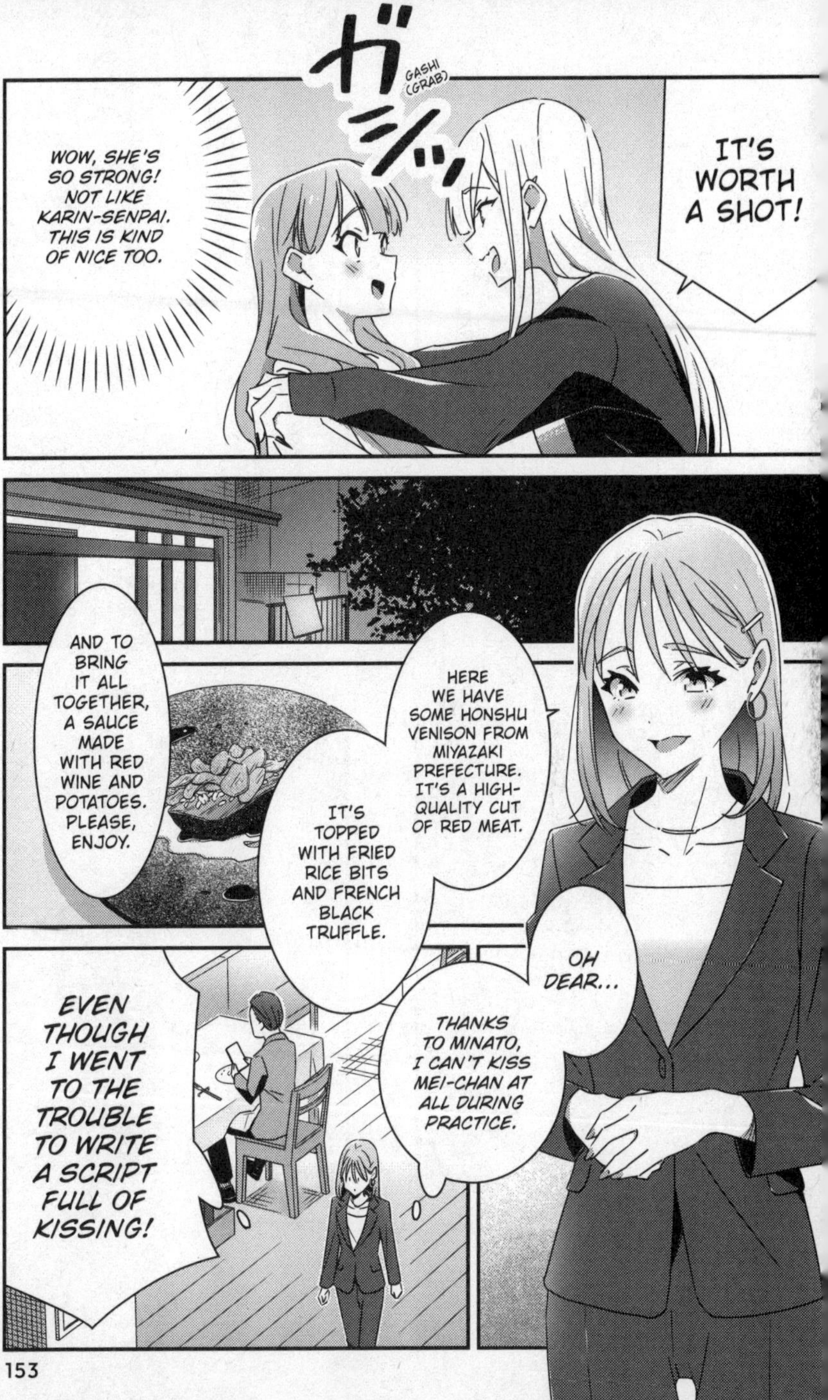
IT'S WORTH A SHOT!
GASHI (GRAB)
WOW, SHE'S SO STRONG! NOT LIKE KARIN-SENPAI. THIS IS KIND OF NICE TOO.
HERE WE HAVE SOME HONSHU VENISON FROM MIYAZAKI PREFECTURE. IT'S A HIGH-QUALITY CUT OF RED MEAT.
IT'S TOPPED WITH FRIED RICE BITS AND FRENCH BLACK TRUFFLE.
AND TO BRING IT ALL TOGETHER, A SAUCE MADE WITH RED WINE AND POTATOES. PLEASE, ENJOY.
OH DEAR...
THANKS TO MINATO, I CAN'T KISS MEI-CHAN AT ALL DURING PRACTICE.
EVEN THOUGH I WENT TO THE TROUBLE TO WRITE A SCRIPT FULL OF KISSING!

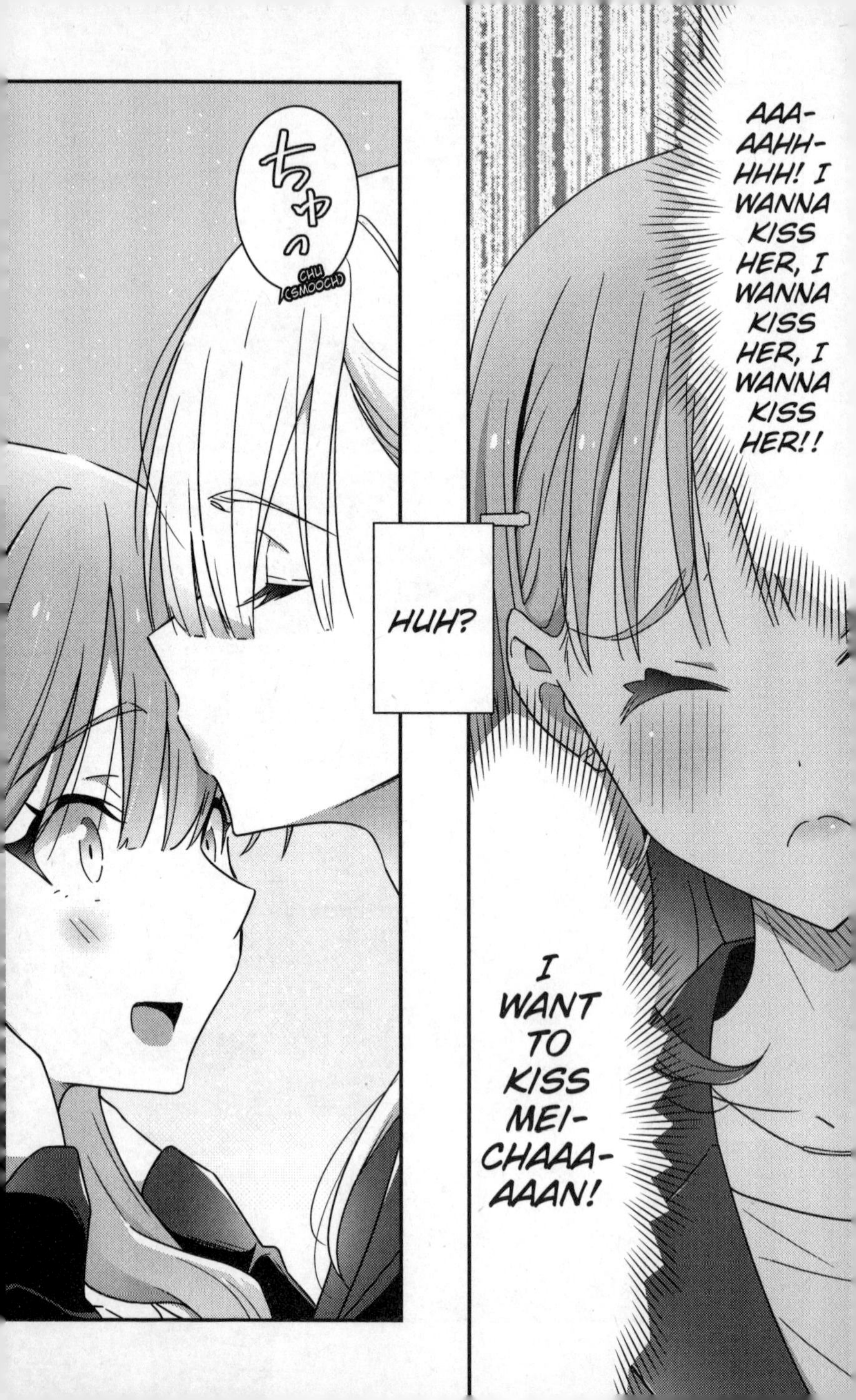
AAA-AAHH-HHH! I WANNA KISS HER, I WANNA KISS HER, I WANNA KISS HER!!
I WANT TO KISS MEI-CHAAAA-AAAN!
ちゅっ
CHU (SMOOCH)
HUH?

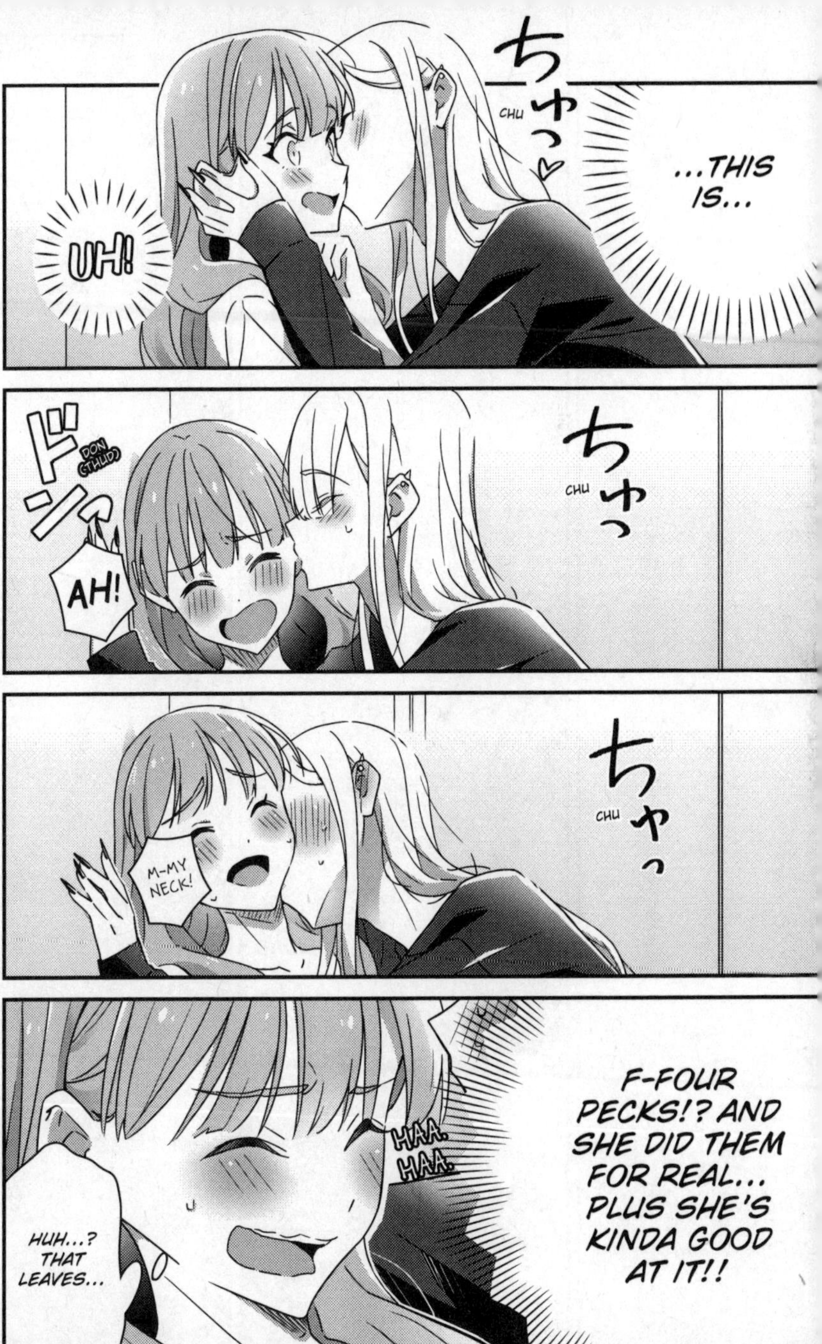
...THIS IS...
ちゅっ
CHU
UH!
ちゅっ
CHU
ドンッ
DON (THUD)
AH!
ちゃっ
CHU
M-MY NECK!
F-FOUR PECKS!? AND SHE DID THEM FOR REAL... PLUS SHE'S KINDA GOOD AT IT!!
HAA. HAA.
HUH...? THAT LEAVES...

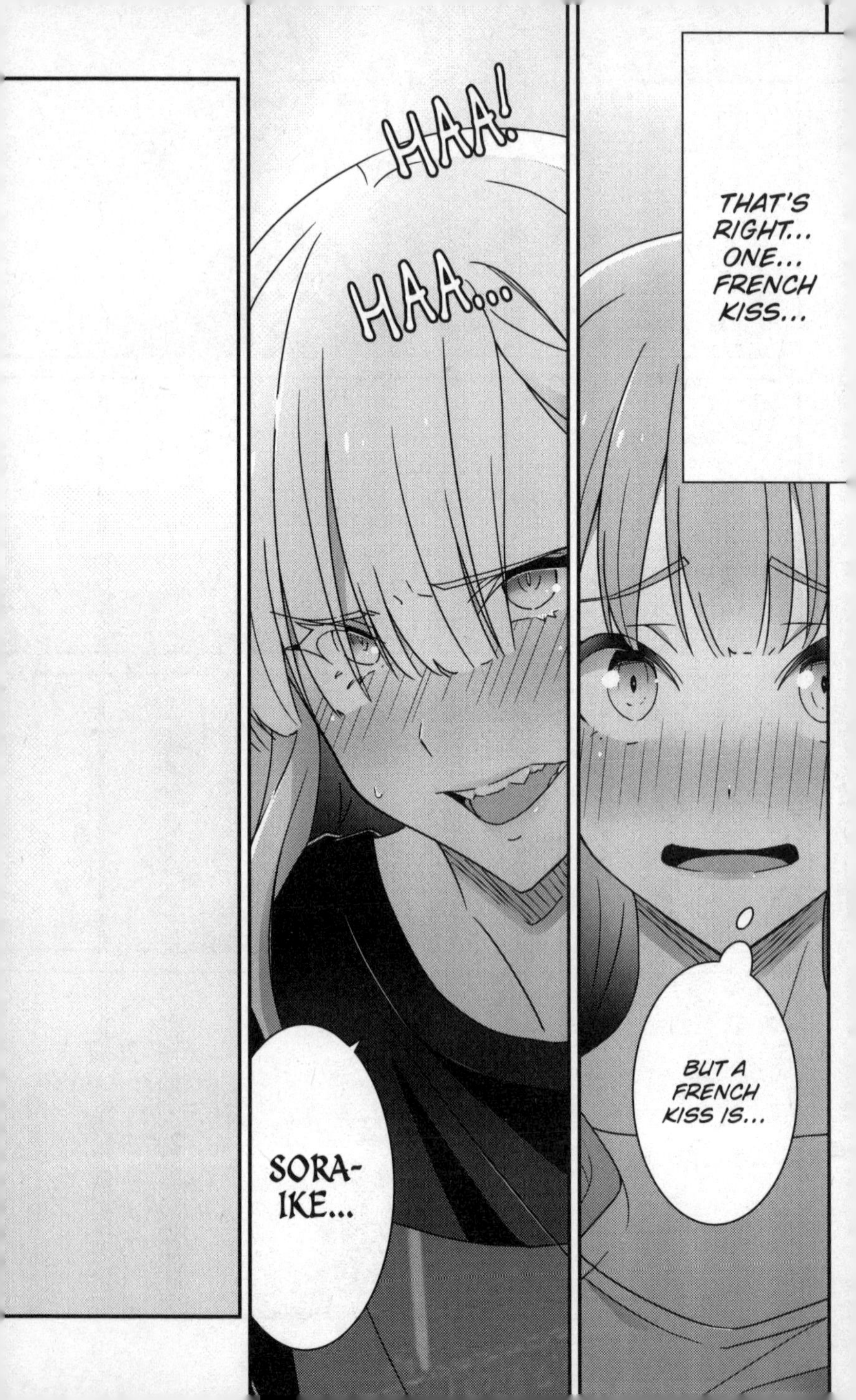
THAT'S RIGHT... ONE... FRENCH KISS...
BUT A FRENCH KISS IS...
HAA!
HAA...
SORA-IKE...

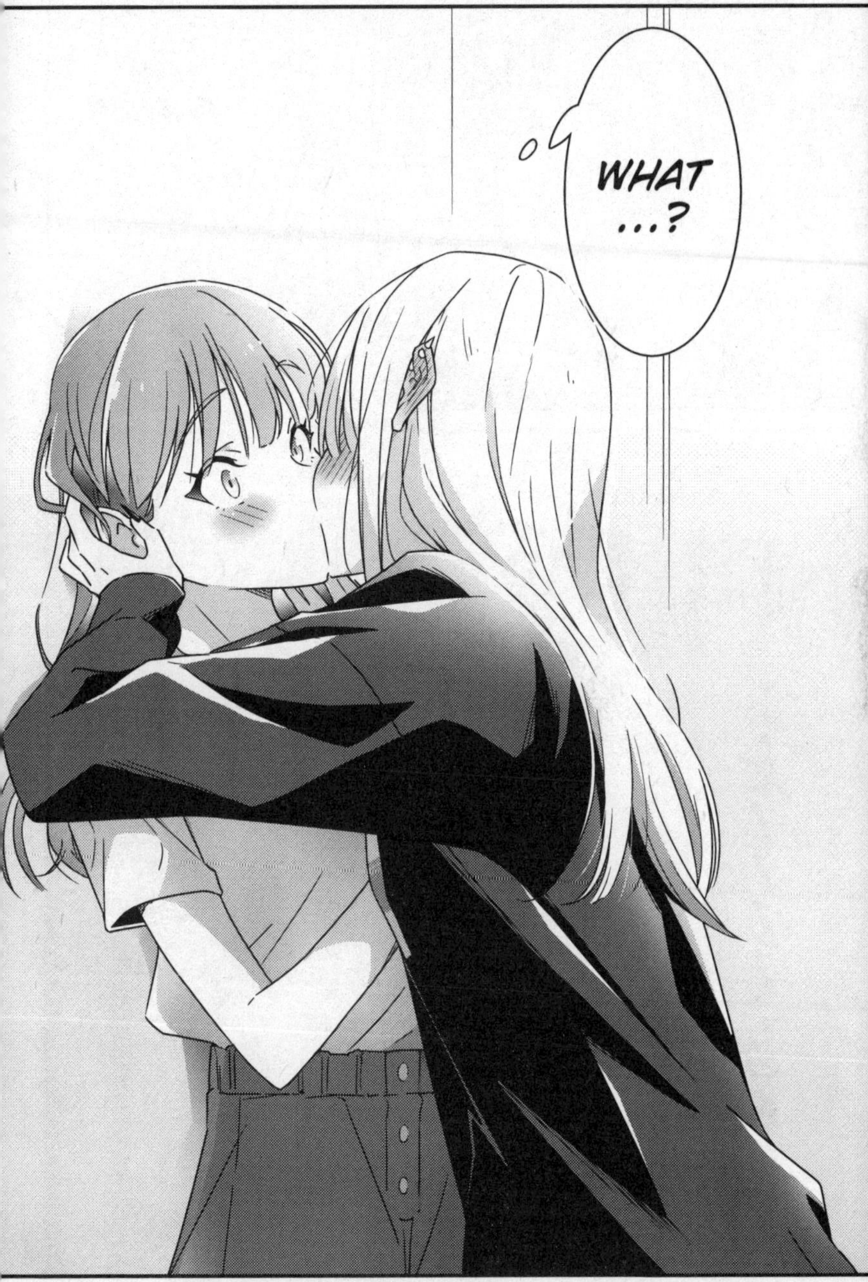
WHAT ...?

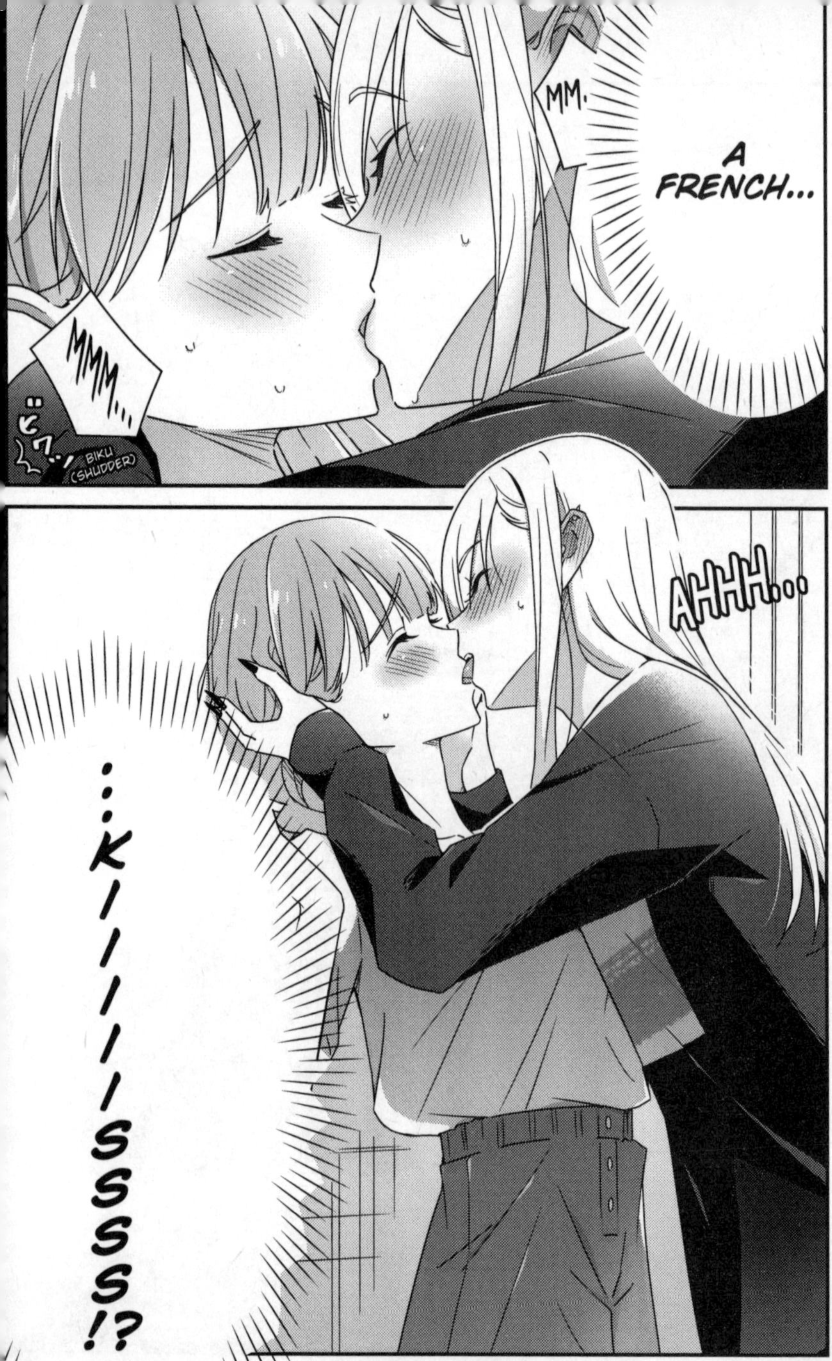
A FRENCH...
MM.
MMM...
ビクッ
BIKU (SHUDDER)
AHHH...
...KIIIIISSSSS!?

Translation Notes

♥ ♥ ♥ ♥ ♥ ♥ ♥ ♥ ♥ ♡ ♥ ♥ ♥ ♥ ♥ ♥ ♥ ♥ ♥ ♡ ♥ ♥ ♥ ♥ ♥ ♥ ♥ ♥ ♥

Page 117 - The performer is reading the poem "*Ame ni mo makezu*" by twentieth-century Japanese poet Kenji Miyazawa. This poem is translated under many titles, including "Be Not Defeated by the Rain."

Page 142 - Karin offers to make **bento boxes**, a type of packed lunch often eaten on outings. They can include anything, though most commonly they will have rice, meat, and pickled vegetables separated into sections within a box.

Page 145 - Riri's rabbit **Fluffina** is called *Mofumi* in the Japanese, derived from *mofumofu*, meaning "fluffy," and the character "*mi*," meaning "beauty," commonly used in girls' names.

Page 152 - The **King Game** is a popular Japanese party game. In it, the players all draw lots, one of which is labeled with "king" and the rest with numbers. The "king" player then gives an order, specifying numbers to perform the action but not knowing who has each number. It is similar to truth or dare and often played at mixers.

♥   ♥

Honorifics

♥ ♥ ♥ ♥ ♥ ♥ ♥ ♥ ♡ ♥ ♥ ♥ ♥ ♥ ♥ ♥ ♥ ♥ ♡ ♥ ♥ ♥ ♥ ♥ ♥ ♥ ♥ ♥

No honorific: Indicates familiarity or closeness; considered rude to use without permission.

-san: The Japanese equivalent of Mr./Mrs./Miss. If a situation calls for politeness, this is the fail-safe honorific.

-chan: An affectionate honorific indicating familiarity used mostly in reference to girls; also used in reference to cute persons or animals regardless of gender.

-senpai: A term commonly used to respectfully refer to upperclassmen in school or seniors at work. Its antonym, used for underclassmen, is *kouhai*.

-sama: Extremely formal and conveys an enormous amount of respect for the addressee.

-(o)nii: Literally means "older brother" but can refer to unrelated boys under thirty.

-(o)nee: Literally means "older sister" but can be used as a term of endearment or respect for an unrelated girl one looks up to.

♥

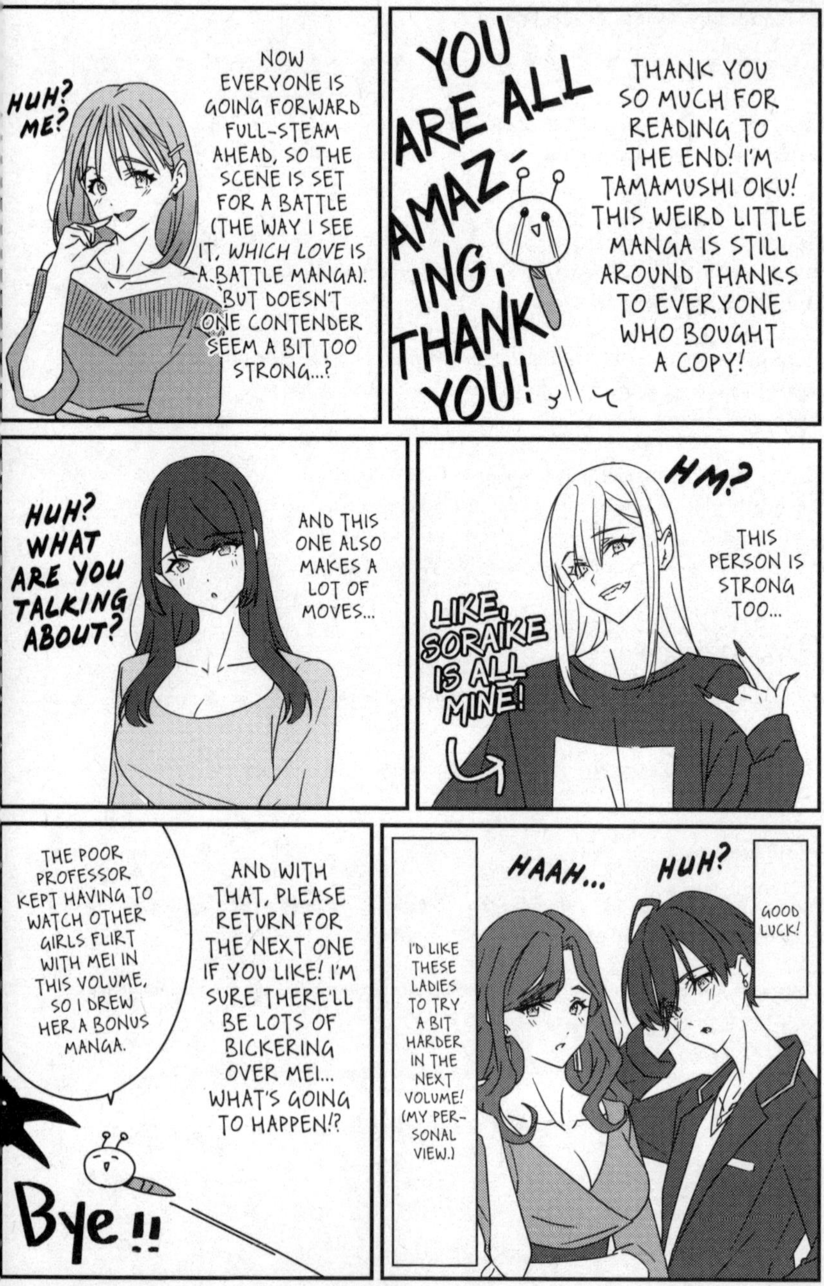
THANK YOU SO MUCH FOR READING TO THE END! I'M TAMAMUSHI OKU! THIS WEIRD LITTLE MANGA IS STILL AROUND THANKS TO EVERYONE WHO BOUGHT A COPY!
YOU ARE ALL AMAZING, THANK YOU!
NOW EVERYONE IS GOING FORWARD FULL-STEAM AHEAD, SO THE SCENE IS SET FOR A BATTLE (THE WAY I SEE IT, *WHICH LOVE* IS A BATTLE MANGA). BUT DOESN'T ONE CONTENDER SEEM A BIT TOO STRONG...?
HUH? ME?
HM?
THIS PERSON IS STRONG TOO...
LIKE, SORAIKE IS ALL MINE!
AND THIS ONE ALSO MAKES A LOT OF MOVES...
HUH? WHAT ARE YOU TALKING ABOUT?
GOOD LUCK!
HUH?
HAAH...
I'D LIKE THESE LADIES TO TRY A BIT HARDER IN THE NEXT VOLUME! (MY PERSONAL VIEW.)
AND WITH THAT, PLEASE RETURN FOR THE NEXT ONE IF YOU LIKE! I'M SURE THERE'LL BE LOTS OF BICKERING OVER MEI... WHAT'S GOING TO HAPPEN!?
THE POOR PROFESSOR KEPT HAVING TO WATCH OTHER GIRLS FLIRT WITH MEI IN THIS VOLUME, SO I DREW HER A BONUS MANGA.
Bye!!

THANK YOU SO MUCH TO THE READERS AND EVERYONE INVOLVED IN PRODUCTION! I APPRECIATE IT!

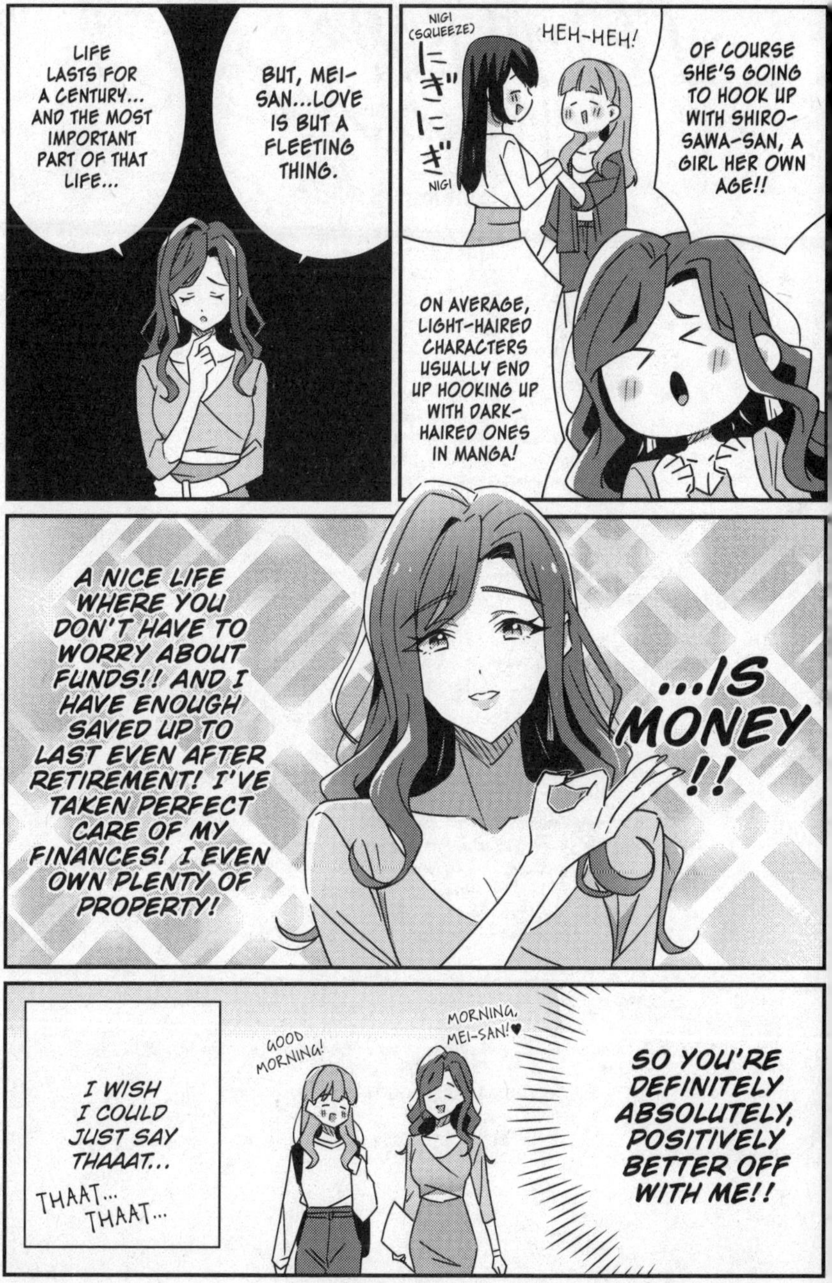
OF COURSE SHE'S GOING TO HOOK UP WITH SHIRO-SAWA-SAN, A GIRL HER OWN AGE!!
HEH-HEH!
NIGI (SQUEEZE)
にぎにぎ
NIGI
ON AVERAGE, LIGHT-HAIRED CHARACTERS USUALLY END UP HOOKING UP WITH DARK-HAIRED ONES IN MANGA!
BUT, MEI-SAN...LOVE IS BUT A FLEETING THING.
LIFE LASTS FOR A CENTURY... AND THE MOST IMPORTANT PART OF THAT LIFE...
...IS MONEY!!
A NICE LIFE WHERE YOU DON'T HAVE TO WORRY ABOUT FUNDS!! AND I HAVE ENOUGH SAVED UP TO LAST EVEN AFTER RETIREMENT! I'VE TAKEN PERFECT CARE OF MY FINANCES! I EVEN OWN PLENTY OF PROPERTY!
SO YOU'RE DEFINITELY ABSOLUTELY, POSITIVELY BETTER OFF WITH ME!!
MORNING, MEI-SAN!♥
GOOD MORNING!
I WISH I COULD JUST SAY THAAAT...
THAAT... THAAT...

I Don't Know Which Is Love

2

Tamamushi Oku

Translation: **LEIGHANN HARVEY** ✣ Lettering: **ELENA PIZARRO**

DORE GA KOI KA GA WAKARANAI Vol. 2
©Oku Tamamushi 2022
First published in Japan in 2022 by KADOKAWA CORPORATION, Tokyo.
English translation rights arranged with KADOKAWA CORPORATION, Tokyo,
through TUTTLE-MORI AGENCY, INC., Tokyo.

English translation © 2024 by Yen Press, LLC

Yen Press
150 West 30th Street, 19th Floor
New York, NY 10001

Visit us at yenpress.com ❤ facebook.com/yenpress ❤ twitter.com/yenpress
❤ yenpress.tumblr.com ❤ instagram.com/yenpress

First Yen Press Edition: January 2024
Edited by Yen Press Editorial: Fortune Soleil, Thomas McAlister
Designed by Yen Press Design: Wendy Chan

Yen Press is an imprint of Yen Press, LLC.
The Yen Press name and logo are trademarks of Yen Press, LLC.

The publisher is not responsible for websites (or their content) that are not owned by the publisher.

Library of Congress Control Number: 2023938740

ISBNs: 978-1-9753-8789-1 (paperback)
978-1-9753-8790-7 (ebook)

1 3 5 7 9 10 8 6 4 2

WOR

Printed in the United States of America